D0131239

A CONCISE HISTORY OF
WESTERN ARCHITECTURE

R. FURNEAUX JORDAN

A CONCISE HISTORY OF
WESTERN
ARCHITECTURE

HARCOURT, BRACE & WORLD, INC.

To E.M.F.J.

First American Edition 1970

Library of Congress Catalog Card Number: 79-99555

Printed in Great Britain by Jarrold and Sons Ltd, Norwich

CONTENTS

PREFACE

This book is an attempt, in a very small compass, to look at the main trends of Western architecture from the dawn of history to the present day. Even more, it is an attempt to show how the actual structure and forms of architecture were almost always the product of time and space – of circumstance more than will. Man's thoughts and actions – his religion, politics, art, technology and aspirations, as well as landscape, geology and climate are the things from which an architecture is born. The art of a civilization, rightly interpreted, is a very precise reflec- tion of the society which produced it. This is an iron law concerning man and all his artefacts. True, the artist, by reason of his taste or skill may give some special twist or charm to the thing he is designing, and may design it a little better or worse than the next man; what he can never do is to produce something not of his own era. He cannot be elsewhere either in time or space. In architec- ture, an art tied to practical purposes and executed always within severe practical limits, this dialectical law is more marked than in any other art. To some extent the painter, poet, composer, sculptor – although in- evitably a child of his time serving his own generation – can withdraw to some sort of ivory tower; the architect never. Architecture is the product of a hundred circum- stances. It would be an arid task to study the architecture without at least also glancing at the circumstances.

R.F.J.

Chapter One
INTRODUCTORY

All European culture, not least its architecture, had its
beginnings outside Europe. Prehistoric man had spread
widely over much of the habitable world. He was
thin on the ground but he was there. And yet, through
many thousands of years – whether hunter, shepherd or
fisherman – he had never organized himself into any kind
of community larger than the family or the group of
families we call a tribe. His energy was concentrated upon
survival in a hard world, following his flocks from
pasture to pasture, picking berries as he went. He had the
marvellous uninhibited talent of a child when painting
his cave, the resourcefulness of a savage when building
his hut. He invented many things – spears, fish-hooks,
baskets, pots, canoes – but, never settling, he never
invented the town.

Only when man could free himself from this thraldom
to the hunter-fisher economy could anything like
'civilization', and therefore architecture, come into being.
This liberation was the first revolution in the story of man.
It came, to start with, in the great river valleys and in their
deltas, where the alluvial soil was black and fertile, and
one could build with reeds. If we plot the first civiliza-
tions upon a world map we shall find, not that civilization spreads outwards from a centre, but rather that it
comes into existence at more than one point, that there
are several tiny caterpillars of culture upon the globe . . .
the valleys of the Tigris and Euphrates in Mesopotamia,
of the Nile in Egypt, of the Indus in north-west India
and of the Yangtse in China. They all had one thing in

common, a mastery of irrigation. Each of these valleys – most of all the Nile – when the annual snows melted in the mountains hundreds of miles away, was flooded. The silt-bearing water crept inch by inch over the level fields depositing its precious load. When man learnt how to control this flood, with dykes, ditches and water-wheels, then his corn seed was returned to him several hundred-fold. It was possible for one man to grow corn for many, and the many were freed for other tasks. They might even leave the soil and come together in cities.

It is especially in cities that mind can sharpen itself upon mind, that ideas and techniques can be exchanged and sold. So in the Nile Valley (as also in Mesopotamia and far away in China), first in the Delta and then in Upper Egypt, there came into history the city. And with the city there came also into history not only priests and kings, but lawyers and scribes, doctors, astronomers and mathematicians, prostitutes and actors, merchants, potters, artists and architects. It was the beginning of all things.

As sixteenth-century Spain and England accepted the challenge of the sea and of a New World, as ancient Rome accepted the challenge of a continent and built an empire, so Egypt accepted the challenge of reeds and swamps and hot sand and flood, and built the first nation. Other people came into existence in not dis-similar ways, but Egypt was unique. To live in the Nile Valley was to be enclosed, from birth to death, within a geography and a routine of extraordinary simplicity. There were few things to impress themselves upon the Egyptian mind; such as they were, however, their psychological impact was terrific. There was the Nile itself – source of all life; there was the mysterious regularity of sun, moon and stars; there was fertility and the grave. It was out of the fear and mystery of these things that the Egyptians made their complex hierarchy of gods, and their strange religion. In the service of that religion they made their art and their architecture.

Egyptian theology, with its deified pharaohs and strange animal-headed gods, was complicated. The most important thing was the belief that survival after death depended upon the preservation of the body. Immortality was only for privileged royal and priestly beings, except that a servant might hope to be a servant in the world beyond the stars, in eternal servitude to his master. At the day of resurrection the spirit or *Ka* of the dead man would enter once more into his body; the body must be there, intact, ready for that moment. In prehistoric times the fact that the dry desert sand had helped to preserve the body may have suggested the idea of what came to be called 'the good burial'. For three thousand years that idea was an obsession. Embalming became a high skill, one of the most important sciences in the world's first civilization. It followed logically, once the corpse was embalmed or mummified, that it must also be preserved in an impregnable tomb. This was more difficult. The impregnability of the tomb became the problem, and indeed the basis, of Egyptian architecture.

Impregnability had to be provided in more than one form, security for the cadaver, and security for the dead man's possessions – his wives, his furniture, his food and his jewels. The accumulated *objets d'art* of Ancient Egypt, with which the world's museums are filled, were once in tombs, awaiting a second existence at the resurrection. The tomb was not only an impregnable monument; it was a storehouse, a chapel and a work of art.

The Egyptian tomb had to be not only durable, it had to look durable. Apart from prehistoric graves – which, however, already contained jars for food, ointment and entrails – the earliest historic tombs were the *mastabas* of

1 Reconstruction of the tomb-complex of Zoser at Saqqara (c. 2680 BC), showing the Step Pyramid surrounded by ritual buildings, all within a stone-faced wall: (a) entrance; (b) hall of pillars; (c) ceremonial court; (d) store-houses; (e) double-throne and (f) shrines of Upper and Lower Egypt; (g) and (h) south and north buildings and courts, possibly symbolizing the administration of Upper and Lower Egypt; (i) mortuary temple; (j) south tomb. The Pharaoh's tomb lies under the pyramid

2 Saqqara. Columns in the shape of papyrus – with tulip-shaped flowers and ridged stem – in the north court (h, in Ill. 1); the builders did not yet trust stone enough to make them free-standing. Symbolic of Lower Egypt, the papyrus became a common decorative motif

the I–III Dynasties of the Archaic Period (c. 3200–c. 2700 B C). They were mainly near Memphis, a little south of Cairo, capital of the Old Memphite Nome. These *mastaba* tombs were small with stepped sides and a flat top (their name coming from the Arabic for a bench of the type found outside the doors of Arab houses). They were almost solid but somewhere in the heart of the mass of mud-brick or masonry was a series of rooms, including the burial chamber containing the sarcophagus of the dead, with all his impedimenta. Externally there was a recess simulating a blocked-up door. Through this false door the *Ka* or soul could return to the body. This recess also served as a small chapel where offerings could be made to the dead, and where the priest could say prayers for the repose of the soul.

The *mastaba* was faced with limestone blocks brought from the mountains bordering the Nile Valley. These were finely and accurately cut for their place in the sloping walls. Functionally, therefore, the *mastaba* was designed to achieve permanence. Aesthetically it was designed to look permanent in an impressive way. Technically it involved metal tools, mathematics, transport and organized labour. It was, in fact – for all its apparent simplicity – *architecture*. It was also the germ of a great development. It was clearly the embryo of the pyramids, while the little recess or chapel was to be developed eventually, in Upper Egypt, into the great mortuary temples of Thebes on the west bank of the Nile at Luxor. The fine stone-cutting of the *mastaba* was the start of a masonry tradition which was to run like a golden thread through all the architecture of Europe.

The first 'pyramid' was built as early as c. 2680 B C, at Sakkara, between Memphis and the Nile. It was a large-scale development of the *mastaba*, not truly pyramidical in form. Known as the Step Pyramid, it is some 200 feet high; it was the tomb of the Pharaoh Zoser of the III Dynasty, and formed part of a large and very sophisticated group of buildings. Most of these are in effect sham – simply façades on solid rubble cores – but the mere fact that they are of stone is of tremendous importance. A double throne symbolized Zoser's rule over Upper and Lower Egypt, and a number of features exist in duplicate to represent the two kingdoms. At the heart of all, in a small sealed chamber next to the pyramid, was the grim seated statue of Zoser, once with malachite eyes (this is now in the Cairo Museum). A civilization has here come to maturity. Layout, plan, vista and setting, as well as painting and sculp‑ ture, have become part of architecture. The Step Pyramid itself has long since lost its facing, but was once a clear‑cut giant's staircase to Heaven. The whole group was contrived, considered, designed. We know the name of the architect. He was Imhotep. His technical skill was great, but it was the creative imagination that was now recognized for the first time as a divine attribute of man. Imhotep was made a High Priest of Re the Sun God, and was assured of honour in this world, and of immortality in the next. In later ages he was revered as a sage and as the patron god of medicine.

A little to the north of Memphis, on the rocky plateau of Giza, was the royal cemetery – an orderly arrangement of windless courts paved with green basalt, rows of pyramids of many sizes, *mastaba* tombs for the burial of courtiers, austere and unadorned funerary temples cut with beautiful precision, underground passages and, almost always, wherever one might be, the sharp apex of a pyramid against the blue sky or the stars. There, with their golden furniture, jewels and spices around them, kings and queens, princes and princesses, were buried. There, during the IV Dynasty, the three largest pyramidal tombs were built by three pharaohs, Cheops, Chephren and Mykerinus: each pyramid was a symbol of eternal life and of eternal servitude to the king.

The largest (*c.*2575 BC) was built by Cheops. It was in every sense a climax, historically and aesthetically.

3, 4 Giza. Below, the pyramids of Cheops (c.2575 BC, foreground), Chephren and Mykerinus; mastaba tombs, for the courtiers, are visible at the right. Above, the mortuary temple by the Nile where Chephren's body was embalmed. Its severe masonry is charac‑ teristic of the IV Dynasty: the piers are now free‑standing

Although Imhotep's work at Sakkara was a brilliant revolution – virtually the creation of architecture as an art – it was only one of a series – Sakkara, Medum, Dashur, leading to the apotheosis of Giza. This Great Pyramid contained six and a quarter million tons of stone. It was 480 feet high before the apex stones were lost. Each side of the square base was 760 feet, with a mathematical error of about 0·03 per cent. Each polished block weighed about two and a half tons. The joints between them were one-fiftieth of an inch – jeweller's work unexcelled by the builders of the Parthenon.

Almost more impressive were the actual mechanics of construction. Herodotus says that 100,000 men worked for twenty years fed on a diet of onions. The blocks of stone, some of them 20 feet by 6 feet, would be brought from the quarry by barge at the height of the Nile flood, but they had to be handled at both ends of the journey and then dragged up a ramp to the Pyramid site, a hundred feet above the river. Wedges, rockers, levers, cradles and sledges were all used. The missing element was the wheel – no carts, no pulleys, no cranes.

5 Building the pyramid of Mykerinus at Giza (a conjectural reconstruction). Four rubble ramps were built, progressively higher, around the stone casing of the pyramid. Up three of these teams of men dragged stone, brought from the Nile, on sledges; by the fourth the crews descended. Once the capstone was in place, the ramps would be gradually removed and the stone facing – visible at the side – polished

The Great Pyramid is a valid symbol of a culture. The mystical meaning of the measurements and proportions is unknown; it is certain, however, that here we have mathematics not as a mere tool of the engineer, but as a mystique, an end in itself. God is a mathematician. It is this Greek attitude to mathematics as art that would seem to have come into the world with the tomb of Cheops.

The pyramids mark the culmination of the Old Kingdom – monolithic, immutable, austere, puritanical. There followed an interregnum and a 'dark age' – the VII to X Dynasties. Then once more, about 2000 B C, Egypt emerges into history. With the rise of the Middle Kingdom pharaohs a new capital was established at Thebes, 300 miles south of Memphis. In 1370 B C, Amenhotep IV (Akhenaten) was to build a new city at Amarna (now Tel-el-Amarna) to the north of Thebes, but the Theban area remained in effect the metropolitan province of Egypt until its absorption in the Roman Empire two thousand years later. We now enter upon the age of the great temples.

6 *Instead of pyramids, later pharaohs built mortuary temples at Thebes. Such was the Ramesseum of Rameses II (XIX Dynasty), seen here from the court looking towards the pillared hall. The court was decorated with reliefs and colossal statues of the pharaoh as the god Osiris (see also Ill. 13). The squat pillars beyond have both papyrus and lotus-bud capitals*

13

This development in the *use* of architecture signifies no corresponding change in life or religion. The 'good burial', the preservation of the material things of this life for use in the next, was still the basis of all belief. The fact is, however, that functionally both the *mastaba* tomb and the pyramid had been a failure. Their massive impregnability, so far from protecting the tomb, had advertised its existence. Pilfering and sacrilege had been rampant.

Nevertheless the dead must still be buried with all their possessions, and there must still be a sacred place for sacrificial offerings and prayers. In short the tomb must now be hidden. The offering niche, once a mere recess in the *mastaba* wall, had already become a considerable, but nevertheless subordinate, chapel of the pyramid. It now assumed overwhelming importance. A number of the great temples of the Theban Empire were really funerary chapels (i.e. mortuary temples) related to the tombs of the deified pharaohs buried deep in the Theban hills. Here and there, as at Deir el-Bahari, the temptation to give the mountain tomb some great architectural frontispiece – still to combine tomb and temple – was irresistible. On the whole, however, the new system worked. The temples, on a vast scale, were built near the river, while the dead kings were sealed in their deep tombs. Some may be there still. As is well known, the tomb of the boy king, TutankhAmun, with its amassed treasures, was substantially intact until 1922.

There are many beautiful single temples throughout the Nile Valley, but at Karnak there is a whole complex of temples, all originally contained within a sacred compound, with a sacred lake bearing a colony of ibis. The compound was approached from the Nile by an avenue of carved couchant rams. These temples were built through the centuries by a whole series of pharaohs. There is nothing comparable in the Western world unless we think of each Roman emperor adding a forum to Rome, or the cathedrals being added to through some four or five centuries. The main core around which the

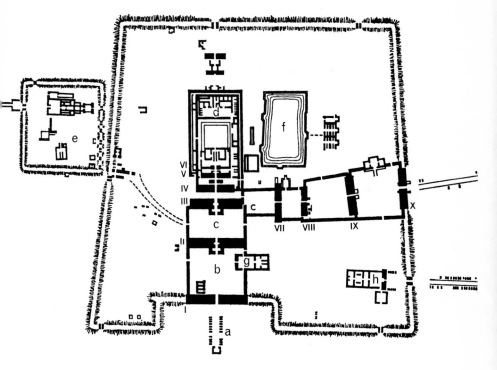

rest grew was the great Temple of Amun, begun in the XII Dynasty (1991–1786 BC). Other pharaohs added temples, pylons or temple courts until the end of Egypt's history. The dead but deified pharaoh, absorbed into the other gods, would be worshipped. His interest, therefore, was personal.

The typical temple, of which that of Amun was merely a large version, had usually an outer court open to the sky but with columns round, as in a cloister; then, beyond that, a large columned hall followed by the sanctuary; then beyond that again a rabbit-warren of rooms where the priests lived and planned their ceremony. The central room of this inner complex was the shrine, the holy of holies where the cult statue was kept. The temple rooms all looked inwards upon courts, and were lit – if at all – by a small shaft of sunlight penetrating a small hole in the flat stone roof. The enclosing wall (the

7 Precincts of the Temple of Amun at Karnak (XII Dynasty and after). Approaching from the Nile by the avenue of rams (a), one enters the Temple of Amun proper, which stretches from the great courtyard (b) through the hypostyle hall (c, see also Ills. 8–10) past the sanctuary to the festival hall of Tuthmosis III (d). The length is interrupted by pylons (I–VI), added by successive pharaohs. Further pylons on another axis (VII–X) lead towards the Temple of Mut, standing in a separate enclosure like that of Monthu (e). Next to the Temple of Amun are the sacred lake (f) and a temple added by Rameses III (g). The precincts are completely walled

temenos) therefore had no windows; moreover it was double so that the whole temple was surrounded by a totally inaccessible security corridor. All the columns, all the walls, were completely covered with incised pictures and hieroglyphs – hymns to the deities and statements of self-glorification by the pharaohs.

The avenue of rams – which began at the landing-stage – the entrance, the court, and the columned hall were all planned with strict symmetry, on a single axis. As so often throughout history – whenever planning is in the grand manner – the real basis of it is the *procession*. The central doorways, for instance, have their lintels most curiously cut away so that banners and standards could pass through unlowered. Flanking each doorway were the pylons. These pairs of pylons are the most prominent feature of every Egyptian temple. At Karnak they are 140 feet high – near-solid masses of masonry, slotted for masts flying pennons, and bearing in very low relief epic accounts of the glory of pharaoh, about eight times life size. Symmetry and grandeur have become part of architecture.

We are led by this symmetry and grandeur all the way from the avenue of rams into the outer court, and from the court into the hypostyle hall. This hall is of great significance. It is a columned hall. The cylindrical columns are very massive, and are closely spaced so that single slabs can bridge from one column to another. The vistas and the glimpses from one side of the hall to the

8–10 Hypostyle hall, Karnak (XIX Dynasty). Below, plan and section looking along the main axis: the more massive central columns, with papyrus capitals, support a higher roof with clerestory lighting at the sides. The lower pillars have lotus-bud capitals (compare Ill. 6, of the same date).
Opposite, a view across the hall along a–a, showing the clerestory with its stone grilles. One sees the Egyptian treatment of masonry – columns and walls of tremendous weight and mass covered with slightly incised figures and hieroglyphs, so delicate that they do not detract from the functional mass

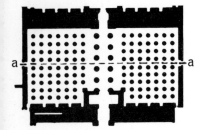

other are mysterious and dramatic. The hall is 320 feet by 160 feet. Down the centre is an avenue of 12 columns, each 69 feet high and nearly 12 feet in diameter. These have bell-shaped capitals based on the lotus blossom. On either side of this central avenue or 'nave' of columns, are other columned areas, each with 60 columns, 42 feet high and 9 feet in diameter. Since the central avenue has columns higher than those of the area on either side, the roof of the central area is some 20 feet higher than the roof of the side halls. This means that there is a vertical wall between the higher and the lower roof, and that this can be pierced by windows – actually by large stone grilles. These admit daylight into the hall high up. This method of lighting – where one part of a building rises higher than another part – is called 'clerestory lighting'. It is found again and again in history, as for instance in the nave of a cathedral when it rises above the aisles. It is an effective method. It keeps the source and glare of light high up, above the eye, and yet lights brilliantly the central area of a large building. In the case of the hypostyle hall at Karnak it must have been particularly dramatic – shafts of brilliant sunlight penetrating the shadowy forest of columns. Here and there the light would catch the richly painted hieroglyphics and carvings, while the outer parts of the hall would be in almost complete shadow. Mystery, light, colour and drama have here been added to the history of architecture.

The simple geometrical forms of Egyptian architecture, clean and clear-cut, unadorned except for reliefs and incised hieroglyphs, bore a perfect relationship to the landscape. They were in contrast to the peerless sky and the level desert. They were an echo of the rock formations in the mountains beyond the Valley. This, in early days, may have been chance. By the time of the XVIII Dynasty (1570–1314 BC) there is little doubt but that the Egyptians had become conscious, aesthetically conscious, of the relationship of architecture to landscape. The proof lies in the temple of Hatshepsut at Deir el-Bahari.

Queen Hatshepsut reigned over Egypt for many years in her own right, and – like Catherine the Great or Maria Theresa – left her mark. Her mortuary temple in the mountains at Deir el-Bahari is a remarkable piece of architecture. In general its arrangement is not dissimilar to the usual temple layout – avenue, forecourt, columns, inner shrine and so on – but the fact that it is set against a cliff, at the foot of a fine mountain bluff, alters its whole character. It is on rising ground. The processional avenue and the approach end in an impressive series of ramps. The ramps lead up from one platform to another. The main avenue of sphinxes ran from the Nile to the foot of the first ramp. On the platform between the top of this first ramp and the foot of the next one, the sphinxes were of red granite. The platform was probably planted with cedar trees. There are carved pictures of these trees, their roots in baskets, being carried on shoulder poles, each by four slaves, brought from the Land of Punt, across the Red Sea . . . one of Egypt's very few forays into the outer world.

11 Mortuary temple of Queen Hatshepsut at Deir el-Bahari (XVIII Dynasty). Due to the site, the traditional temple areas are on different levels, approached by ramps. The plain, severe forms were clearly designed as a foil to the rocky mountains above them – beyond which lies the Valley of the Kings

12 The larger of the two rock-cut temples of Rameses II at Abu Simbel (XIX Dynasty), before its removal to higher ground. The stupendous façade consisted of four seated statues of the pharaoh, each 65 feet high. The temple, hollowed out of the rock, was entered between the two pairs of figures

The platforms were fronted by colonnades, on the back wall of which are incised and painted reliefs telling of the Queen's divine birth, her expeditions and architectural achievements. From the upper platform there is a wide view of the Nile, but Deir el-Bahari can also be approached by a mountain path from the Valley of the Kings where the Queen herself was buried.

The main point about Deir el-Bahari, however, is the deliberate simplicity of its architecture, its complete subordination to the dramatic landscape. A few strong horizontal lines contrast with the verticality of the cliff. The broad pattern of light and shade in the colonnades reads from far off. Richness, ornament and sculpture are almost wholly omitted since they could never compete with the surroundings. An understanding of architecture in landscape must be added to those things which Egypt passed on to Europe.

If the temple at the foot of the mountain was to be part of the landscape, two courses were open to the builder. The first, as at Deir el-Bahari, was to design with a few strong lines, such as would hold their own against the overwhelming precipice above them, and to avoid all sculptural ornament. The other course was to produce a sculptural architecture on such a grandiose scale that it, too, would hold its own. This seemingly impossible task was undertaken at Abu Simbel on the Upper Nile by carving the actual face of the mountain. The two temples at Abu Simbel were built in the XIX Dynasty by Rameses II, about 1250 B C. The larger of the two was certainly stupendous, holding its own not only against the mountain side, but also when seen from far off across the river. A forecourt led to a great façade, 119 feet wide and 100 feet high. This façade was carved with four colossal seated statues ot Rameses, each 65 feet high – made possible only by cutting them out of the living rock. Beyond this façade one passed into a vestibule with eight columns representing the King in the likeness of the god Osiris; beyond that was a columned hall and then the sanctuary – a complete temple underneath a mountain. It was really the application of the technique of tomb building to the making of a temple. (The formation of a modern reservoir has involved cutting out the temple in blocks, and removing it, to be reconstructed at a higher level above the water.)

Egyptian building perfectly mirrors its creators. More than any architecture there has ever been, it was free from all extraneous influences such as an alien culture. As we see it, however, it is misleading. It appears to us as if it were wholly an architecture of death. The palaces and the houses have all vanished centuries ago. All we know of them must be deduced from the paintings and the contents of the tombs.

The house, an affair of reeds, hanging mats and wooden columns, must have had a certain airy elegance. The gardens were formal. The jewel boxes, the bracelets

13 Just inside the large temple at Abu Simbel (Ill. 12), statues cut from the living rock represent Rameses II as Osiris, the god of the dead

14 Model of an Egyptian house, from the tomb of Meket-re at Thebes (c. 2000 BC). A deep, shady portico with painted papyrus columns looks out on a small walled garden where trees surround a pool: as in all hot climates, water and shade were highly prized

of lapis lazuli, turquoise and gold, the stone vases, the gazelles and dogs in pink alabaster, the golden discs for gaming, the carved barges for sailing among the flamingoes on artificial lakes, the fragments of lovely beds, chairs and stools, the use of quartz and faience – all these things were of an elegance appropriate to the dappled sunlight of verandahs, shadowy rooms and the tinkle of fountains – the first architecture of an aristocracy. If in style, structure and ornament Egypt's direct or specific contribution to any European style was negligible, it laid the foundation of an attitude to architecture which was durable.

The culture and influence of Classical Greece became the basis of a whole Hellenic world. It is found in the territories invaded by Alexander the Great, throughout Magna Graecia and ultimately in the Roman Empire. The great Classical Age, however, consisting virtually of the two generations of Athenian history dominated by Pericles in the fifth century BC, has been likened to the perihelion of a comet – a long, slow preparation through a thousand archaic years, a short blaze of achievement, then the long, slow decline.

The story of modern man begins for us when the Greek first enters upon the stage of history. Civilization began centuries earlier, but it is not until the Periclean Age that we find intellect and the rule of law. That age was a creative moment. As Lewis Mumford has written: 'The mind remains delicately suspended; the eye looks round, discriminates, inquires, beholds the natural world and passes at a bound from sprawling fantasy to continent, self-defining knowledge.'

For thirty centuries the Egyptian craftsman had carved the same hierarchic figures – the same eye, same nose, same loincloth, same torso: a simple exercise repeated to the point of technical perfection. Then, already, even in Archaic times, the Greek sculptor is observing and analysing. Even the most Archaic Greek statue is carved by Pygmalion; it is about to breathe, not because it is realistic but because it is instinct with life. Unlike the carefully delineated pharaohs on the walls at Luxor, it is more than a glorified hieroglyph.

So too with the theatre. If, with the passing of tyranny, custom had become law, then with the tragedies of Aeschylus and Sophocles what had once been ritual and myth became drama. To the single actor – originally the priest – first one and then more were added, giving rise to the clash of mind upon mind, and the spectacle of man at war with destiny. Greek drama remained formal and sacerdotal, with the priests always enthroned in the 'stalls', and was ultimately absorbed into the history of both the theatre and the church, only to be liberated once again in the time of Shakespeare.

And as with sculpture and drama, so with thought. It was Plato who laid down the ideal condition for government – that a philosopher should be a king and a king should be a philosopher. This condition was fulfilled under Solon, when law and order replaced custom. Nature and society began to be understood. Dislike of *hubris* – intellectual pride – and the precept 'know thyself', became the axioms of Greek thought; the ideal was the balanced mind, 'nothing to excess'.

The Greeks were not unaware of the problems of their culture. Violence was curbed but it existed. Slavery was basic to the economy. Cruelty was disliked but disregarded. Homosexuality and infanticide were defended with cold reason. The stunted role of women undermined the integrity of life. The Greeks were always conscious of the nearness of the primitive – hence their aloofness. In so far as they were aware of a world beyond the Aegean, it was a wholly barbaric world. The hosts of Persia or the ancient dynasties of Egypt were beyond the pale. Greek democracy, when it came to the point, reduced itself to the votes of a few thousand Greekborn adult males.

In the last analysis, however, Greek wisdom was an attitude to the human mind and the human body. The Greeks had rejected the gods of Egypt, without adopting the monotheism of the Jews. They conceived the gods of Olympus not only as embodying the powers of nature, but also as beings anatomically perfect while possessed of human frailty. As such they made statues of them, and for those statues they made shrines, the temples. The Greeks overcame the basic crudity of their theology by sublimating the deities in superb sculptures, by idealizing the human body itself, and by enshrining the functions of the whole Olympic hierarchy in poetry, myth, drama and architecture. Greece is a peninsula of jagged bays and headlands, of inlets running far into the mainland, each inlet separated from the next by the mountains. The climate produced rigorous and athletic men; the marble was almost an invitation to carve them as if they were gods.

The Greeks were a maritime people only in the sense that they traded a little – as far as Spain to the west and the Euxine to the east – made poetry out of their wine-dark sea, and would rather sail round the coast from city to city than cross the mountains. However they looked inwards upon Hellas rather than out upon the great world. They could never, like the Romans, have organized an empire. Even more did they look inwards upon the city itself – isolated upon its own arm of the sea. When threatened from without, as in the wars with the Persians, the Greek cities could band together, but it was the city states such as Athens, Sparta and Corinth that were the object of patriotism and effort. Greek architecture was civic rather than national. It was upon the public works of Athens, not of Greece, that the Periclean Age expended its genius. That genius was compounded of the virtue of perfectionism and the vice of self-absorption.

As with sculpture, drama, law and philosophy, so with architecture: absolute perfection was sought, but only within clearly defined limits. The Greeks, for instance, were never engineers. Architecture is divided into two great families – the trabeated and the arcuated, beamed and arched; Greek architecture is trabeated. With all its refinement the Greek temple, structurally, was no advance upon Karnak or Stonehenge. The Greeks knew the arch but they never exploited it. They never attempted to cover a large space with vaults or a dome as the Romans were to do. They were fascinated by the meticulous fitting together of stone blocks, but they were not otherwise interested in structure. Their skill in handling stone, their obsession with mathematics as a mystical thing – an end, not a means – their strangely crude but strangely poetic religion, their adoration of the human body with the consequent elevation of sculpture to the status of a dominant art . . . these were the elements from which Greek architecture derived.

A Greek town, at almost any date, must have been just a collection of white-walled houses with flat roofs or tiled roofs of low pitch, like the temple. Each house looked inward upon a small court, and presented an almost windowless wall to the street – the timeless house of all hot countries where there is seclusion of women. Politics were an affair of the market place – the agora – and drama an affair of the open-air theatre. This left only the temple as a medium for an architecture which had almost all the attributes of the human anatomy – proportion, balance, grace, precision and subtlety; but which was also marmoreal and sculptural.

15 *The Palace of Minos at Knossos (c.1600 BC) had an elaborate staircase, the first in the world with regular flights and landings. The supporting columns, with their unusual downward taper, are a hallmark of Cretan architecture*

The origins of Greek architecture are uncertain, and drawn from more than one source. The Ionic column – that decorative but irrational affair with curious spiral volutes as its capital – is found in an archaic form in many lands. From the sea-girt kingdom of Crete, from the beautifully decorated apartments of the Palace of Minos at Knossos, there came to Greece the great gift of precision and refinement. The Cretan palaces were vast and unfortified, spreading out irregularly around a central court and including workshops and storehouses. There was an ornamental façade at the west; the rooms were usually frescoed, the wooden columns brightly painted. About 1450 BC, Knossos was conquered by the Mycenaean war-lords of the Peloponnese: through them, Cretan influence passed to the mainland.

The whole basic concept of the columned temple probably came from the house of the Mycenaean chieftain. Mycenaean palaces were more formal in plan than those of Crete, and stood in citadels, on strategic hills. Within the walls were a number of buildings, religious and domestic. (There is a parallel in the conglomeration of church, chapel, tombs and palace for the ancient kings of Ireland, on the Great Rock of Cashel.) Outside the citadel were the royal tombs, of

16 *The throne room at Knossos, built by the Mycenaeans after their conquest c. 1450 BC. The high-backed throne is original: the wall-painting, with its refined but stiff drawing of wingless griffins and plants, is a copy based on fragments*

17 *The Treasury of Atreus at Mycenae (13th century B C), a 'tholos' or bee-hive tomb some 50 feet across and high. The stone courses of the vast dome are smoothly corbelled out, one over the other, and the doors have triangular heads: the true principle of the arch – the wedge-shaped voussoir – was not yet understood*

18 *Isometric reconstruction of the palace at Mycenae. A staircase in two flights (a) led to the throne room (b) and the great court (c). Beyond this lay the megaron (d), a single room with four columns round a central hearth, approached through a columned portico and vestibule. (As at Knossos, Ill. 15, the columns all taper downward)*

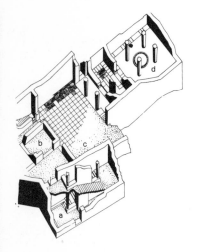

which the most famous is the so-called Treasury of Atreus at Mycenae. A walled passage leads to a beehive-shaped chamber about 50 by 50 feet, which rises to a corbelled vault made of tiers of carefully cut, slightly overlapping stones. The span of the largest of these beehive tombs (*tholoi*) was only exceeded by that of the Pantheon, over a thousand years later. Among the buildings within the Mycenaean citadel was the chieftain's own house – the *megaron* – much like Homer's descrip-tion of the house of Odysseus. It was a single simple room with a central hearth, preceded by a vestibule and – most significantly – an outer portico with columns. When a 'house' had to be built for the statue of the god or goddess, the prototype was this chieftain's house, a rectangular room with a portico. The architect and the sculptor might, in the course of centuries, transmute this wooden house into a marble shrine, but basically it remained a house, never a place of assembly, never a church, and almost always upon a high place. The temple was always set apart from the town, not only by being put in a sacred enclosure, but usually also upon a headland, a citadel or acropolis.

The rectangular temple with low-pitched roof and surrounding colonnade – the peristyle – thus became the basic form of the Greek temple. There were many variations upon the theme. On the Acropolis, above the city of Athens, is the most famous group of buildings in the world. Those temples are in two styles, the Doric and Ionic. These are the names given to the two kinds of 'order' used: this term refers to the whole unit – the column with its base below and entablature above. There are three main 'orders' – Doric, Ionic and Corinthian. The Doric Order, plainest of all, has a simple moulded capital and no base (the Romans later made it more slender and added a base); the Ionic Order has a slimmer column, with, as we have seen, a capital consisting of two linked volutes; the Corinthian, with its richly carved capital bristling with acanthus leaves, was used far more by the Romans than the Greeks. The details and proportions of the 'orders' were minutely prescribed in the first century A D by the Roman architect Vitruvius, rather as if they had been laid down by God. They became the vocabulary of the language of classical architecture. During the last four or five hundred years thousands of architects have been obsessed by these

19 Pottery model of a shrine from Argos (late 8th century B C): a single room fronted by a portico of two columns, it marks a stage in the evolution from house to temple

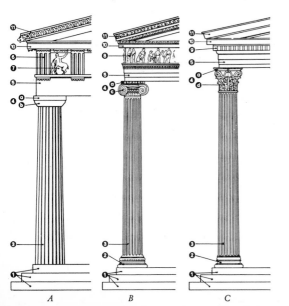

20 The Classical Greek orders: A, Doric; B, Ionic; C, Corinthian. (1) Stylobate; (2) attic base; (3) shaft; (4) capital; (4a) abacus; (4b) echinus; (4c) Ionic volute; (4d) Corinthian volute with acanthus leaves; (5) architrave; (6) triglyph; (7) metope; (8) frieze; (9) dentils; (10) facia; (11) cyma

21, 22 *The Doric Order at Paestum.*
Below, a corner of the Archaic 'Basilica' (mid-6th century BC). The columns have an exaggerated taper – an early use of entasis – and spreading capitals. Virtually everything above the architrave has been destroyed.

Opposite, the 'Temple of Neptune', built a century later. Though still heavy compared with the Parthenon (Ill. 29), it includes some of the same refinements: all the horizontals are slightly curved. The three temples at Paestum were originally plastered, to hide flaws in the local travertine stone

'orders', sometimes to the exclusion of intelligent design. The Greeks, however, used them with flexibility, discretion and great artistry.

The Greeks believed themselves to be a blend of two races. They may have been right. One race was Dorian, the other Ionian. The Dorians were a tribe of northern shepherds from as far away as the Steppes – hardy, rigorous, practical – who had come south in a series of migrations. The Ionians came over the sea from Asia Minor; they were Oriental, sensuous, effeminate, colourful. Character was, as always, reflected in architecture. In bringing together on the Acropolis these two styles of temple building – the plain, sturdy Doric and the

elegant, ornamented Ionic – the Athenians believed that they were giving expression to the two poles of their nature, luxury and abstinence.

It is in the Greek colonies in Sicily and on the Italian coast below Naples that we find the Doric Order in its sternest form. The Temple of Concord at Agrigento (*c*.500–470 BC) and the three temples at Paestum – the so-called Basilica and Temples of Ceres and Neptune, dating from the mid-sixth to the mid-fifth century BC – are the best-preserved examples. They are, in a sense, archaic – having few of the refinements of the Parthenon Doric – but they do have a splendid, almost primeval strength. The columns are stout, the capitals huge, and all the stones ponderous. The effect is overwhelming.

When we seek the Ionic style in isolation we turn to the Ionian Greek colonies of Asia Minor. At Ephesus the first great temple of the goddess Artemis (the Roman Diana) was designed as early as *c*.540 BC, and then rebuilt in 356 BC, more or less on the original foundations. The temple was nearly 400 feet long, the columns over 50 feet high. The workmanship and carving were technically refined; it was richly ornamented, probably brilliant with colour.

23 Reconstruction of the vast Archaic Temple of Artemis at Ephesus (begun c.540 BC), looking across the portico: a triumph of engineering – the columns were some 60 feet high and widely spaced – as well as a rich display of the ornate Ionic Order

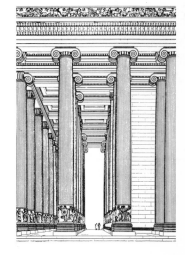

When we turn to Athens in the fifth century B C, there is loss as well as gain. The drama of the primeval has gone but here, on its own terms, civilization has been sharpened to a point of perfection. On the Acropolis, ancient and sacred ground, there were earlier buildings. They were ruined in the Persian Wars, and Socrates would have seen them as stones blackened by smoke. Then, under Pericles, the stupendous effort was made.

The Acropolis itself – that high rock outside the city – had its sides built up and its top flattened to form a kind of podium for the temples. This separation of the temples from the town was deliberate. As shrines they normally had no place in the street, as had the Roman temple or the Christian church. Equally important, however, was the fact that the temples could be *seen* from the streets, rising above the wall of the sacred enclosure – a continual reminder of the gods, like the medieval bell chiming the hours for prayer. This distant view of the temple had a profound influence upon its form. It was designed so that it should be 'read' from far off. Forgetting its minutiae, we may think of the temple –

24 Plan showing the major buildings on the Acropolis at Athens (see pp. 33–5), and the Theatre of Dionysus below (h). From the Propylaea at the west (a), flanked by the Pinacotheca (b) and Temple of Nikè Apteros (c), the Sacred Way led toward a colossal statue of Athene (d). The Erechtheum (e) stands partly on the site of the goddess's old temple (f), which was replaced by the Parthenon (g)

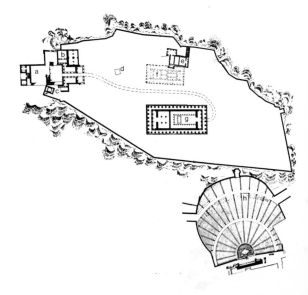

specially the bold and simple Doric peristyle of the Parthenon – as a series of alternating bands of light and dark formed by the columns and the shade between them. Of course there was delicate ornament on the Parthenon but it was not intended to be seen, and could not be seen, except from near to. It was the intermediate scale of richness, neither delicate nor bold – the Gothic pinnacle or the Roman Corinthian Order – that would have been useless on the Acropolis.

It is sometimes said that the Greeks were not town-planners. In that they had no formally laid out cities in the grand manner, such as Rome or Paris, this may be true. Such self-conscious magnificence is the attribute of an imperial capital rather than of a small city state. In a higher sense, however, the Greeks were superb designers of cities. We see this in the careful way – geometric but not formal – that they arranged the agora and the temple groups in cities such as Miletus or Priene. The buildings on the Acropolis would seem at first sight to be almost haphazard in their placing. They were certainly not formally planned, as the Romans might

25 The Acropolis at Athens stands on a natural hill, much built up to form a platform. Here one can see, from left to right, the Propylaea, the Erechtheum and the Parthenon. The simple form of the Greek temple made it 'read' well from far off

33

26 Model reconstruction of the Athenian Acropolis, c. 400 B C. This shows the steep approach, with the Propylaea screening the full drama of the scene until the visitor had reached the summit and stood with the Parthenon on his right and the Erechtheum on his left. At the entrance the little Temple of Nikè Apteros acts as a foil to the larger buildings

have liked; but their arrangement and balance and relationship are in fact extremely skilful. As one beheld them from the entrance to the Acropolis, that is from the Propylaea, there was no symmetry. There was balance. There was the large simple mass of the Parthenon on the right, on the left the much smaller but more complex and intricate Erechtheum. Between these two the composition was resolved by the enormous statue of Athene – her flashing spear and helmet visible to sailors out on the Aegean. Finally, the Parthenon, an example of clear-cut sculptural precision, was itself so placed that it could never be seen except against the sky . . . an astonishing piece of town planning, never to be repeated.

One ascended the Acropolis by a ramp to the Propylaea. This building, designed by Mnesicles in 437 B C, is not a temple. It is a glorified gateway or porch – a covered hall with a Doric portico facing the ramp, and another opening out onto the Acropolis. It had an adjoining wing, the Pinacotheca or painted gallery. Near by, perched on a podium, was the little Temple of Nikè Apteros – the Wingless Victory – designed by Callicrates in 426 B C. This was an exquisite Ionic temple

in miniature, a gem less than 13 feet long, forming a foil to the large mass of the Parthenon when both are seen from far off.

Although the buildings on the Acropolis could be seen from a distance, it was only when one had passed through the Propylaea onto the plateau that one could see them all, at a single glance, and could then appreciate the whole drama of the scene. It was brilliant stage management.

The most venerable temple was always the Erechtheum, built by Mnesicles in 421 BC on the site of an older temple. The new Erechtheum was still connected with the most sacred myths and housed the most sacred relics. Nearly all the Greek temples – although variable in size – were rectangular and had a surrounding peristyle. The Erechtheum is unique. It is small and yet contains a number of rooms. It is irregular in its massing; it was never finished, which partly explains its unusual form. Erechtheus, Poseidon and Athene all have their separate shrines there. (Athene's second shrine – the Parthenon – was rather an upstart affair compared with this holy of holies.) It makes use of the Ionic Order three times,

27, 28 *View and plan of the Erechtheum in Athens, begun by Mnesicles in 421 BC. The temple contained shrines of Athene (in the large room to the east, right) and other gods. Attached to it are three Ionic colonnades of different size, and a rostrum with female figures ('caryatids') instead of columns. The ruins in the foreground, above, are those of the ancient temple of Athene (f, in Ill. 24)*

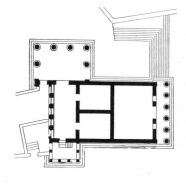

in three different sizes. Its most remarkable feature is the so-called Caryatid Portico, not truly a portico at all, but a rostrum. Sculptured maidens, 7 feet 9 inches high, take the place of columns. The obvious inherent difficulty is skilfully overcome. The sculptor has carved his maidens in such an easy pose that the marble entablature which they carry on their heads seems no burden. The Caryatid Portico is a very ornate *tour de force* which, had the Erechtheum ever been finished, might have been a jewel in the centre of a long blank wall.

The Parthenon, like the Erechtheum, replaced an older temple, but on a new site a little to the south of the older one. The Parthenon was dedicated to Athene Parthenos – the virgin Athene who had been miraculously born, adult and fully armed, from the head of Zeus. It was begun in 447 B C, by the architects Ictinus and Callicrates. Phidias was the master sculptor.

The stylobate, or stepped platform, on which the Parthenon stands is 228 feet long and 101 feet wide. The peristyle which ran all round the temple consisted of 56 columns, all of the Doric Order. There are eight columns at each end (instead of the usual six), leaving a space opposite the central entrance. There were 17 columns on each side (the south side is now incomplete), giving a central column suggestive of 'side' or no entrance. The portico at each end was two columns deep, giving greater shelter at the entrance. The shrine

30 North porch of the Erechtheum (at the top in Ill. 28). Slender Ionic columns, 25 feet high, are unusually widely spaced, giving an airy effect. Above them in the frieze white marble figures were attached to a grey stone background

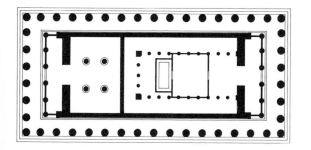

29, 31 View of the Parthenon from the north-west (opposite), and plan. Begun in 447 B C by Ictinus and Callicrates, its simplicity is deceptive (see p. 40). Within the temple the shrine faced east, divided by columns into nave and ambulatory (Ill. 32). A columned room at the west end – left – served as a treasury

32 *Reconstruction of the sanctuary in the Parthenon, looking towards the gold and ivory statue of Athene by Phidias. An ambulatory was screened off by a double tier of Doric columns. The lighting arrangements and roofing are unknown: here the artist suggests a coffered wooden ceiling, and sunlight entering by the eastern door alone*

or *naos* of the older and archaic Parthenon had been 100 Greek feet long and had, therefore, been called the Hecatompedon; this name was transferred to the *naos* of the new temple. This was about 63 feet wide, probably with columned aisles. It contained, in roughly the position where the altar stands in a Christian church, the 40-foot statue of the goddess Athene in ivory and gold by Phidias. Also enclosed in the *cella*, in addition to the *naos*, the temple had another room, about 63 by 44 feet. This was called the *parthenon* and gave its name to the entire building. The word means virgin, and this room may have been the home of the virgins who cared for the temple and tended its lamps. It was also the hieratic treasury of the Acropolis, its doors being closed with a bronze grille.

The Parthenon has no windows. How was it lit? This has always been a controversial matter. Since the seventeenth century the building has been too ruinous to allow any theory to be tested. There are, however, three such theories. The hypethral theory is that there was a large rectangular hole in the roof immediately above the shrine. This seems unlikely. There are no signs of any arrangement in the floor for draining off rain-water – relatively little though there might be in Athens. Also the hole would cause an ugly break in the roof line of a building which had, above all things, to be aesthetically perfect. The second theory is that the roof of the Parthenon, and of other temples, was of timber with thin roofing slabs of Parian marble or alabaster. These, though not transparent, would be sufficiently translucent to give a diffused glow within the shrine. Many such roofing slabs exist and this is an attractive theory assuming that there was no ceiling below the roof. The third theory is that the great eastern doors were left open and that the Greek sunshine gave all the light needed – the horizontal beams of the rising sun shining directly upon the golden statue. In spite of these dim and holy mysteries of the shrine, it was on the outside of the Parthenon that the Greek genius discovered itself.

The beauty of a ruin being adventitious, the significance of the Parthenon today lies only in its power to clarify the limitations and ideals of Hellenism. The limitations were severe, the ideals sublime. In essence the Parthenon was simple, in detail complex. In essence it was just a veranda of columns around a rectangular hall. It was not large and its roof, probably only of timber, has long since vanished. Structurally it was primitive, in every other way it was sophisticated.

Athens was a very small place. The Greeks, rejecting richness and size, chose perfection – a counterpart of the *polis*, the tiny city state, with inchoate empires all around. It was upon the simple carcass of the marble hall that they expended their skill. They kept the basic

33 View across the west end of the Parthenon, with the boldly fluted Doric columns of the peristyle on the left, and engaged columns in the cella wall on the right. Round the top of this wall – originally shaded by a coffered ceiling of which a fragment remains at the end – ran the famous frieze of the Panathenaic procession

simplicity, but made of it a vast web of geometric elaboration. This was much more than the supposed correction of optical illusions, much more than the refinement of form. It was the expression of mathematics as a thing divine. It was in this marriage of mathematics and feeling, of precision and sensuality, that the Greeks invented beauty.

The circle, the ellipse, the parabola: these are the elements that comprise this deceptively 'rectangular' building. It is a rectangle without right angles. This is the approach of the sculptor rather than the architect. Could Ictinus have carved his temple out of one block of marble he would have fulfilled an ideal. As it is the blocks were ground one on another, with water and marble dust between them, until a hair joint had been achieved. Every horizontal line – steps, cornice and so on – has a barely perceptible upward curve, with a radius of as much as two miles. The simple, unadorned and sturdy columns not only taper but, to prevent any appearance of sag, they also bulge by eleven-sixteenths of an inch – the *entasis*. The columns all tip very slightly inwards so that their central axes, if extended upwards, would meet a mile above the earth. The corner columns, where the sky is seen between them and the diffusion of light might make them seem further apart, are fraction-ally nearer together . . . and so on. No two marble blocks are identical, each has its mirror image only on the other side of the temple. The whole building tends subtly towards the pyramidal – grace tending towards strength.

Apart from the long-vanished Athene of the shrine, Phidias's sculptures were in three 'movements', all integral with the architecture. First, were the statues in the pediments – the birth of Athene at one end of the temple, and Athene's contest with Poseidon for the soil of Attica at the other end. These pediment sculptures are over life-size; they are in the round and stood out against the shadow which they cast on the wall behind

them. Like the columns themselves they were large enough to 'read' from the streets of the city.

Second, and next in scale, were the carvings on the metopes – the slabs which, alternately with solid blocks, formed a frieze above the columns and below the cornice. The metope sculptures, showing struggles such as the battle between the Centaurs and the Lapiths, are slightly less than life-size and in high relief; they were intended to 'read' only after one had climbed the steps of the Propylaea, and could view them across, say, the width of the Acropolis.

Third, the famous Parthenon frieze. This, not to be confused with the metope carvings just referred to, was placed at the top of the wall of the cella. It could not, therefore, be seen until it was meant to be seen – as one stood under the colonnade and looked up at the wall itself. Thus it could be in very low relief. The whole frieze has as its subject the Panathenaic procession towards the ancient image of the goddess Athene kept in the Erechtheum and the ceremony at the shrine. The most famous figures are the lightly prancing cavalry; the most beautiful are the gods seated in easy conversation over the eastern doorway.

34 The Theatre of Dionysus in Athens (c.330 BC) was the first great theatre in the world, with perfect vision and acoustics for an audience of 30,000. The present stage arrangement is Hellenistic: originally there would have been a narrower stage (at the top), adequate for the small cast of a Greek play, and a circular orchestra where the chorus performed, between actors and audience

Deep in the crevices of the carving tiny traces of colour have been found. All the sculptures were certainly highly coloured, as were all the shrines and sarcophagi of the Mediterranean world for a thousand years. The whole temple may even have been coloured. Those pale gods may once have borne the touch of Madame Tussaud. This is inescapable. The mouldering and moonlit ruin – pagan or medieval – was a product of the Romantic Movement. What the modern tourist thinks as he mounts the Acropolis, what were the thoughts of the generation of Byron or Chateaubriand, are things that would have been as utterly incomprehensible to the Periclean Greek with his precise mind as he is to us.

At the foot of the Acropolis is the Theatre of Dionysus, dating from 330 BC. The theatre at Epidauros (350 BC) is perhaps more beautiful and better preserved, but the Theatre of Dionysus is the prototype of all Greek theatres and indeed the ancestor, by way of Rome, of all the theatres in the world. The Greeks neither needed nor attempted to build a covered theatre. It would have been beyond their structural means to construct a roof of such enormous span. Nor did they attempt to build up an auditorium of steeply raked seats on a substructure of arches and vaults, as did the Romans. Instead, the Greeks chose a naturally sloping site. Once again, in fact, as in the temples, they aimed at perfection within their own limits. Out of doors, on marble seats, with perfect vision and perfect acoustics, the Theatre of Dionysus seated thirty thousand spectators. The stage, with a wall behind it, was narrow, but was sufficient for the very limited number of actors. In front of the stage was the *orkestra*, where the chorus commented on the action of the play. The front seats were splendid marble thrones for the use of the entire priesthood. Except for the absence of scenery, all the essentials of the theatre as we know it were present in the Theatre of Dionysus.

35 One of the seats of honour in the front row of the Theatre of Dionysus. The vast majority of the audience sat on the tiers of marble steps, visible in the background, built on the sloping hillside

We shall never quite know what it was that caused a small Latin tribe to conquer the world and to build that empire from which we are all come – our laws, our learning, our religion, our roads, our agriculture and our architecture. At its height, by the third century A D, the Roman Empire stretched from somewhere in Scotland, north of Hadrian's Wall, right across to the Persian Gulf. It embraced much of Arabia and North Africa. These were not ephemeral conquests. This was the Empire which Rome – with roads, law, garrisons and a postal system – organized and exploited, and for which it built cities.

What were the qualities of such superb administrators. 'The Roman', said Seneca, 'came into the world with a sword in one hand and a spade in the other.' The Roman was everything that the Greek was not. The Greek and the Roman were at opposite poles. Where Greece failed, Rome was destined to succeed, while the Roman was to fail where the Greek had been most brilliant. The Athenian was inward-looking, contemptuous of the non-Hellene; the Roman legionary marched to the ends of the earth, first conquering and then absorbing the subject peoples, until not even the emperors were necessarily Roman.

The Greco-Roman relationship was one of the great love-hates of history. The Roman despised the Greek as effeminate and tricky, and yet all Roman intellectual life, from the nursery to the university, was saturated with Greek thought. Roman architecture adopted the

36 Detail of a model of Rome c. A D 300, looking from the Capitoline Hill towards the Colosseum, with the Palatine Hill on the right. From the Colosseum (1), the Sacred Way led past the Temple of Venus and Roma (2), the Basilica of Maxentius (3), the House of the Vestals (4), the Temple of Antoninus and Faustina (5) and the Temple of Castor and Pollux (6). Off it to the south lay the Temple of Augustus (7), the Basilica Julia (8) and the Temple of Saturn (9). To the north stood the Basilica AEmiliana (10) and the Curia (11). The Imperial forums lay beyond, built by Vespasian (12), Nerva (13), Caesar (14), Augustus (15) and Trajan (16). In the foreground is the Temple of Jupiter Capitolinus (17). The public buildings have colonnades; the private houses are plain

45

trappings of the Greek style – columns, pediments, cornices, etc. – and yet, so unimportant is 'style' compared with culture, the two architectures express the extremes of human thought.

The Greek was a deeply religious artist. His greatest architectural achievement was the temple – the carved shrine. The Roman, on the other hand, saw architecture primarily as structure; he was absorbed by the enclosure of space, of large floor areas, by means of vaults or domes – feats of engineering in stone, brick or concrete. The Roman was also the greatest vulgarian of history, lavish in his use of ornament, carving, mosaic, paint and gilding. These things, all too often, concealed the splendid simplicity of the underlying structure. Like our own dams or silos, the utilitarian structures – bridges, roads and aqueducts – are some of the Roman Empire's finest monuments, exemplifying its finest qualities.

The contrast between the Greek temple and the Roman temple reveals the whole character of a people. The Greek temple, as we have seen, was a shrine, aloof and isolated. The Roman temple, like some Baroque

37 The Maison Carrée at Nîmes (c. 16 BC) is the best-preserved Roman temple. With its portico – of Corinthian columns – only on the entrance side and its big flight of steps it emphasizes the response of the Roman temple of town-planning: civic architecture in the street rather than the Greek acropolis

church, was a feature in the street; it had a façade with a great flight of steps leading to a richly carved Corinthian portico. One was a tribute to the deity; the other was an expression of imperial pride, an urban monument. Such pride is a quality of empire builders. It was, in its most monumental form, one of the greatest things that Rome left to the world. The Greeks also had a wonderful sense of town planning, but of a different kind – restrained and exquisite as we have already seen in our analysis of the buildings of the Acropolis. The Greek town of Miletus has been called 'one of the most splendid city plans ever made', combining great artistry with the use of a basic grid. On analysis, however, we find that the Greek work of the fourth century BC is extremely modest – an agora and a colonnaded street. A further extension of the town on an imperial scale belongs to the second century and is Hellenistic; it is symmetrical and formal. All the rest is Roman. The Roman gave to history not only engineering as the basis of architecture, but also town-planning as a conscious and monumental art. The Roman virtually invented the capital

38 *Looking along the Roman forum from the Basilica Julia (8, in Ill. 36) towards the Colosseum; three columns from the Temple of Castor and Pollux (6) still stand, on the right. On the left, the Temple of Antoninus and Faustina (5), transformed into a church: it stands directly on the Sacred Way and, like the Maison Carrée, has a portico only at the front*

city. Rome itself was the first of a long line culminating in Vienna, Paris and Washington. And with that out-ward expression of imperialism there came also into art the 'grand manner' – the formal axis, the triumphal arch, the culminating palace, the avenue, the fountains and all the symmetrical attributes of power and vanity.

With this emergence into history of the capital city, there came also the innumerable types of building of which a city is made: palaces, theatres, temples, courts, tenements, libraries, villas and so on. The Seven Hills of Rome were covered with them. With their carvings and their gilding many were intensely vulgar; many, with their large internal spaces, demanded the highest skill of the engineer.

The Roman was seldom either serene, refined or exalted. In Roman art and architecture we look for other qualities. We may expect to find fine, dignified and even grandiose planning; large, daring and efficient structures; lavish ornament of all kind. The Greeks of the Classical age produced a little architecture and a little sculpture, all of the highest order; Imperial Rome produced vast quantities of both, mostly second-rate.

Large areas of ancient Rome were slums. Huge gim-crack tenement blocks frequently collapsed, burying the inhabitants in the ruins. Each of the more important emperors, however, left his mark upon the city. This was only partly due to the policy of 'bread and circuses', the pacification of the mob by doles and entertainments. No doubt the amphitheatres, theatres, arenas and public baths in Rome, like the victories abroad, increased the

39 The surviving north aisle of the Basilica of Maxentius in the Roman forum, finished sometime after AD 313. It consists of three vast niches with coffered tunnel vaults, which buttressed the high groin vaults of the central hall (see Ill. 40). The decorative facing has vanished, exposing the brick and mortar which form the core of most great Roman and Byzantine buildings

40 *Reconstruction of the Basilica of Maxentius (see Ill. 39), looking towards the western apse. The nave is covered by three massive coffered groin vaults, making large clerestory windows possible – a scheme similar to that in the thermae (Ills. 43, 44). Aisles are formed by piercing the big lateral buttresses*

prestige of the imperial power, but the emperors also liked to set the seal of their own magnificence upon the city. The triumphal arches, the equestrian statues, the paved and colonnaded forums, the temples and the courts were for posterity.

Rome, for all this grandeur, was a piecemeal city: its grandeur was mainly due to a series of pretentious additions planned by each emperor with too little regard for the work of his predecessor. Rome's wonderful site, the hills north of the Tiber, prevented any great system of symmetry. Each of the six imperial forums must be judged in isolation. Rome could never have been seen as a whole, and is now so ruinous – it became a quarry for later builders – that it can be seen only through the imagination. We can still trace, however, the outline of the larger forums and many of the buildings. Some of the triumphal arches remain, as do the columns of Trajan and Hadrian. The Pantheon, the Colosseum and the great thermae were all virtually indestructible. They have been mutilated and stripped, but their basic structure remains as Rome's precious gift to the world. A substantial portion survives of the great Basilica Nova of Maxentius, finished by Constantine after AD 313. It was groin-vaulted in three vast bays, buttressed by massive partitions in the aisles. One of these aisles still stands complete, with deeply coffered transverse tunnel vaults.

The Romans needed large buildings. They liked the massive and the durable, stone, brick and mass concrete. They were fortunate in having Pozzolana cement, the best in the world. Their architecture had as its basis the round arch, and they exploited it fully. The arch is a way of using small stones to span a wide area. A temporary arch of timber called 'centering' is fitted between the walls, and a number of wedge-shaped stones – voussoirs – are placed on it. When the last voussoir – the keystone – is in position the arch is complete and the timber centering may be removed. Only the crushing strength of the material, capable of disintegrating under its own weight, sets a limit to the span of the arch. The Romans frequently built arches with spans of over 80 feet.

A series of arches may be built side by side. This, obviously, will form a semi-circular roof – a tunnel vault. This is the most elementary form of vault. Equally, if over a circular space a number of arches are built, all meeting at the centre, the result is a dome. A cross-section through a dome at any point is an arch. Arches, arcades, vaults and domes are all variations upon the theme of the arch. This theme, whatever stylistic changes there might be, was the basis of European architecture.

A beam exerts a direct downward pressure. Not so the arch. The Arabs have a saying that 'the arch never sleeps'. It exerts outward thrust, always trying to push the wall over. Any arch, vault or dome must have this outward thrust opposed by a counter-force such as another arch, a thick wall or a buttress. In Gothic architecture the buttress became an important decorative feature, but decorative or not its principle must always be there even if, as in Roman architecture, it is hidden somewhere in the structure. This system of thrust and counter-thrust, while giving wonderful scope to the planner, is also one of the limitations of arcuated building. A continuous tunnel vault exerts tremendous thrust along its base and must rest on a suitably thick wall; this

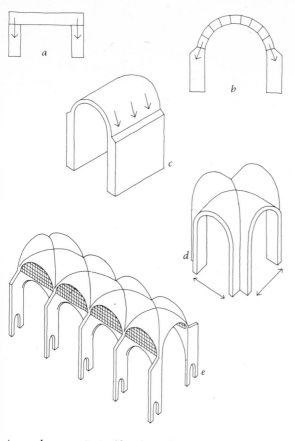

is cumbersome in itself and an obstruction to adequate windows. It creates an architecture of weight and gloom, exemplified in the Romanesque style of the pilgrimage roads (see p. 103).

The Romans, however, discovered the more ingenious method known as the groin vault. This consists of two *intersecting* tunnel vaults over a square bay; it solved five problems: 1, it concentrated the thrust at the four corners of the vaulting bay; 2, it made possible, in theory, the total abolition of the wall except for buttresses at the four corners; 3, it enabled large windows to be inserted high up under the arches of the vaults – the clerestory; 4, it enabled the timber centering used for one bay of vaulting to be dismantled and used again for the next bay; 5, it enabled several square bays to open one from the other. The main halls of the great thermae usually consisted of three square vaulting bays, each about 80 feet, giving a rectangular hall 80 feet wide and 240 feet long, splendidly lit, and with side aisles in addition, filling the space between the buttresses. All the main structural elements of the great cathedrals – nave, aisles, vaults, clerestory – as we find them a thousand years later, were now inherent in European architecture.

The Roman thermae were not mere public baths; they were an essential part of public life, centres for business, exercise and culture during the day, centres for pleasure during the night. Agrippa, Trajan, Caracalla and Diocletian all gave large thermae in the larger provincial cities – no less than eleven in the North African city of Timgad. The vaulted halls, the main architectural legacy of the thermae, were only the core of a vast complex of rooms and courts. The Thermae of Caracalla, for instance, were a fifth of a mile across. They were laid out in a small park with a running track, a grandstand and a wrestling arena. While the main hall, off which the *tepidarium* opened, had three bays of vaulting, the hot

42, 43 Thermae of Caracalla, Rome (AD 211–17): air view from the west, and plan (opposite). The air view may easily be collated with the plan: the semicircular area in the foreground is the site of the calidarium (5). The ruins still show the massiveness of Roman structure. The highly symmetrical nature of the plan, as well as its vastness, is clear. Its chief features (opposite) are: (1) main entrance, between rows of small baths and shops; (2) entrance halls; (3) frigidarium; (4) central hall, with tepidarium to the south; (5) calidarium; (6) private baths; (7) sudatoria; (8) open peristyles; (9) gymnasia; (10) park with trees; (11) stadium; (12) lecture halls and libraries; (13) reservoirs; (14) Marcian aqueduct

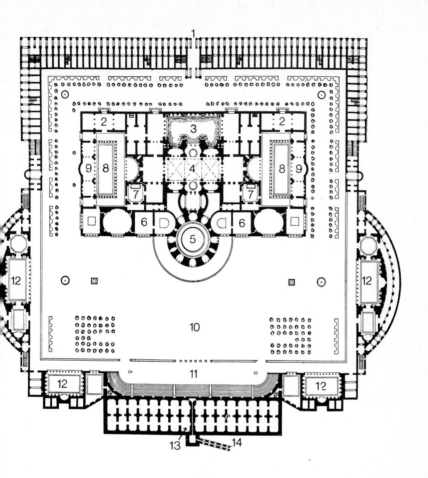

bath (*calidarium*) was domed. This dome we must envisage as gorgeously painted and filled with steam. The heating was achieved by forcing hot air through brick flues built under the floor and in the thickness of the walls. The cold bath – the *frigidarium* – was as elaborate as the others in its decoration, but was open to the sky. The thermae needed a big water supply. Of the fourteen aqueducts bringing water across the Campagna to Rome, one was wholly reserved for the Thermae of Caracalla. The subsidiary rooms included small theatres, libraries, lecture halls, as well as many private bath-rooms, massage-rooms and dining-halls. There

53

44 The tepidarium of the Thermae of Diocletian (AD 302) converted by Michelangelo into a church, Sta Maria degli Angeli in Rome shows clearly the scale and structure, as well as the lighting, of such Roman vaulted halls as the Basilica of Maxentius (Ills. 39, 40) and the central hall of the Thermae of Caracalla (4, in Ill. 43)

were two gymnasia for the training of youths. The plan was highly formal and rigidly symmetrical at the absurd cost of duplicating every item of accommodation on either side of the main axis. Symmetry must have been thought of as synonymous with grandeur.

The Roman vaulted hall gave Europe its first large scientific structure. It was a seminal building. The thermae also show the first functional plan of a multi-purpose building. A replica of the hall of the Thermae of Caracalla could be seen until recently in the now-demolished concourse of Pennsylvania Station, New York (1906–10). The Thermae of Agrippa (20 BC) have vanished, so have the Thermae of Trajan. The Thermae of Diocletian (AD 302), accommodating three thousand bathers, were similar to the Thermae of Caracalla; the vaulted hall may still be seen, converted by Michelangelo in the sixteenth century into the Church of Sta Maria degli Angeli.

In devising the groin vault the Romans went a long way towards solving the problem of a highly architectural, fireproof roof over a large area. There remained one limitation. The fact that the arches on all four sides of the vaulting bay had all to rise to the same height – to give a level roof line – necessitated square vaulting bays, and this imposed a system of planning on a square module. It was left to the builders of St-Denis in the eleventh century to make the breakthrough, to build steeply pointed arches over short spans, less steeply pointed arches over wide spans, thus giving complete flexibility of plan. Meanwhile, however, despite this tyranny of the square bay, the Romans were able to build on a very large scale.

The Romans also developed the arcuated system in the dome. The essential problem of dome building, however, they never solved. Just as building vaults only over square bays inhibited the plan so building domes only over circular spaces also inhibited the plan. In the dome of the Pantheon the Romans gave to their Byzantine successors a magnificent inspiration, but they left it to Byzantium to solve the problem of effectively placing a circular dome over a square. On its own terms, the Pantheon (as rebuilt AD 120–4) has one of the five great domes of the world, with Hagia Sophia in Byzantium,

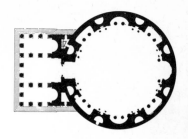

45, 46 Plan and section of the Pantheon in Rome (AD 120–4; to different scales), an absolute circle with an attached portico. The thick walls are cut into at a low level by niches and recesses, but their mass is carried up around the base of the vast coffered dome. The big open 'eye' at the top lights the room, while reducing the weight, and therefore the thrust, of the dome

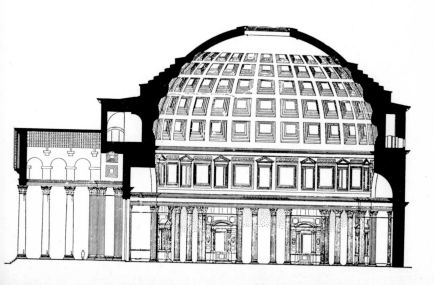

the Duomo in Florence, St Peter's in Rome and St Paul's in London. Hagia Sophia covered the greatest floor area but was not impressive externally; the later domes of Florence, Rome and London – being surmounted by lanterns – have dramatic skylines, but have to have their tremendous outward thrust countered by being chained in at the base. The most impressive of domes, as well as the simplest, is the Pantheon.

The Pantheon is a circular temple, 142 feet 6 inches in diameter. Its internal height is exactly the same, and the dome is semi-circular. In other words, a sphere 142 feet 6 inches in diameter would fit exactly inside the Pantheon. It was dedicated to the deities of the seven planets. Its spherical form is symbolic of the cosmos. The great 'eye' in the dome, 27 feet across, is the only source of light, and was symbolic of the sun; the bronze

stars originally set in each coffer were the stars of heaven. Externally the dome was once covered with golden tiles so that seen from the surrounding hills it again symbolized the sun. When the priest sacrificed a beast upon the central altar, the smoke wound upwards to the 'eye', while the single shaft of sunlight cast all shadows downwards. If the halls of the thermae were among the most gaudy interiors of the ancient world, the Pantheon is among the most solemn of all time. In spite of its simplicity – or because of it – the Pantheon was no solution to the essential problem of dome build‑ ing. The rotunda, though large, is the simplest form ever invented, and with that simplicity the Romans were content. The rotunda has a wall 20 feet thick and only in the lower part – far below the line of the dome's thrust – is it cut into by recesses for altars or statues. The wall's

48 *The Pantheon, stripped of its marble sheathing and the gilded tiles which once covered the dome, is now less impressive externally than internally. The portico with its giant unfluted Corinthian columns is characteristically Roman – but must always have been awkward in relation to the rotunda*

full thickness is taken up above the dome's springing level so that the thrust can be met by piling mass and weight at the dome's base, while the apex is lightened by the simple expedient of omitting it altogether, that is, by means of the central 'eye'. The whole problem, within the limits of a dome over a circle, is thus met in the most direct manner.

The arch, in its development as vault and dome, gave us such monuments as the thermae or the Pantheon. As a simple arch it gave us such highly functional things as bridges and aqueducts. The finest is probably the Pont du Gard near Nîmes in southern France (*c.*AD 14).

It was 900 feet long and carried the water channel across the valley, 180 feet above the river Gard, on three ranges of arches. Its strictly utilitarian character is shown by the fact that the projecting stones which were used to support the centering and scaffolding were never cut back. This was engineering rather than 'architecture'; the Romans would have been astonished could they have known that it would be regarded as one of their finest works. Thanks to the thermae and the fountains, Rome's water consumption was about the same as that of Victorian London, but of the many aqueducts supplying the city only fragments now remain. A substantial part

49 *The Pont du Gard, built about AD 14, carried the water supply of the city of Nîmes in a channel some 180 feet above the river. This virtuoso use of arches – the bridge still stands to its full height – is the finest Roman display of pure engineering*

of the Segovian Aqueduct in Spain (AD 10) does, however, survive: it is another splendid range of arches built under the Emperor Augustus.

The most obvious use of the arch is as a single monument, the triumphal arch. Indeed, it may be said that the Romans had a pathological obsession with the arch, as there was to be a Byzantine obsession with the dome and a Gothic one with the tower. One Roman emperor after another built a triumphal arch to his own glory. The Arch of Trajan at Ancona (AD 113) stands simply and proudly on the quay; it commands the eye whether from land or sea. The triumphal arches in Rome are more elaborate and often their ornate realism obscures the nobility of the basic arcuated form. It must be admitted that, in the end, it was the Emperor Napoleon who in 1807 built the finest triumphal arch of all, the Arc de Triomphe in Paris.

A much more important use of the arch was in the hidden structure. While the palaces and villas on the Palatine are now only a legend, their foundations exist as vaulted cellars. Prior to the invention of the steel girder it was the arch or vault alone that could carry a superstructure, and it was this function of the arch that made possible the Roman theatre. The Greek theatre, such as the Theatre of Dionysus in Athens, was a wonderful auditorium, never excelled. But, as we have seen (pp. 42–3) it was necessarily built on a sloping site since the Greeks knew of no way in which the raked seating could be supported except on the solid earth. The Romans could build their theatres and amphitheatres wherever it suited them, the seating supported by range upon range of arches.

Both the theatre and the amphitheatre or arena were important in Roman architecture and culture. The arenas were not – as is popularly supposed – wholly given over to throwing Christians to lions. The persecutions were occasional episodes. The arenas were more often used for violent and dangerous sports, tattoos,

50 *The Arch of Trajan at Ancona (AD 113) was purely decorative and ceremonial, standing in isolation on the end of the quay. While simpler than the arches in Rome, it has the same features: a central opening with flanking features framed by columns, and an 'attic' stage above the cornice. The tripartite division of the triumphal arch gave architecture a new motif (see, e.g. Ills. 199, 201, 204)*

naval displays – for which purpose they could be flooded – and for gigantic spectacles, often sadistic and obscene. Equally the theatres were not devoted entirely to bawdy comedies; serious drama, including the great Greek plays, was performed to full houses. The theatres themselves were a step forward in the long story that runs from the simple outdoor arenas of ancient Crete to the modern opera house.

The Romans turned the plain *skena* wall which had backed the Greek stage into an elaborate set piece with columns, niches and statuary, although it still lacked any naturalistic scenery. They enlarged the stage and greatly increased the backstage accommodation to cope with elaborate productions. Restaurants, foyers and promenades were now a major part of the theatre plan.

Almost all the larger Roman cities – Verona, Pompeii, Nîmes, Arles, Pula – had big amphitheatres and a theatre as well; even small towns, such as Verulamium (St Albans) in Britain, had at least one theatre. Jerash in Jordan (AD 100) is a good provincial example. It had stepped stone seating supported on vaults, an orchestral area, actors' entrance from the wings, and a large stage with an ornate back wall. There was a timber roof, but this was apparently only over the stage. (We recall that, even in a northern climate, the cheaper seats of the Elizabethan theatres were not covered.) The Jerash theatre seated four thousand five hundred, about twice as many as the Paris Opera House. Aspendus in Asia Minor has a similar theatre in good preservation, but the most magnificent is that at Orange in Provence, built about AD 50. This seated seven thousand. The diameter of its half-circle is 340 feet. The stage was 203 feet wide and 45 feet deep. The great surrounding wall was 116 feet high. There are still stone corbels on this wall to support the masts from which was slung the *velarium* or awning, for shading the seats. The wall at the back of the stage was most elaborate – a kind of Roman Baroque – and the central niche still holds a white marble statue of Augustus. The most complete ornate stage wall (*scaenae frons*) survives at Sabratha in North Africa.

51 The stage at Sabratha in Libya (c. AD 200) was backed by three tiers of coloured stone columns. Actors entered through three passages marked by taller columns, such as the one visible on the right. Below the stage – whose raised front is curved and decorated with reliefs – is the semi-circular orchestra; around it stone seats rise on vaulted corridors. Large halls on either side of the stage served as foyers

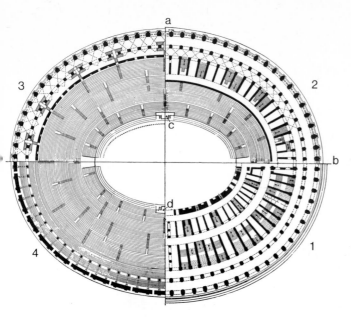

The largest of the amphitheatres was the Colosseum in Rome. It was begun by Vespasian in AD 70 and finished by Domitian twelve years later. Much of it is in ruins, but enough is preserved to enable one to envisage the whole building. It is a big ellipse 620 feet by 513 feet, and rises on a flat site where there was once a lake, between the Esquiline and the Caelian hills. All the stone seating had therefore to be built up on a most elaborate series of vaulted corridors, some concentric with the ellipse and some radial, and some containing the exit staircases. In the intervals the audience could stroll in the vaulted corridors, looking down upon the street below. The amphitheatre seated fifty thousand, but could be cleared in a few minutes. The seats were divided by horizontal gangways into four classes – the two lower being for those of patrician rank. The imperial box was at one end of the arena, the gladiators' entrance at the opposite end. The arena itself was 287 feet by 180 feet. Beneath it was a maze of rooms – stores, dressing-rooms, animals' dens and so on. With the floor of the arena now removed many of these can be seen. The

52, 53 Colosseum, Rome (AD 70–82): plan and half-section. The composite plan of the four storeys (1–4) shows the position of the emperor's entrance (a), gladiators' entrances (b), emperor's box (c) and consul's box (d). Both plan and section show clearly the system of radial walls which supported the seating, and provided access corridors and promenades. The section (across the right half of the plan) also shows the position of the masts – top right – which supported the velarium shading the imperial box

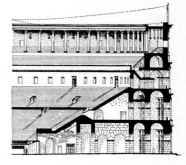

54 *Colosseum, Rome. Note the use of superimposed orders, each with its own entablature, in the form of half-columns attached to piers, and pilasters on a plain wall. Behind the arches were promenades*

55, 56 *Opposite, above: at Petra (c.AD 120) the upper pediment of the rock-cut 'Treasury' opens in an unorthodox way to frame a kind of circular temple with an ornate top – playing with shapes and motifs in a way that looks forward to Baroque (Ill. 241).*
Below: Timgad, built c.AD 100 on a typical Roman grid plan. From the triumphal arch the colonnaded main street runs eastward, bisecting the town. In the southern half lie the forum (top left in the picture) and theatre

velarium, slung from masts, was moved round as the hot afternoon wore on; it is said that sailors manipulated the ropes. In fact this *velarium* may have done little more than shade the imperial box.

The outer wall of the Colosseum is 157 feet high, and is divided into four storeys. The lower three each have eighty arched openings, separated by Roman versions of the orders – Tuscan (plain and unfluted), at the bottom, then Ionic, then Composite. The solid wall of the top stage is articulated by pilasters. The structure is of mass concrete faced with brick, the brick casing actually forming the shuttering into which the concrete was poured. The Colosseum is equally impressive as a structure and as a piece of planning for large crowds.

Some of the most exotic Roman architecture is in the outlying cities of the Empire, more in the Eastern provinces, where old cultures existed, than in the bleak, barbaric lands of Western Europe. Jerash and Petra in Jordan, Baalbek in Lebanon, Timgad in North Africa and, above all, Palmyra . . . all these show an imposition of the Roman style upon an existing Greek or oriental culture. The result is a heady mixture, and in many of these towns there are architectural features such as broken pediments and curving walls which were not seen again until the rise of Baroque in seventeenth century Rome. The theatre at Jerash has already been mentioned. Petra – the 'rose red city, half as old as time' – is older than Rome, but its dramatic tombs, cut from the actual rock, are late Roman, extremely rich and stylized; so too is the town gateway, where Corinthian columns are used purely as sculptural decoration.

Palmyra was an oasis city, first a camp, then a settlement on one of the Asian caravan routes, then finally a wealthy Roman town. It reached the peak of its great prosperity about AD 270. Rose Macaulay wrote in *The Pleasure of Ruins*: 'What we see today, the fabulous ochre-coloured colonnades, the Temple of the Sun with its pillared court, the great fields of ruins like a garden of broken daffodils, lying within the long low shattered line of Justinian's wall, is Graeco-Roman

57 *A main street at Palmyra, in Syria, lined with Corinthian colonnades (late 2nd century). The brackets held bronze statuettes*

of the more florid period.' There was a big marble-paved forum. The surrounding streets were colonnaded and the vista at the end of each was focused upon either a triumphal arch or another colonnade. The columns gave shade to the footwalks. Many of them have projecting stone brackets about two-thirds of the way up. These bore bronze statues, and may also have had mats hung from them to give additional shade to the shops. This gorgeous and lively scene owed much to the Emperor Severus whose empress was a Syrian.

Baalbek (the Greek Heliopolis or City of the Sun) is rich in marble and is magnificently sited, with the temples on rising ground. It was built mainly in the time of Caracalla, and has two of the finest temples outside Rome. The better preserved of the two, the so-called Temple of Bacchus (late second century), has one of the most complete Roman interiors to have survived. The portico has a ceiling made of solid blocks of marble of incredible richness. The less well preserved temple, that of Jupiter, has monolithic columns 65 feet high and 7 feet in diameter. It was the crowning feature of a vast town-planning sequence; a huge hexagonal court and a propylaea with bronze gates were only a part of it. A ramp led down to a crypt beneath the altar where a sacrificial beast could be kept ready for slaughter. The interior of the temple was described by a French traveller in the nineteenth century as 'groaning beneath the weight of its own luxuriance'.

In the face of such buildings as the Pantheon, the Colosseum or these Asiatic temples, the Roman house must take second place. Under the pressure of increasing population, in certain cities – notably Rome and its port of Ostia – large tenements of brick with as many as six storeys were built. Though these might easily become squalid rabbit-warrens, they were a rational solution to the problem of housing large numbers where building-land was expensive. Unlike the typical Roman villa, they had windows to the street.

Any simple Mediterranean town of today, on the other hand, may give some idea of what the middle-class Roman house looked like: white walls, no windows to the street, a flat roof and sometimes an inner court. At its best it was simple, cool and secluded. In Pompeii,

58 Reconstruction of the 'Temple of Bacchus' at Baalbek (late 2nd century). The walls have two tiers of niches linked by giant Corinthian half-columns supporting a coffered wooden ceiling. In the shrine, up a flight of steps at the far end, this arrangement was repeated with columns of green marble, and crowned by a broken pediment

where many wealthy Romans had their villas, some houses were more elaborate than others, but were still basically of this type. Apart from the forum, the theatre and other public buildings, Pompeii was a town of narrow streets, the stone paving worn into grooves by the chariot wheels. Each house, or each back-to-back group of houses, filled a block. There was a door and, if the owner was a shopkeeper, an open shop to the street; otherwise all the rooms looked inwards. It all dates from sometime before AD 79, the year when the Vesuvian eruption both buried and preserved the town. Luxurious villas, such as the House of the Vettii, the House of Pansa or the House of the Faun might have several internal courtyards – the peristyle with a colonnaded cloister around it, and the atrium with a central pool – around which the public rooms, for services and enter-tainment, and the family rooms were grouped. The total effect as one entered from the street was that of a long shaded vista slashed across with sunlight. The decoration of these rooms – richly coloured panels framing painted fantasies in the likeness of arbours, little temples or dancing nymphs – was among the more charming of the sophisticated styles of history. 'Pompeian' rooms

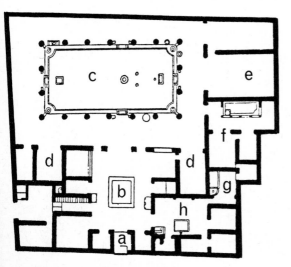

62 *Detail of a model of Hadrian's Villa (c.AD 130). Many of its features were symbolic: thus the pattern for the 'Poikile' (6) was the philosophers' meeting-place in Athens; the 'Canopus' Canal (10) – lined with copies of the Erechtheum caryatids – led to an 'Egyptian' shrine, the Serapeum. At the hub of the scheme was the palace (1) with its courts, of which the most remarkable is the Piazza d'Oro (2); around it were libraries (3), the curious circular Naval Theatre (4), the 'Philosophers' Hall' (5), a stadium (7), baths (8) and storerooms (9)*

are found among the rich interiors both of the First Empire in France, and of Georgian and Regency England.

In Rome itself the Golden House of Nero (except for some galleries) and the other palaces have all vanished. Only outside Rome, where Hadrian's Villa (c.AD 130) stretches for over a mile near Tivoli, are there pools, fountains, courts, Greek sculpture and the ruins of colonnades, libraries and music-rooms. Here the great Emperor, creator of the Pantheon, who almost realized the Greek ideal of the philosopher-king, passed his last serene years.

Chapter Four

THE BYZANTINE EMPIRE

The logical sequel to Roman architecture is Early
Christian. But the story of architecture in the West
forms such a continuous whole that it seems preferable
not to disturb it. I have therefore chosen to deal with
Byzantine architecture (a combination, to put it very
briefly, of Roman and Eastern currents) before going on
to the developments in the West that were to lead via
Carolingian and Romanesque to Gothic.

On 25 July in AD 306, outside the walls of York,
Constantine was acclaimed Emperor of the World, his
legionaries raising him aloft upon a shield. Seven years
later, in the Edict of Milan, Constantine gave freedom
and official standing to the Christian Church. Although
Constantine was baptized only on his deathbed, he
proclaimed himself the Thirteenth Apostle and believed
that after death he would be absorbed into the Trinity.
His choice of a saviour and messiah, out of all the multi-
farious deities available to him, was opportunist and
political. It secured for him the loyalty of the army and
the people. Even so, with the subject tribes pressing hard
upon the frontiers of a dying Empire, Rome herself was
in peril, and in 334 Constantine decided to move his
capital from Rome to the old Hellenic town of Byzantium upon the shores of the Bosphorus. It was a most
momentous decision.

The new city which 'arose like an exhalation in the
night' was renamed Constantinople, but the culture of
which it was the heart will always be known as Byzantine.
That city was founded upon a key strategic site, the

meeting-place of all the maritime and caravan routes of the ancient world. Cities as far apart as Venice and Kiev were within its immediate orbit, while Peking was within its knowledge. It was intended to be a great Latin and Christian capital. Although governed by emperors of many races calling themselves Roman – Romaioi – the Latin elements were in fact soon submerged by the existing Greek culture. But Christian it remained from the fourth century to the fifteenth, from the arrival of Constantine until it fell to the Turks in 1453. That fall seemed to some men to be the end of the world.

Byzantium inherited the artistry of the Greek world – almost all individual artists were Greek – and married to it the structural and engineering genius of Rome. It could escape neither the colour nor the mysticism of the East. All this Byzantium exploited to the glory of the Church which was intent, both in its liturgy and its architecture, upon showing that the teachings of Jesus had been transmuted into an institution which was imperial, powerful, hierarchical, sacerdotal and divine. The result was one of the great architectures of history.

The key, the sign manual, of Byzantine architecture is the dome. To understand this we must glance at those basic structural forms of Roman architecture, one of which travelled westwards to be ultimately developed into the cathedrals of medieval Europe; while the other travelled eastwards to be developed into the domed churches of the Byzantine Empire.

Roman architecture was rich and complex, but two main elements may be detached from the total picture. Among the various great halls that the Romans built there are two basic types – the rectangular and the circular. Whatever stylistic changes might transform Roman architecture during the thousand years that followed upon the fall of the Empire, it is obvious that the long-aisled basilica and the vaulted hall of the thermae – both rectangular – contained in embryo almost all the structural elements of the Gothic cathedral. The basilica and the vaulted hall merged to make medieval architecture, an architecture of the long perspective, of the long vista, of the repetitive rhythm of vaulting bays, all leading to the dim and distant mystery of the sacrament concealed within the chancel.

The Byzantine story is quite different. Gothic and Byzantine architecture are best clarified by opposing them to one another: they are contrasts in structure, plan and decoration. Rome, however, is still the starting-point. A more impressive achievement than the Roman handling of the rectangular hall was the circular hall. The greatest dome the Romans built was the Pantheon, internally at least one of the truly great buildings of history (see pp. 55-7). The Pantheon – a complete circle lit by a circular eye at its apex – must have had a tremendous emotional appeal to an imperial and hierarchic mind. It was cosmic. It was built by Hadrian but must have been admired by Constantine. It was pagan and Roman, and yet also was a perfect expression of the Byzantine mind.

The Pantheon was not the only Roman building which the Byzantine architects must have studied with more than academic interest. Another was the so-called Temple of Minerva Medica, a pagan nymphaeum of AD 260, with a dome 80 feet in diameter. The Minerva Medica, however, was not a square but a decagon, involving only tiny pendentives at each of its ten corners. Ribs within the thickness of the dome concentrated the thrust on to the ten massive piers, so that between those ten piers there need be virtually no wall, and ten spacious apses could open out from the central area, a Roman foreshadowing of Byzantine achievement.

Some Roman domed buildings – mausolea, thermae – had been turned into Christian churches, and a few new domed churches had been built: the most interesting is the fourth-century S. Lorenzo at Milan (since rebuilt), which seems to foreshadow S. Vitale. But in the West the dome never became an accepted architectural

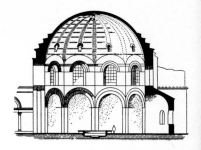

63, 64 *Minerva Medica, Rome (AD 260 and later): plan, and section along the entrance axis. The original design appears in black on the plan. The concrete dome rested on a decagon, buttressed by nine small apses; pendentives, however embryonic, were there. (The apses proved inadequate, and buttresses – at the top in the plan – and large exedrae were added)*

feature. Even in the East, the precedents before Justinian are few and most of them (e.g. Constantine's
Church of the Resurrection at Jerusalem) dodged the
real issue by being roofed with wood rather than stone.

The story of Byzantine architecture, therefore, involves
first the solution of the structural problems inherent in
dome building; second, the discovery of a decorative
system suitable for such buildings; third, the integration
of plan and liturgy, or what we would call 'function'.
In fact, of course, as in any great architecture, the final
solution is a unity wherein structure, decoration and
function are indissolubly one.

Magnificent as was the Pantheon, it pointed only too
clearly to its own limitations. A dome is arcuated; it
exerts thrust and therefore needs abutment. Unlike the
intersecting vault – Roman or Gothic – where the thrust
is concentrated at the four corners of each vaulting bay,
the dome exerts continuous thrust all round its base, and
needs continuous abutment. The Pantheon was just a
giant igloo with walls 20 feet thick, designed to meet the
outward push of its dome. The circular Pantheon is
magnificently simple; but it is not planning. *The circle is
the least flexible of all plan forms* – incapable of development
to meet the functional requirements of, for example, a
more elaborate ritual.

The structural and planning problem of the Byzantine
architect was, therefore, quite simply that of building
circular domes over square spaces. Once that was done,
then, clearly, the sides of the square could be penetrated
by arches and open out into other squares, other areas on
the plan. Square could open out into square, each topped
by its own dome. This gave the planner much greater
flexibility. The arrangement of the various spaces – the
central area, the semi-domed apse, the vaulted aisles and
so on – is in fact one of the great charms of Byzantine
building. How was it done?

When one draws a circle inside a square, four roughly
triangular areas are left over at the corners. When a dome

was built over a square it was these four corners that had somehow to be bridged – whether in stone, brick or concrete. On a small scale various devices were used – a simple stone slab from wall to wall might serve. On a big scale something more truly structural was needed. The solution was eventually found in the 'pendentive'. The pendentive is, as it were, a small triangular segment of dome rising from each corner of the square; these four segments meet to form a circle upon which the true dome may then be built: the transformation from square to

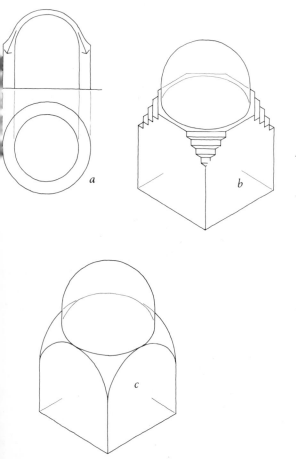

65 A dome, like an arch, exerts pressure downwards and outwards all round its circumference. The simplest support is therefore circular (a). As with a tunnel vault, the wall must resist continuous thrust, and can only be cut into well below the line of thrust (see Ill. 46).

The problem of placing a dome over a square, thus liberating the wall and the plan, can be solved in two ways. In the first, the corners are bridged with straight stone slabs (b) or a series of small arches – 'squinches' – until an octagonal base is formed (see Conques, Ill. 95). In the second, curved triangular segments (c) – 'pendentives' – are inserted into the spaces between the four arches that form the square. This is the Byzantine solution, seen for instance at Hagia Sophia (Ill. 71)

circle has been achieved. The pendentive is as much the key to Byzantine architecture as are the ribbed vault and buttress to Gothic. Once the architect has this key then the way is open to all permutations and combinations of dome building.

The dominating central dome always attracted the Byzantine builder, but once this method of setting a dome on a square had been arrived at there were alternatives. Instead of one central dome, a whole series of square bays each with its own dome could be set alongside each other, producing a cluster of domes. The Byzantine domed bay then became almost comparable to the Gothic vaulted bay; always, however, it remained large – Roman in scale. Three large domed bays are enough to span the 180-foot length of St Mark's, Venice, while ten vaulted bays are needed to span the length of the nave at York Minster. The one object of the Gothic builder was to get rid of weight and mass, to let in light, to arrive at the most delicate possible structure – what the modern engineer calls 'point loading'. Not so the Byzantine architect. He preferred Roman weight. He supported his building on a few large masses rather than upon many columns. Compare the plans of, say, Hagia Sophia or St Mark's with those of late Gothic cathedrals; the 'blacks' on the Byzantine plans are few and big, while on the Gothic plans they are many and small.

What one might call the archetypal Byzantine plans are therefore: 1, the single central dome with all secondary spaces such as aisles and apses completely subordinate to it – this we see on a big scale at Hagia Sophia; 2, the Greek cross with more or less equal arms, covered by domes – this we see in St Mark's, Venice.

A structural system produces a decorative system. The structural system of Byzantine architecture gave large masses below and curved surfaces above – the smooth soffits or under-surfaces of domes and unribbed vaults. The ribs, the richly moulded piers, the mullions and tracery of Gothic do not exist east of Venice, hardly east

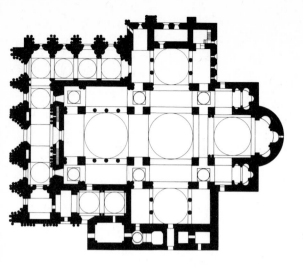

66 *St Mark's, Venice (begun 1063) shows how the mass and scale of Roman work persisted in the typical Byzantine Greek cross plan. Vast domes cover the crossing and the four roughly equal limbs; at their intersection they rest on massive piers (see Ill. 88). A low narthex surrounds the western end*

of Milan. The Byzantine system needed a 'covering' material which could be laid upon the massive walls and upon the soffits of the domes. The Byzantine architects did not invent such a system; they took it from the Romans and transformed it for their own purpose: for the walls a sheathing of marble, for the domes and vaults, mosaic. In details like colonnaded screens, there was much fine Byzantine carving, on the main structure very little.

The Byzantine Empire was rich in marbles – a miraculous quarry of whites, greys and greens. Mosaic may be of glass or marble. It consists of millions of tiny cubes, each about a centimetre across. The surface to be decorated during the day's work is covered with cement; each cube is then pressed into position by the craftsman's thumb while the cement is still wet. The glory of mosaic is threefold. First, it can form a continuous covering, almost as if it were molten, running over curved surfaces and round corners; second, the irregularities of the mosaic surface demand the simplest drawing – any attempt at naturalism is disastrous, and it was this which gave such a wonderfully hieratic and stylized quality to the figures of Byzantine art; third, the slightly different angles at which the tiny cubes are placed cause the whole surface to catch the light here and there, so that there is scintillation amidst the gloom. The small windows in the dome gave that minimum of light needed for this effect.

Thus does Byzantine architecture emerge with the qualities of a great style – the integration of structure and decoration. But what of that other element in architecture – function? What was it all for? Churches are no less functional than laboratories; certain things happen inside them for which they must be designed. The liturgy of the Byzantine Church and the Byzantine plan were also – like the structure and decoration – an integrated unity. This has been disputed; it has been said that the highly centralized plan – as at Ravenna or Hagia Sophia – provided a central area beneath the dome, but that the altar was thereby relegated to a minor place in a small apse. This is to misunderstand the Byzantine liturgy, to confuse it with the Western or Roman liturgy where the climax, the elevation of the sacrament, takes place at the end of that long vista of nave and chancel. This climax, however, was *not* the supreme moment of the Byzantine ceremony.

Visualize the space beneath the dome of Hagia Sophia in Constantinople. That space, uninterrupted by steps or columns, is 250 feet long and over 100 feet wide. Far above it the mosaic saints and the Christ Pantocrator glow dimly. The people crowd into the surrounding aisles and galleries. The marble floor of the vast central area is empty. There is a droning of priests. Behind curtains in the distant apse the sacramental rites – the 'Great Mystery' – are being secretly performed. The Patriarch, the clergy and the acolytes make their proces-sional entrance. Minutes later the Imperial and Divine Household also take up their position beneath the dome. By the time of Justinian, in the sixth century, the whole ritual had been elevated to the status of a divine ballet.

The marble floor, formerly empty, blossomed with encrusted robes. The supreme moment is when Patriarch and Emperor exchange the Kiss of Peace and share the chalice. This is what the dome was built for. It was a quite specific function.

The first great church of Hagia Sophia was built by Constantine in 360, but was burnt to the ground in the riots of 532. It was rebuilt with incredible speed so that in 537 Justinian was able to dedicate it to the Holy Wisdom with the words: 'Solomon, I have vanquished thee'. (It should be remembered, however, that the brick carcass of a Byzantine building could be completed and put into use long before the surface decoration of marble or mosaic was begun.)

Hagia Sophia is a vast rectangle, 250 feet by 220 feet, with an inner and an outer narthex, or porch, and

67 Hagia Sophia, Istanbul (537). One sees how the semi-domes at each end (left and right) and the massive buttresses at the side (foreground) support the central dome, and how the dome itself, braced by forty miniature buttresses, could have a ring of windows round its base. The Islamic minarets were added later

79

formerly an atrium or forecourt. The main body of the church has surrounding aisles, 50 feet wide, vaulted and galleried. These aisles are separated from the central area by very beautiful colonnaded screens – each column a single marble shaft. The aisles reduce the central liturgical area to 250 feet by 107 feet. The dome is 107 feet in diameter, but the space it covers is extended to east and west by large semi-domes. These in turn open out into the semi-circular spaces called exedrae. The main dome is seated upon a square, supported by four pendentives and four great arches. These four arches have their thrust taken to the east and west by the semi-domes just described and to the north and south by four huge buttresses, each 60 feet by 25 feet, which emerge externally above the roofs of the aisles.

The whole arrangement can be understood only by reference to the plan and diagram. It has been likened to a mass of soap bubbles rising out of each other. The semi-domes resist the thrust of the main dome, and then their thrust eventually reaches the ground over 100 feet from the first point of impact. It is a miraculous feat of engineering. It could have ended in aesthetic chaos had not all the semi-domes and main arches been sprung from a single horizontal line running round the whole interior. Below this line all the walls were sheathed in marble, above this line all was mosaic. This gave unity.

The big dome – 180 feet above the floor – is actually ribbed. This is unusual in Byzantine work, but it does enable the thrust of the dome to pass down forty ribs, and enables forty small windows to be placed between the ribs, at the base of the dome. This circle of diffused light made the blue and gold mosaic glitter. It was also the origin of the saying of Procopius that the dome of Hagia Sophia was suspended by a chain from heaven.

The object of the architects, Anthemius of Tralles and Isidore of Miletus, was to build an interior both moving and functional. The spaces of Hagia Sophia – arena, aisles, exedrae, conches, vaults and domes – all open outwards and upwards, one from the other, giving changing vistas, glimpses; everything is mysterious and half-hidden, yet everything is revealed. Procopius has described it for us in its contradictions: light and gloom, space and mass, mystery and clarity. The vaults float, the

69 Plan of Hagia Sophia, Istanbul. The great central dome is buttressed by two half-domes, which are in turn supported by apses to the north and south. In addition great buttresses stretch out from the four central piers (Ill. 67). This structural system of curves is then set into a square; vaulted aisles pierce the buttresses and open into the nave through colonnades (Ill. 70)

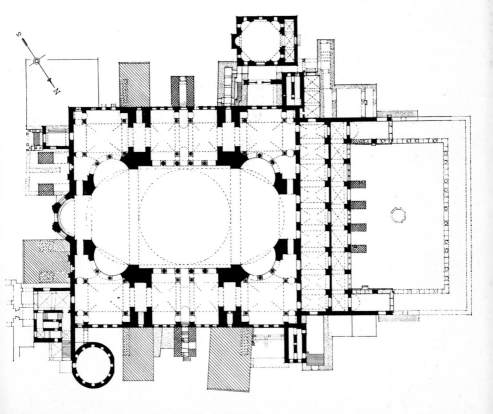

columns perform a choral dance, the central dome hangs from the sky. Procopius also described the colours: the mosaics, the shimmer of grey marble on the walls, the greenish, the blue and the yellow-veined marble shafts, the crisp carving on the capitals, the mother-of-pearl, the dangling golden lamps.

Hagia Sophia was the logical conclusion of the Byzantine system – structural, decorative, functional. In the other churches of Constantinople and of the Empire at large the function could not, of course, be exactly that of Hagia Sophia, since the Emperor did not appear in them. But it became normal for the clergy to occupy the whole of the nave and for the congregation to be crowded into the aisles, the galleries and the narthex. The central dome thus retained the same liturgical meaning that it had in the imperial cathedral, since it was beneath it that the climax of the Eucharist took place.

70, 71 The effect of the interior of Hagia Sophia, with the dim light glinting on mosaics and the mystery of one space opening into another, is difficult to convey by photographs. The aisles are separated from the central area by screens of columns (right) – single shafts of marble said to have come from the Temple of Artemis at Ephesus. The cushion-shaped capitals are carved mainly with the drill, giving a crisp, staccato effect. The general view (opposite) shows clearly the geometry of placing a circular dome over a square, with the big pendentives as fine areas for display of mosaic

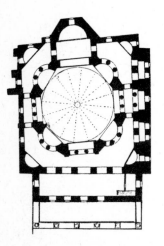

72, 73 Interior and plan of SS. Sergius and Bacchus, Istanbul. This church – slightly earlier than Hagia Sophia – is an octagon surrounded, except on the east side, by a roughly square aisle. The domed central area is only 52 feet across, so that the pendentives bridging the eight corners are quite small. They are true pendentives, nevertheless. The eight spaces between the piers are closed by triplets of arches alternately straight and curved

None of Justinian's other churches attempted to rival Hagia Sophia in magnificence, but several of them are related to it in design. SS. Sergius and Bacchus, also in Constantinople, was begun some years before Hagia Sophia. It made full use of the lovely Byzantine concept of the surrounding aisle. The main central area, which rises above the aisles, is a domed octagon only 52 feet across, leaving the remaining space for the circumambient aisle. This aisle opens out into the central area through colonnades: the whole charm of the constantly changing vista is exploited. Nevertheless, the dome is still built only over an octagon, not over a square: the great structural step had yet to be taken.

74, 75 *Interior and plan of S. Vitale, Ravenna (547). Like SS. Sergius and Bacchus, the central domed area is octagonal. Here, however, the surrounding aisle is also octagonal, and the openings between it and the central area are all curved in plan. This produces a still subtler interpenetration of spaces*

The same is true of S. Vitale in Ravenna. This church is an octagon over 100 feet across. Like SS. Sergius and Bacchus it has a surrounding aisle – vaulted and galleried – leaving an octagonal central area just over half the total diameter. This central area is taken up higher than the aisles and then domed. Certain structural issues were evaded rather than solved. The pendentives at the corners of an octagon are negligible compared with those at the corners of a square. The dome itself was built of hollow clay pots – the bottom of one pot inside the mouth of the next below it – giving a dome of such lightness as to almost eliminate the problem of thrust. (This device was used thirteen hundred years later by

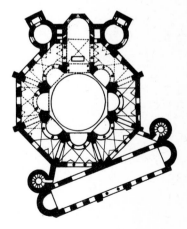

76 S. Vitale, Ravenna. In this detail one is looking across the choir, past marble columns whose capitals are carved with the drill (cp. Ill. 70), towards the mosaic showing the Emperor Justinian with his court. All the surfaces are either marble or mosaic

John Soane in the Bank of England, London.) The glory of S. Vitale lies in its mosaics. On one side of the chancel are huge figures of Justinian and his courtiers; opposite are the Empress Theodora and her ladies. These mosaics are supreme works of art. Worthy of them are the coloured marble shafts with their white capitals. These capitals are carved more with the drill than with the chisel, giving a staccato crispness of light and shade.

St Irene at Constantinople (begun in 532, but restored after 564 and again in 740) follows Hagia Sophia in its general scheme. The eighth-century rebuilding added a drum beneath the central dome, probably the first instance of that feature.

A fifth major church built by Justinian has entirely disappeared and is known only through Procopius' description. It was, however, probably the most influential of them all: the Holy Apostles at Constantinople. Its plan was a Greek cross with domes over each arm and a fifth over the crossing. It was copied almost immediately in the rebuilt church of St John at Ephesus, which had an extra dome at the end of the west arm, producing a nave with two bays.

77, 78 *St Irene at Istanbul (begun 532, restored 564 and 740) is virtually a smaller version of Hagia Sophia. The major differences are (a) that it has two domes instead of one, thus giving the interior a more longitudinal movement, and (b) that the eastern dome has a low drum, the result of 8th-century alterations. Note at the east end the early arrangement of tiered stone seats for the clergy*

These great churches of Justinian had a propaganda purpose as well as a utilitarian or ritualistic one. Procopius devoted a whole book to the *Buildings*. They stood for political authority and religious orthodoxy, and they set a dominant pattern for architecture for as long as the Byzantine Empire lasted, and beyond (the Blue Mosque of 1609–16 is an almost exact copy of Hagia Sophia). Their hallmark, as has been said, was the dome, but this did not mean the exclusion of all other types of design. The Eastern Empire before Justinian had been prolific in architectural invention, and the variety of church plans continues to be surprising right down to the Arab invasion. It is impossible here to do more than indicate a few of them, without pausing to trace the relation between one school and another.

Constantine's Church of the Nativity at Bethlehem (before 333) had combined a double-aisled basilica with an octagonal east end. St Mary at Ephesus (early fifth century) had a nave and transepts, both with aisles, and a long chancel with double aisles. St John of Studion at Constantinople (founded 463) is likewise a fairly conventional basilica. The first church of St John at Ephesus was more elaborate, with aisled transepts and double-aisled chancel all centering on the shrine of the saint under the crossing.

Egypt during the fifth century produced several churches in which a basilican nave was combined with a trefoil east end of three apses serving as chancel and transepts. The Nativity at Bethlehem was remodelled in this way in the sixth century. Syria and Palestine were areas of bold experiment, including very early churches with quatrefoil plans (again seeming to look forward to SS. Sergius and Bacchus and S. Vitale) and the amazing fifth-century Martyrium of Qalat-Siman, with long arms meeting at a central octagon. In Anatolia, longitudinal and central-space churches were combined.

Such regional variations were not entirely obliterated by the new trends set by the capital. One finds differen

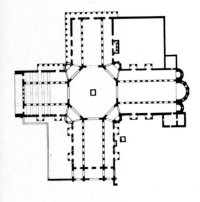

79 *Plan of the Martyrium, Qalat-Siman (470): a highly unusual design with four long aisled arms converging upon a central octagon*

elements of Justinian's churches assimilated in different areas, depending largely on the religious or political situation at the time. In Mesopotamia and Coptic Egypt austere versions of the old basilica, without domes, persisted. In the Balkans, on the other hand, the dome was eagerly taken up and developed in a rather provincial way. St Donat at Zara (early ninth century) has been called 'a cousin several times removed' of SS. Sergius and Bacchus; while in the kingdom of Greater Bulgaria centred on Ochrid there evolved during the ninth century a type of high barrel-vaulted hall-church with a dome over the crossing.

By far the most architecturally fertile of the provinces of the Byzantine Empire during the seventh to eleventh centuries (in fact it was for part of that time politically independent) was Armenia. Some of the leading intellectuals and artists of the Byzantine world were Armenian; one of them, Trdat, was in charge of Hagia Sophia when it had to be repaired in 989.

Armenian churches mostly embodied some form of central planning surmounted by a dome on a drum. They are usually fairly small in scale. The palace church of Zwartnots, built between 641 and 666, was a brilliant variation on the idea of SS. Sergius and Bacchus. It had a circular exterior and a quatrefoil inner arcade rising through three storeys, leading to a high dome on a drum. The roughly contemporary church of the Holy Apostles at Mschet, the ancient capital of Georgia, was another version of the quatrefoil – four arms meeting at a central dome with four square chapels in the corners. Trdat himself designed Ani Cathedral, a longitudinal church of three bays, but given a central emphasis by a dome over the middle bay. The dome has collapsed, but several other progressive features are still to be seen there, including the pointed arch. Where most Byzantine churches are notable for their mosaics, Armenian ones excel in sculpture. That of the churches in the old royal city of Aght'amar is particularly fine. Armenian

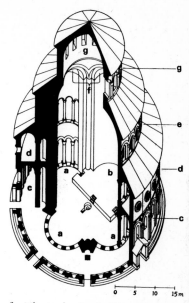

80 The circular church of Zwartnots, in Armenia (641–66), was another version of the central-space plan with circumambient aisle (see Ills. 72–5 and 101). In the quatrefoil centre one solid-walled lobe held the altar (b) while the other three (a) rose through the arcade (c), gallery (d) and clerestory (e). The dome rested on four arches (f) and a high, windowed drum (g)

81 The Church of the Holy Cross at Aghtʿamar (915–21) represents one of the many Armenian variations on the central plan. The four arms supporting the octagonal drum are square on the exterior, apsed inside. In the corners are smaller niches, visible on the outside as small polygonal forms. The use of reliefs in bands and circles is characteristic of Armenia

82 The Little Metropole Cathedral, Athens (c.1250), is on a very small scale, but it is full of delightful carving and ornament, much of it removed from earlier Greek buildings

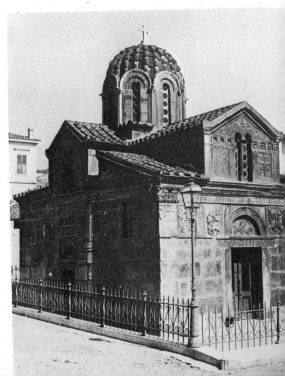

influence was strong in the neighbouring lands of Anatolia and Georgia, where it persisted until the thirteenth century. Armenia itself ceased to exist politically in the early eleventh century and has only recently been recognized for the astonishing architectural centre that it was.

The eleventh century brought new types of plan, deriving from earlier models but offering new scope for spatial and decorative effects. In the Balkans domes crowned tall octagonal drums (their height made possible by the generally small size of the buildings). Nea Moni, on the island of Chios (1042–56), contains a church with a dome on an octagonal drum, which in turn rests on a square; the east end opens into three apsidal chapels. It is a simple and impressive design, especially when seen with its original mosaics and marble veneer. Most popular of all was the quincunx or cross-in-square plan: a square divided into nine bays with the central 'cross' articulated by domes. This occurs, for instance, at Hosios Lukas and all over Greece from the eleventh century onwards. Many of these churches are on the scale of parish churches in the West. In Athens the Little Metropole Cathedral (c. 1250) is the smallest 'cathedral'

83 The Monastery of Nea Moni on the Island of Chios (1042–56) has a fine church with very tall arches carrying the dome over a complex plan. The exteriors of Byzantine churches are always subservient to their interiors. Here the mosaics and carved capitals are exceptionally rich

91

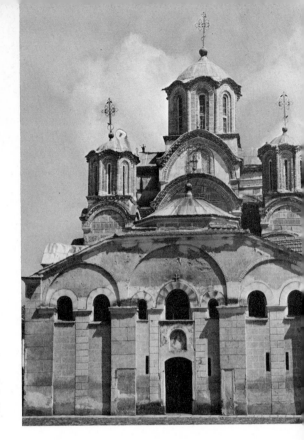

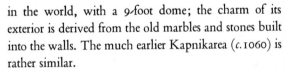

84, 85 *St John the Baptist, Gračanica (1321), above, and the Holy Apostles at Salonika (1312–15), below, both show the outstanding characteristics of this late phase of Byzantine work: very tall proportions and small domes on polygonal drums*

in the world, with a 9-foot dome; the charm of its exterior is derived from the old marbles and stones built into the walls. The much earlier Kapnikarea (*c.*1060) is rather similar.

In 1204 Constantinople was sacked by the Crusaders. Although it later recovered its autonomy, and although painting and mosaic recovered their vitality, architecture from this time onward became conservative and repetitious. A church such as the Holy Apostles at Salonika (1312–15) is still based on a variant of the cross-in-square plan, though its spaces are in fact organized in a novel and complex way. The church at Gračanica, in Serbia (1321) takes these ideas even further. Both the interior elevations and the exterior drums of the domes are given unprecedentedly tall proportions.

Finally, a brief note on two areas outside the Byzantine Empire. One is Russia. Christianity was officially adopted at Kiev in 988. The great cathedral of Kiev, the masonry of which still substantially survives, was built early in the eleventh century on a plan based on the quincunx but expanded to accommodate extra aisles. From Kiev Byzantine Christianity and Byzantine architecture spread to Novgorod and eventually to Moscow, where the earliest of the Kremlin cathedrals, the Dormition (1475–9), though designed by a Renaissance Italian, kept the same quincunx plan and five domes. St Basil's, of 1555–60, is a last exotic fantasy on themes that began in Byzantium a thousand years before.

The other postscript is Venice, the only city of the West in direct contact with the Eastern Empire. St

86, 87 *In Russia, the style of Kiev Cathedral (1037–46, reconstruction above) was basically that of Salonika. The fantasy of St Basil's in Moscow (1555–60, below) shows Byzantine architecture in its final exhaustion*

88, 89 *The Byzantine style in Western Europe. Above, St Mark's in Venice (begun 1063); below, St-Front at Périgueux (began c. 1120, rebuilt). Both have Greek cross plans covered by domes, with windows in these domes; both have, at the crossing, massive piers pierced with arches. St Mark's is fully Byzantine and was no doubt the model for the more Romanesque St-Front*

Mark's (begun 1063) is in all important respects a purely Byzantine church, low in proportion, clad in marble veneer, its five domes gleaming with mosaic. From Venice Byzantine inspiration travelled west weakly and sporadically. In the thirteenth-century S. Antonio ('Il Santo') at Padua the Byzantine system of dome construction was applied to a basically Gothic plan with nave, transepts and chancel with ambulatory. In Romanesque France, the churches of Anjou and Angoulême Cathedral seem to have absorbed some Byzantine influence, though more as a solution to the problem of vaulting than as an aesthetic style. The only consistently Byzantine example is St-Front at Périgueux, which follows St Mark's in being a Greek cross covered by five domes; but the whole church was rebuilt in the nineteenth century, the chancel-arm to a completely new design, so that the original extent of its Byzantine qualities is hard to assess. Neither S. Antonio nor St-Front ever had any mosaic or anything approaching Byzantine decoration. It is St Mark's that must be regarded as the Western outpost of the Byzantine spirit.

Chapter Five

WESTERN CHRISTENDOM:
I ROMANESQUE

The architectural link between Imperial Rome and medieval Christendom is known as 'Early Christian'. The earliest Christians in Rome met in houses, hired halls or, under pressure of persecution, in the catacombs. It was there that pagan rites were adapted to Christian needs and that the teachings of Jesus were transmuted into a 'Church'. The first actual churches – mainly in the fourth and fifth centuries – were built when persecution eased or after the Edict of Milan (AD 313) whereby the Church won peace at the cost of subordination to the secular power. Some of these early churches, much changed, survive in Rome; they were the germ of Western building through over a thousand years.

The word 'basilica' is confusing. The pagan basilica was a concourse, a place of assembly, a *bourse*. The word did not imply any specific architectural form. The Basilica of Constantine, for instance, was a big vaulted hall like one of the halls of the thermae; the Basilica of Trajan, much larger, had only a timber roof. It was in

90 Plan of the Basilica of Trajan, Rome (98–112): (a) entrance, (b) altars surrounded by tribunals in apses, (c) libraries, (d) Trajan's Column. While the double apses, continuous aisles and lateral entrance do not appear in Early Christian churches, the basic concept of a large assembly hall with nave and aisles was clearly established

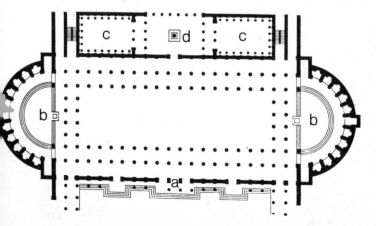

91 *Restored interior of the Basilica of Trajan, Rome: double aisles, a colonnaded gallery, clerestory lighting and an open timber roof*

fact virtually a nave with columned aisles. It was cheap and well lit; it had good sight lines. In other words it was an excellent prototype for the earliest and simplest Christian churches. In these first churches it was essential that everyone should see the celebrant at the altar but, as yet, no large eastern limb for choir or ritual was needed, only a simple semi-circular apse for the altar. Architectural elaboration was deliberately eschewed. The long aisled basilica met the case well and thus became the basic form of the Early Christian church.

S. Clemente, Rome, dates from the twelfth century, but was built over the remains of a fourth-century basilica. In addition to the nave and aisles it still retains the atrium or forecourt with ablutionary fountain, and a large narthex or porch where the penitents and the un-baptized could hear the service. The original Basilica of St Peter (*c*.330) was built by Constantine, but the present church has wiped out all traces of the earlier one. S. Paolo fuori le Mura is a nineteenth-century copy of the fourth-century basilica, but probably gives an impres-sive idea of the original. Sta Maria Maggiore was founded by Sixtus III in A D 432, but is now embedded in the larger Baroque church.

92 *Section of Old St Peter's, Rome (c.330). Like the Basilica of Trajan, above, the church had double aisles and timber roofs; but in it, as in other Early Christian churches, the elevation was of two storeys only – arcade and clerestory. There was a transept at the far end, with a single apse opening directly off it*

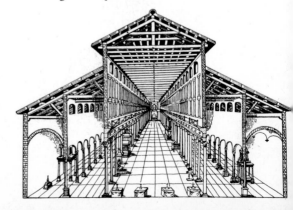

We have already seen how the inspiration of the Roman dome passed eastwards to suffer a sea-change into Byzantine architecture. We now have to see how the long basilican plan passed westwards to be transformed ultimately into the Gothic cathedral. This transformation must be traced in terms of plan, structure and decoration. The basilican plan consisted of no more than the nave, two aisles and the apse. But when we glance at a basilican church such as, say, S. Clemente, we see immediately the line of the *cancelli*, the marble balustrade fencing off nearly half the nave for the use of priests and

93, 94 S. Clemente, Rome (12th century, built over a 4th-century basilica): plan, and view of the chancel. An atrium (a) leads into a simple rectangular church with nave and aisles and, in its original form, a single eastern apse. To the west of the altar (b) is the choir (c), enclosed by 'cancelli' (d) and flanked by the Gospel ambo (e) and Epistle ambo (f). This encroachment of the choir upon the nave is clear in the photograph above

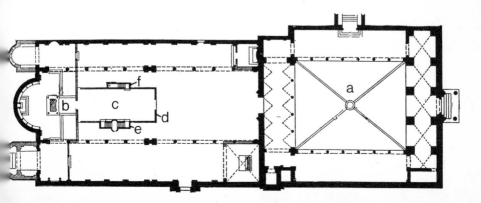

choir and forming, in fact, a 'chancel'. Already then, at some early date, ritual had overflowed from the apse into the nave. In the centuries yet to come the nave – however elaborately it might be vaulted – remained an aisled hall normally reserved for the laity. It was the little apse which expanded until in the end we have such miracles of planning as the chevet of chapels around the east end of French cathedrals, or the long chancel and Lady Chapel of England. The story of the church plan, therefore, from the fourth to the fourteenth century is really the story of its eastern limb.

If the basilica was the germ of the medieval nave – as a columned hall with clerestory – it was the Roman vault that inspired medieval structure. Medieval architecture developed from the attempt to cover a large space with a fireproof roof made of stones no larger than could be carried by a pack-horse. This process will take us from the bold eleventh-century arches of, say Ste-Foy at Conques, to the airy fantasies of such sixteenth-century Gothic as St Anne at Annaberg, Louviers or Henry VII's Chapel at Westminster.

This long story is usually divided into two 'styles' – Romanesque and Gothic. It is true that the Romanesque style (in England, 'Norman') used the semi-circular arch and was heavy and thick walled, whereas Gothic, using the pointed arch, achieved flexibility and lightness. All the same, the development was continuous and our subdivisions into styles would have been incomprehensible to the medieval builder. The builders at Durham, when they began work in 1093, were undoubtedly building in the Romanesque style; some six years later, when they had reached the vaults over the choir and its aisles they were tentatively exploring the pointed arch and rib vault – a moment of useful innovation but not, for them, a conscious stylistic development. It was, in fact, to be another thirty years before pointed arches and rib vaults would be consciously exploited at St-Denis, thereby creating a new style.

95, 96 Romanesque achievement and Gothic virtuosity: above, Ste-Foy at Conques (begun c.1050; see also p. 113) with high tunnel-vaulted nave, and crossing covered by a lantern on squinches; below, St Anne, Annaberg (begun 1499; see also p. 154) – the functional stone vault transformed into a fantastic pattern of ribs

The 'Dark Ages' may have been neither so dark nor so barbarous as was once supposed. Western Europe, nevertheless, has little to offer between the departure of the legions in the fifth century and the coronation of Charlemagne in 800. In southern Europe the great monastic establishments were an assurance that civiliza-tion might survive the fall of Rome; in the north, however, such little architecture as there was is found mainly within the remote sphere of the Irish missionaries. The asceticism of the hermits in the desert outside Alexandria found its way to that wild Atlantic world, to return eastwards, bringing Christianity to Britain and to Scandinavia. In Ireland there were such things as the seventh-century Gallarus Oratory near Dingle, or the spectacular corbelled domes of the monastery at Skellig Michael. The Hall of the Kings at Tara was probably an aisled basilica, with the throne in an apse. In Britain there was the fairly advanced masonry of the Northum-brian churches at Jarrow and Hexham, both about 680, and such ambitious buildings as Brixworth, with two rows of arches constructed of Roman bricks on principles derived from Roman remains. In Gaul there are scanty remains of a few basilican churches – indistinguishable from simple Mithraic temples – and there is the remark-able sixth-century domed baptistery at Venasque. Clovis

100 *Abbey gatehouse, Lorsch (c.800)*

101 *Palatine Chapel, Aachen (792–805). Based on S. Vitale at Ravenna (Ill. 74), it set the pattern for palace chapels. The ground floor was public while the gallery, for the Emperor, communicated with the palace*

had accepted a barbarous form of Christianity as early as 496. Charles Martel, in the eighth century, had secured France forever against Islam.

But it is not until the age of Charlemagne that we can find a new chapter in architecture. The gatehouse of the Rhineland abbey of Lorsch (eighth century) has almost pure Corinthian columns and pilasters as part of a vivid design. In Charlemagne's palace at Aachen (Aix-la-Chapelle) it would seem as if Western Christendom was hesitating between Byzantium and Rome, between the dome and the basilica. The palace has a large octagonal chapel with fine marble work. It was designed in 792 and is still singularly complete. Its designer was a northerner, Odo of Metz, who looked East, to the church of S. Vitale at Ravenna, for inspiration. The great hall of the palace, on the other hand, like that at Tara, was an entirely Western aisled basilica with Charlemagne's throne in a apse.

What, we may ask, compelled the West on the whole to ignore the Byzantine dome in favour of the basilica? Did liturgy dictate architecture, or *vice versa*? We have already seen (pp. 78–9) how the hierarchical nature of the Byzantine Church demanded a central dome. The monastic nature of the Western Church called for a different plan. Apart from Charlemagne's Palatine Chapel, the West sought inspiration in the Roman basilica. The basilica, after all, still had something of the glamour of the ancient Constantinian Church.

As Roman rule disintegrated and first the bishops and then the great abbots became the civilizing elements, architecture changed radically. With the emergence of the big churches a new architecture crystallized into the style that we call Romanesque. This architecture derived three things from Rome: from the basilica it got length; from the thermae the groin vault; and from Roman building in general it got the semi-circular arch. It made of these things a new kind of building . . . strong, articulated, heavy, logical and yet mystical.

Whereas the basilica had been long and low, the Romanesque church was tall and vigorous, piercing the skyline with its towers. Whereas the Roman column had been a single shaft, and the Roman arch had a smooth undersurface, the Romanesque pier and arch were heavily moulded, articulated. Strong lines emphasized the structural forces within the building. Ornament was sparse. This was no longer a Mediterranean style of marble veneer; it was a northern style of masonry.

The walls of a Romanesque building are thick. An arch, door, or window, penetrating a thick wall, would have a very broad undersurface. In Byzantine architecture this might be a good background for mosaic. In actual building it created difficulties. The timber centering or 'false work' had to be both elaborate and strong; it had also to be supported from the floor on scaffolding. *The urge to lighten this timber centering was a*

102 Maria Laach (1093–1156): the quintessential Romanesque church, incorporating the Western themes of long nave, transept and steep-roofed towers. The towers in the foreground mark a western choir, not uncommon in German Romanesque

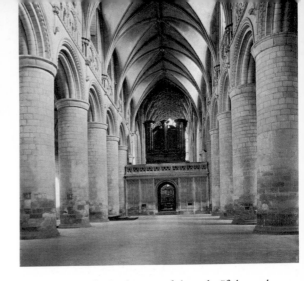

103 *Arches in the nave of Gloucester Cathedral (c.1087) spring from big cylindrical piers, almost unornamented and bearing no relation to the classical column. The vaults are Gothic*

104 *Diagram showing the difference between two arcades, the first with square piers and unmoulded arches, the second moulded, i.e. with the mouldings of the arches articulated to correspond with those of the piers. Wider timber centering – the curved framework of wood under the arch – is needed for the former*

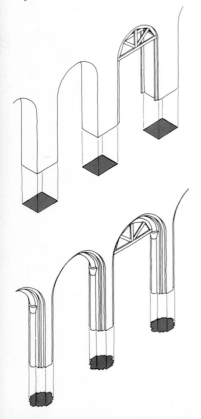

major factor in the development of the style. If the arch was, however, built as a series of rings, then only the lower or inner ring needed centering. In itself this then acted as centering for the remaining rings, until the whole arch, to the thickness of the wall, was complete as a series of concentric mouldings.

Here and there – as in the nave arcades of English Benedictine churches (e.g. Tewkesbury and Gloucester, c.1087) the moulded arch springs from a cylindrical pier. The effect is clumsy, the design unresolved. If, however, each ring has a corresponding moulding in the support-ing pier, then that pier is articulated to accord with the arch above: one part of a building responds to another part. Also, the lines of thrust in the arch are, as it were, carried visually to the ground. This articulated or com-pound Romanesque pier replaced the Roman column with profound effect. It can be seen at its simplest in, say, S. Ambrogio at Milan (late eleventh century), in Ste-Foy at Conques (begun c.1050), or at Mainz Cathedral (altered in 1181). This compound pier was of course destined to be refined into the moulded pier of the Gothic cathedral.

The basic section of a Romanesque church – high nave and lean-to aisles – had, in embryonic form, been inherent in the basilica. This was two-tiered, with an arcade below dividing the nave from the aisles, and clerestory windows in the plain wall above. In many areas, notably in Germany, Romanesque churches retained this arrangement. A different type of two-tier elevation appears in the churches on the pilgrimage roads to Santiago de Compostela, and in central France: here the clerestory is eliminated and the heavy tunnel vault rests directly on the triforium. The builders obviously did not want to risk weakening the wall by piercing it; the result in such churches as Conques, Santiago itself, and Clermont-Ferrand is a massive, dark interior. The triforium or 'dark storey' could be anything from a proper gallery above the aisle, opening into the nave, to a blind arcade on solid wall. The three-tier arrangement – arcade, triforium, clerestory – is found all over Europe and was standard in England.

105, 106 Two-storey elevations (in both cases, looking west in the nave). At Quedlinburg in Saxony (early 12th century, above) the triforium is reduced to a blank wall between arcade and clerestory. The piers are alternately square and cylindrical (see p. 118), the latter, unlike those at Gloucester, being obvious echoes of classical columns. Nave and aisles are covered by flat wooden roofs.

At Santiago de Compostela (c. 1075–1150, left) it is the clerestory which has vanished. The triforium is an open gallery; above it spring the tunnel vaults of the nave. Transverse arches dividing the vault into bays rest on shafts which run the full height of the wall. The piers are moulded

107 *Southwell Minster nave (c.1130), a variation within the three-tier elevation. The triforium has arches as wide as those of the arcade below; it also has articulated piers, whereas those of the arcade are cylindrical*

Everywhere the changes were rung on the basic arrangement by varying the relative proportions of the storeys; by varying the subdivisions of the triforium; by choosing between columns and compound piers for the arcade; and of course by using different mouldings and surface decoration. The front moulding or roundel of the pier in the nave arcade might be taken up the full height of the building, to the cross-beam of a wooden roof or to the springing of the vault. This wall-shaft gave strong vertical emphasis, another visual line of force, in a design where verticality was everything.

For the smooth undersurface of the Roman groin vault an even more elaborate centering had been needed than for a simple arch – virtually a timber mould of the whole inside of the building. The halls of the thermae must have been a forest of timber during construction. But in the vaults of the crypt of Auxerre Cathedral (c.1030), for instance, we see how there are arches dividing one vaulting bay from the next. The wooden centering used in one bay could now be dismantled and re-erected in the next bay – a great saving in the cutting of timber. When, however, we look at the abbey at

108 *Auxerre Cathedral crypt (c.1030): the intersections of the cross vault are left as groins, but each bay is separated from the next by a heavy arch*

109 Mainz Cathedral (11th century and after 1181). Giant quadripartite vaults cover the nave in a double-bay system (see p. 118). Unlike the Auxerre crypt, there are simple diagonal ribs to mask the groins and to simplify construction

Pontigny, a hundred years later, or at Mainz or, again, at Durham, there has been a further development. The intersecting edges of the groin vaults are now strengthened by ribs, in themselves each a distinct arch. Centering is necessary to build each of these arches but not, as hitherto, for the whole vaulting bay. The builder had created a lobster-pot of arches, and had only to bridge from arch to arch with small stones. This form of vault with diagonal ribs dividing it into four is the 'quadripartite' vault. It is the first form of the ribbed vault which, with all its ultimate diaphanous complexity, gave Gothic its magic. As a concept, bold and simple, it was Romanesque.

The moulding of the vaulting ribs meant that the stone roof, like all else, was now highly articulated. There was now unity between all parts of the building. And if out of this attempt to reduce the centering there had grown a structural system, then out of this structural system there had also grown a decorative system.

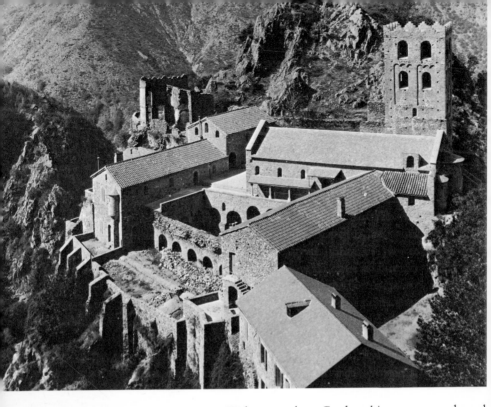

110 *St-Martin-du-Canigou (1001-26), from the south: a noble piece of siting. The monastic buildings are compressed on a rocky spur around the low cloister; to the left is the refectory and to the right the dormitory, joined to the church, which stands between the cloister and the bell tower*

We have seen how Greek architecture was sculptural in that the temple was a vehicle for fine carving, and how Roman and Byzantine were architectures of mass – decoration consisting mainly of marble sheathing or mosaic. But in Romanesque it is the very stones of the structure that are carved, whether with chamfers, mouldings or roundels. Every pier, every arch and rib, the jamb of every door and window, has each stone cut for its place in the building. In the great cathedrals of the thirteenth and fourteenth centuries we have richer mouldings, more complex vaults, but Romanesque had already achieved an integration of function, structure and decoration.

Having glanced at Romanesque in general and noted its emergence from its Roman past as an historical style in its own right, we must now look at a few examples in different countries and under different monastic orders.

111 *The interior of St-Martin-du-Canigou is remarkable for its date in having long tunnel vaults which rest only on a central arch and on eight columns with rough capitals. There is neither gallery nor clerestory*

The earliest buildings to which the term 'Romanesque' is applied are really crude Romanizing structures, in Lombardy, Dalmatia or Catalonia. S. Vincenzo in Prato, Milan (*c*.833), for instance, has vaulting only in the apses, while S. Pietro, Agliate, near Milan (*c*.875) has tunnel vaults, not groin vaults. These churches, like some early basilicas, have only three apses – one central and one at the end of each aisle – but St Donat at Zara in Dalmatia (*c*.876) actually anticipates, in an archaic way, the ambulatory and radiating chapel arrangement. In Catalonia at least two churches, Sta Maria, Amer (949) and Sta Cecilia, Montserrat (*c*.957) are humble buildings with fairly sophisticated vaults. Picturesque and romantic in setting, and carefully restored, is the monastery of St-Martin-du-Canigou in the Pyrenees (*c*.1009). It has long tunnel vaults over nave and aisles, all supported on columnar shafts; the plan is Romanesque, the structure Roman.

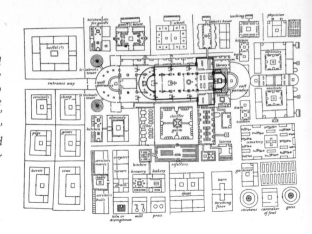

112 Ideal plan for the monastery of St Gall (c.820). In this redrawn version the parts can be identified: the long-aisled church with a transept, apsed ends and round towers at the west; the monastic quarters around the cloister to the south and east of the church; in the western and far southern area, guests' lodgings, stables, workrooms, servants' quarters, a school, etc. A regularized plan for a spiritual, cultural and commercial centre

113, 114 St-Philibert, Tournus (begun c.950). The crypt (plan below) has an ambulatory and radiating chapels. Two rows of slender columns down the centre support the choir floor, on rough groin vaults; the ambulatory is tunnel-vaulted. In the church itself (opposite) the nave, at the left, has transverse tunnel vaults while the aisles, at the right, are groin-vaulted. The small stonework and fairly thick mortar are typical of 'First Romanesque'. All the mouldings are severe and square, decorated only by banded stonework or paint

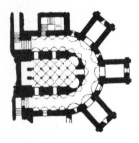

In the Benedictine monastery of St Gall is a manuscript plan dating from c.820. It shows at how early a date the conception of a highly organized large monastery had been realized – on paper. The Benedictine Rule was the most civilizing influence in Europe, not least in architecture. The St Gall plan shows a basilican nave which, with its apses – one eastern and one western – was 325 feet long. Flanking the western apse there are round towers. North and south transepts, together with the extended eastern choir, transformed a basilican plan into a cruciform one. In their junction with the nave they also created the 'crossing' – a focal point over which could ultimately rise a belfry, central tower or Gothic flèche. The St Gall plan shows the church as being the heart of a conglomeration of schools, libraries, workshops, farms and so on. There was also the cloister garth, balancing contemplation with activity. Both socially and architecturally the medieval Church was taking shape.

One church of the 'First Romanesque' period is particularly important: St-Philibert, at Tournus in Burgundy. Begun about 950, its plan includes a westwork, a transept, and a crypt with ambulatory and radiating chapels. Above the crypt this arrangement is repeated. The significance of this development is immeasurable;

here, fully developed seemingly for the first time, was the French chevet. Tournus is also remarkable for its stone vaults, a series of experiments with tunnel vaults (both longitudinal and transverse), quadrant vaults and groin vaults, carried out in the early years of the eleventh and twelfth centuries.

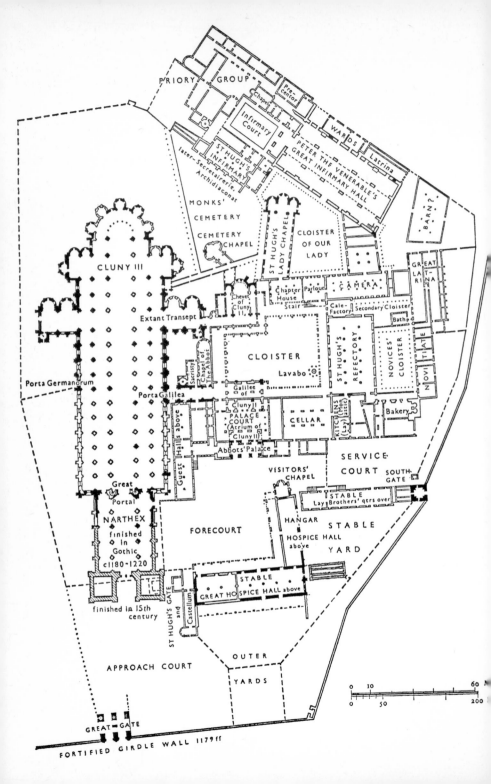

PRIORY GROUP

Pre-Centor

Chapel

Infirmary Court

WARDS

Latrina

ST. HUGH'S INFIRMARY later: Secretairerie, Archidiaconat

PETER THE VENERABLE'S GREAT INFIRMARY HALL

BARN?

MONKS' CEMETERY

CEMETERY CHAPEL

ST HUGH'S LADY CHAPEL

CLOISTER OF OUR LADY

GREAT LATRINA

CLUNY III

Chevet of Cluny II.

Chapter House

Parlour Stair

CAMERA

Cale-Factory

Secondary Cloister

Baths

Extant Transept

Sacristy

Door of The Abbot

Galilee of

ST HUGH'S REFECTORY

NOVICES CLOISTER

NOVITIATE

Porta Germanorum

Porta Galilea

Guest Halls above

CLOISTER

Lavabo

KITCHENS (Lay) Classic

Bakery

Cluny II. PALACE COURT (Atrium of Cluny II)

CELLAR

Abbots' Palace

SERVICE COURT

Great Portal

VISITORS' CHAPEL

SOUTH GATE

STABLE Lay Brothers' qtrs over

NARTHEX finished in Gothic c1180-1220

HANGAR

HOSPICE HALL above

STABLE

FORECOURT

STABLE YARD

finished in 15th century

ST HUGH'S GATE and

Castellum

STABLE GREAT HOSPICE HALL above

APPROACH COURT

OUTER

YARDS

0   10   60 M
0   50   200

GREAT GATE

FORTIFIED GIRDLE WALL 1179 ff

115 *Opposite: plan of the monastery of Cluny in 1157, including projected buildings (showing Professor Conant's latest research). The general grouping is standard (cp. Ill. 112). Near the entrance are stables and guests' quarters; the centre around the cloister is reserved for the abbot, monks and lay-brothers; beyond this the infirmary stands in isolation. In the plan of the church (some 600 feet long) note the double aisles, double transepts with apsed chapels, and the chevet with ambulatory and radiating chapels*

116 *Model of the third church at Cluny (1088–c.1121), from the east. The elements seen in the plan, opposite, are clearly recognizable – apse with chapels, low eastern and larger western transepts with their chapels. In addition there are great towers over the two crossings and over the western transept arms*

One of the great institutions of the Romanesque world – instrumental in bringing the St Gall ideal to fruition – was the Cluniac Order. The monks came to Cluny, in southern Burgundy, in 915, and for three hundred years were a great cultural force. The second abbey church at Cluny, begun about 955, inspired other churches from Spain to Germany. The vast third church was complete by 1121, with a three-storey elevation under a pointed barrel vault, double aisles, twin transepts, and some of the finest of all Romanesque sculpture. The rebuilding was the work of Abbot Hugh of Semur, one of the great builders of all time: he governed the Order for sixty years until his death in 1109, and personally approved the plans for about a thousand churches. Among the great Cluniac priories such churches as

Paray-le-Monial (c.1100) and Autun (c.1120) followed the pattern of Cluny III; Vézelay, contemporary with Autun, was completely different, with high groin vaults and no triforium. A common ideal of magnificence ran through all Cluniac architecture. There were local variations – Burgundian, Provençal, Saxon, Swiss, Lombardic, Spanish and so on. Many Cluniac churches had rich Corinthian carving, and each was noble in its vaulting, its many-towered silhouette, lighting and colour . . . all primarily a setting for the Cluniac psalmody.

Another institution which brought Romanesque architecture to maturity was the pilgrimage. Not yet was Europe a network of pilgrimage routes with every cathedral a shrine, but as early as 844 we hear of Santiago de Compostela in north-western Spain as the shrine of James, son of Zebedee. A generation later pilgrims, in parties of two hundred at a time, were streaming down the roads of France. These roads started at Arles, Le Puy, Vézelay, St-Denis and Chartres where there were

117, 118 Paray-le-Monial (c.1100, above) and Vézelay (c.1120, right) were both Cluniac, but they differ completely in design. Paray-le-Monial is similar to Cluny III, with an ambulatory glimpsed between narrow piers, and pointed transverse arches supporting a tunnel vault. Vézelay, on the other hand, has high groin vaults and round transverse arches, strikingly banded in coloured stone

already churches of note. They converged upon Spain at Roncevaux. On each of the five roads was a great pilgrimage church – St Martin at Tours, St Martial at Limoges, Ste Foy at Conques, St Sernin at Toulouse and, of course, Santiago de Compostela itself.

Those five churches, all finished by the early twelfth century, show Romanesque in its maturity. The church at Conques – perhaps the most beautiful – is the smallest; the others are all of the order of 300 feet long, and have highly developed plans. As forecast a generation earlier by the ambulatory and chapels of St Philibert at Tournus, the aisles have now become processional ways around the whole building, culminating in the shrine behind or beneath the high altar – the last stage of the pilgrimage. Each of these churches shows skill in planning, in stereotomy and vaulting. As we have seen, the typical large pilgrimage church has a two-storey elevation, with massive tunnel vaults springing above the triforium; there is no clerestory, and the interior is dimly lit from the aisle windows. Each was built high, with

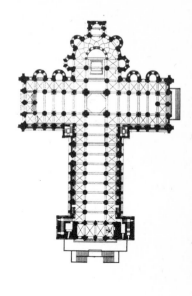

119, 120 Pilgrimage churches. The typical plan appears at Santiago de Compostela (begun c. 1075, above). An aisle runs right round the building, merging with the ambulatory; there are two eastern apses on the transepts, and two towers at the west end. The exterior reflects the plan. In the east end of St Sernin at Toulouse (begun c. 1080, left), the ambulatory and numerous chapels are clearly expressed (cp. Cluny, Ill. 116) building up to the octagonal crossing tower, finished in Gothic times. The church is of brick

towers, and each had perfect acoustics for the Roman chant.

The generation which saw the growth of the Santiago pilgrimage and the earlier work of the Cluniacs also witnessed a spiritual awakening in the monastic world. Carthusians, Premonstratensians and Cistercians were all founded in the forty years between 1080 and 1120. The Cistercians were never 'anti-Cluny', but by the example of their austere life they brought about the decline of the Cluniacs. By the year 1200 there were some seven hundred Cistercian monasteries. The monks chose remote and well-watered sites. Their abbeys were severely plain and uniform all over Europe – a Cistercian monk could feel at home in any of them. Towers, painting and sculpture were excluded. The churches were at first extremely simple. Rebuilding about 1130 gave Cîteaux and Clairvaux new, larger monasteries, still very plain; the churches (both destroyed) had square east ends, and two-storey elevations with clerestories. Pontigny (begun 1140), with its chevet of c. 1185–1210, is probably very like the final form of the great church at Clairvaux. Fontenay (1139–47) is the oldest surviving

121 Pontigny, a Cistercian church whose simplicity contrasts with the more elaborate Cluniac buildings. The late 12th-century chevet with flying buttresses has a continuous outer ring of chapels; there are no towers

122 Fontenay (1139–47), the Cistercian ideal. The piers are articulated, but there is no sculpture and the east end is austerely square. The arcade is slightly pointed, and wall-shafts carry the transverse arches of a pointed tunnel vault

Cistercian complex and must represent St Bernard's wishes. The site is wooded, the buildings spacious within their walled enclosure, also well proportioned and of fine ashlar, but completely unadorned. There are transverse barrel vaults in the aisles, a Cistercian feature found, for example, at Fountains (1135–50) in England.

It is not possible to consider Romanesque architecture in terms of what we now call 'countries'. Clearly, for instance, Normany and England were a single school of architecture. Clearly, also, monastic influence ignored the loose boundaries of Romanesque Europe. As Professor Kenneth Conant has written: 'The Romanesque is a style of fascinating by-ways and local schools. This

123 Jerichow Abbey, Brandenburg (c.1200). A Premonstratensian abbey church, almost wholly of excellent brickwork. It has a raised choir (cp. Ill. 130) and a two-storey elevation below a wooden ceiling

125 Opposite: west front of St-Gilles-du-Gard (c.1170), very Roman with its composition based upon a triumphal arch, its Corinthian columns, fluted pilasters and jambs, classical mouldings around the tympana, and its sculptural style derived from antiquity

has been its charm for many lovers of the arts, and, in consequence, the historians have generally analysed it as a series of quasi-independent regional phenomena. Yet the great movements and chief institutions of Roman-esque times with their architecture were inter-regional."

Many of these regional schools must here be taken for granted, and only one or two considered in detail. Local materials influenced building everywhere. On one sense both Romanesque and Gothic were born of the splendid limestones of France. In the Netherlands and northern Germany the clays ultimately gave us a great school of brick building, while the Romanesque of Italy and Provence acquired its own Mediterranean character through the decorative and sculptural use of marble. The fragmented geological map of England gave a variety of schools – limestone, sandstone, flint, brick – while the importation of Caen stone from Normandy to Norman England gave a material beautifully textured for the carver.

Northern, Roman, Byzantine and even Islamic

elements are found in varying degrees everywhere. Apart from Charlemagne's specifically Byzantine work at Aachen, Byzantine influence is evident in Sicily, where the rulers – in an attempt to rival the Emperor of the East – imported craftsmen from Byzantium. St-Front at Périgueux (c.1120) in Aquitaine is structurally almost wholly Byzantine, the plan almost identical to that of St Mark's in Venice. Angoulême Cathedral (1105–28) and the abbey of Fontevrault (c.1119) are other examples in Aquitaine of Romanesque churches with domes over square bays. Islamic influence, while strongest in Spain, also appears in Sicily and on the French pilgrimage roads into Spain. It is evident, for example, in the doorways and large-cusped arches at Moissac and in the cathedral and St-Michel-d'Aiguille at Le Puy. In Provence on the other hand, true to their tradition, they continued to build handsomely in a Latin way. The façade of the Cluniac priory of St-Gilles-du-Gard (c.1170), and St-Trophîme at Arles, with its late twelfth-century cloister walk, are Provençal examples of Roman simplicity.

124 Above: central apse of Monreale Cathedral, Sicily (begun 1174). The interlacing arches and discs, themselves patterned and forming a rich design on a light ground, show Islamic influence

126 In this detail of the ruins of Notre-Dame at Jumièges (1037-66) we see its two most distinctive features: (a) the double-bay system of the nave (cp. Ills. 105, 109) giving alternate cylindrical piers and compound piers with wall-shafts which carried a flat wooden roof, and (b) one of the two west towers (cp. Ill. 128). At the top is the western crossing-arch

If the Burgundian intellect was uniquely capable of a synthesis of planning, structure and carving, other regional schools made their contributions. Languedoc advanced the progress of vaulting in such great churches – already mentioned – as Conques. Apart from the domed pseudo-Byzantine churches, there was also in Aquitaine a special Loire group which built with surprising maturity such things as the abbey of St-Benoît-sur-Loire as early as 1060; even before 903 St-Martin at Tours may have had vaulted aisles.

The greater Romanesque churches all followed the basilican plan of nave and aisles, though with the addition of transepts and eastern chapels they were by the twelfth century far removed from the original pagan basilicas. In most of them the nave and aisles were separated by rows of uniform columns or piers, but in certain buildings and in certain areas there were variations on this pattern, in the form of alternating supports. These usually consisted of a simple rhythm of thick-thin-thick, with compound piers alternating with columns or with more slender piers. Two bays of the aisle correspond thus to one bay of the nave: all bays could, by this means, be kept square, which was a great help where groin or round-arched rib vaults were used – pending the liberating force of the pointed arch. We find this system all over Europe, in such otherwise diverse buildings as Jumièges in France, Modena and S. Michele at Pavia in Italy and Durham in England. A different system was introduced in St Michael at Hildesheim: to every bay of the nave there were three corresponding bays of the aisle, making a rhythm of two columns, one pier, two columns, one pier, and so on. This triple rhythm became popular throughout Lower Saxony, but in the great churches of the Rhineland it is the double-bay system that we find, lending variety to such a monumental building as the cathedral at Speyer – a royal mausoleum with a fine crypt and with a total length of 435 feet, the same as Chartres.

One of the great phenomena of the medieval world –
second only to its inheritance from the Roman Empire
– was the impact of the Normans. By the beginning of
the eleventh century these intelligent, vigorous Vikings
had been living in France for over a hundred years. They
had become not only French and feudal, but also
patrons of monastic orders and of great master masons.
They created a civilization as far south as Sicily, as far
north as Iceland. The Romanesque of Normandy
became a consistent structural system, applied in turn
in the English cathedrals built with such energy after
the Conquest.

Norman Romanesque – like Norman rule – was
heavy, strong, uncompromising, but also highly articulated. While the mouldings were simple squares and
roundels, the ornament largely abstract and even the
capitals often only plain 'cushions', the architecture was
nevertheless orchestrated masonry of a high order. Every
concentric ring of every arch had a square or a half-
column to correspond to it in the pier below (moulded
arches springing awkwardly from cylindrical piers as at
Gloucester, Malvern and Tewkesbury have been mentioned on p. 102; they may be regarded as an English
Benedictine aberration). Moreover, the sheer richness of
a multiplicity of concentric arches – possible only in a
thick wall – became in itself a kind of ornament, as one
may see in the innumerable doorways of English village
churches. Within the nave, however, apart from mass,
scale and harmony of parts, almost the only concession
to emotion was the strong division between the bays by
the great emphasis put upon the wall-shaft, taken up in
an unbroken vertical band from floor to roof. In this
lay not only the strong articulation of the bays themselves,
but also the germ of that soaring quality, that aspiration,
that was to be the essence of Gothic – though less in
England, paradoxically, than in France.

The Romanesque of Normandy was worked out as
early as c. 1040 at the abbey of Jumièges. There, as we

127 *In Durham Cathedral nave, a much enriched version of the double-bay system supports high rib vaults of c.1130. All the ribs are decorated with typically Norman chevron mouldings; transverse arches, slightly pointed and with heavier mouldings, separate the twin vaulting bays*

have already seen, we find that to keep the bays square on plan there are two bays of the aisle to one of the nave: the wall-shaft is used only on alternate piers. The same system appears at Durham, begun in 1093; but whereas Jumièges never was vaulted (the wall-shafts at most carried transverse arches for a wooden ceiling), at Durham there came the historic moment when, instead of using round arches and the usual vaults, the masons chose to roof the cathedral with rib vaults: the choir was rib-vaulted by 1104, but this vault – owing to faulty infilling – had to be rebuilt. In the nave (*c.*1130) the vaults are of a highly unusual type consisting of two twinned quadripartite vaults per bay, separated by pointed transverse arches. Here were the germs of the Gothic style, though below these vaults Durham was fully Romanesque.

The Norman style of church-building which was brought to England in 1066 typically involved a three-storey elevation and cruciform plan, sometimes with towers. We find this in St-Etienne at Caen, William the Conqueror's own foundation of c.1068. Among the earliest Norman works to survive in England is the north transept of Winchester (c.1079) – very plain, with large-jointed masonry. The flowering of the style is exemplified in the groin-vaulted crypt of Canterbury (c.1100–1120) and in the great naves of Ely and Peterborough.

The story of Italian architecture during the Middle Ages is, on the whole, different. The early churches of Lombardy, from the ninth century, radiated a new building system throughout southern Europe which, as well as the good masonry used in Carolingian buildings at the same time, involved the use of stone vaults. Ornament on the exterior was in the form of pilaster-strips, ending at the top in a row of shallow, blank arches. The style as a whole spread to the Rhineland, then returned to northern Italy in the eleventh century to be embodied

128 West front of St-Etienne, Caen (begun c.1068). Nave and aisles are expressed by the division into wide and narrow bays, separated by flat Norman buttresses. Above the aisles rise two arcaded towers, strikingly high even before the addition of Gothic spires. For the development of this theme, see Ills. 136, 142 and 145

129 Ely Cathedral nave (begun c.1110) shows the three-storey Norman arrangement of arcade, gallery and clerestory with a passage in the thickness of the wall. The capitals are plain cushions. The wall-shafts rise to a vast wooden ceiling. On the right the corner of the crossing, originally square, is canted for the 14th-century octagon (Ill. 164)

in such churches as S. Abbondio and S. Fedele in Como.
At the time there was widespread experimentation with
rib vaults: the magnificent church of S. Ambrogio in
Milan may have had rib vaults before Durham, though
its present vaulting almost certainly dates from after 1117.

The chaotic state of Rome after the fall of the Empire
meant an almost complete cessation of building; while
the cathedrals were built Rome slept. Elsewhere, at
Pisa for instance and at Florence, a style emerged depending much on surface enrichment for its effect. There was
no innovation in plan, no attempt at vaulting. At Pisa
little decorative arcades and rich marble facing are used
throughout, even in the Gothic Baptistery and Campo
Santo. S. Miniato al Monte in Florence is simple,
beautifully proportioned in a classic way, and rich in
marble inlay; it has a wooden roof. Pevsner called it
'a first synthesis of Tuscan intellect and grace with
Roman simplicity and poise'. It is difficult indeed to
believe that S. Miniato was built before the Norman
transept at Winchester.

*131 S. Ambrogio, Milan (choir c.940,
nave begun c.1080). Roman in its
breadth, like S. Miniato, the nave is
however splendidly covered by quadripartite rib vaults, in vast domed-up
square bays. Note the articulated response of the piers to arches and vaults,
and the absence of a clerestory*

*130 Opposite: S. Miniato al Monte,
Florence (c.1073), shows how different southern Romanesque is from
northern. The scale is almost Roman;
the piers are copies of classical columns,
with some re-used antique capitals; the
choir is raised over a crypt; nave and
aisles have open timber roofs; and the
richness of the marble facing, itself
Roman in inspiration, is more evident
than any structural vigour*

123

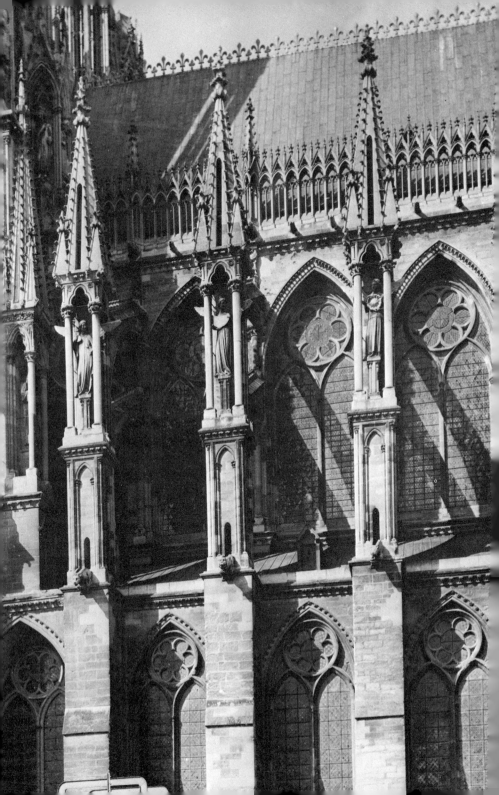

Chapter Six

WESTERN CHRISTENDOM:
II GOTHIC

The Middle Ages, from the time of Charlemagne to the Reformation, are like some vast tapestry, rich and glowing, filled with detail both sublime and squalid. We may think of this tapestry as being woven through seven hundred years; as the work comes to a close the details become more complex, also more precise and defined. What began as a story of pious abbots and fighting chieftains, framed in heavy Romanesque arches, ends with the extreme sophistication of the monastic orders, the heraldic protocol of an aristocracy, the mercantile cities of northern Europe and Italy, and with the splendours and miseries of the Crusades; while through it all runs the golden thread of Gothic art, the discipline of Gothic structure.

Medieval architecture was European but, after the twelfth century, it emanated mainly from France, and has come to be called 'Gothic'. This is no less true because technically there was, in our sense, no such thing as France. There was Brittany, a fief on the fringe of the Celtic world; there was Normandy, expansionist and practical, creating the administrative structure without which no great architecture can exist; there was Burgundy, with its great river system and its big fairs and its long chain of abbeys – a land fervent for building and for travel. There was Aquitaine, which belonged to or was influenced by England during much of the medieval period. And then there was Provence, once a province of the Empire, represented in the Roman Senate, and very Roman in its life and laws, learning

132 Rheims Cathedral nave (designed c.1210). The Gothic style depends on a balance of forces, as against the Romanesque reliance on mass. On the exterior of a Gothic cathedral the system whereby the thrusts are transmitted is frankly exposed. Pointed arches channel the weight of the vault to a few selected points. At these points flying buttresses carry it to the ground; to counter the outward thrust of the vault, they are weighted with heavy pinnacles. The new structural theory went hand in hand with a new aesthetic. Flying buttresses were seen as leaping flights of stone; pinnacles became displays of sculpture and ornament; windows, now safely as wide as the spaces between the buttresses, were filled with patterns of bar-tracery, probably invented here at Rheims in the early years of the century. Most important, all these features were welded into a unity

and art . . . a civilizing link between Antiquity and Christendom.

Above all there was the central domain of the Ile de France. This was the ancient realm of the Capetian monarchy, taking one back almost to the last days of Charlemagne. Hugh Capet, in the tenth century, had been called 'august king of France and Aquitaine'. By making the coronation an eighth sacrament he had been set above all other feudal lords, as 'the eldest son of the Church'. Only slowly did Normandy, Burgundy, Brittany and the rest come under the royal sceptre, but the disputations of the University of Paris decided both the theology and the law of Christendom. As Byzantium in the East had succeeded Rome as a world-capital so Paris did in the West. The Ile de France became a casket wherein civilization was safeguarded. From Paris and the cathedrals of the Ile de France – St-Denis, Laon, Chartres, Amiens, Beauvais, Le Mans and Bourges – the structural and aesthetic principles of Gothic went

133 Loches, one of the great castles of France. The rectangular tower in the centre is the old keep ('donjon') of about 1100. In front of it stand the bastions and curtain walls of the later castle. The slope ('batter') of the wall and the keeled plan of the bastions are sophisti-cations introduced into military archi-tecture by advances in the technique of war

forth, carried across Europe by the great master masons. The centralized nature of the French monarchy, as well as its sacramental prestige, enabled the kings of France to pursue a consistent policy – architectural as well as political – through many generations.

Every part of medieval Europe set its own stamp upon this Gothic architecture. German, Spanish, English are all distinguishable and have each their own history, and yet each is truly only a local variant of the great structural theme evolved by the builders of St-Denis, Sens, Laon and Chartres. In the early twelfth century the Roman-esque churches of, say, Normandy and England, are almost identical; little more than a hundred years later, Amiens and Salisbury must be contrasted rather than compared. And yet, in spite of the differences, the former is a central example, the latter a provincial example of the same style, the Gothic.

Gothic architecture must be seen in a Gothic Europe, a Europe where travel was difficult in summer, impos-sible in winter, but almost always fruitful since journeys were made only for serious reasons – the pilgrimage, the crusade, the commission to build a cathedral. Gothic architecture must also be seen as a product of a caste system, in which each man had his specific place and function. The Church or the monastic orders built cathedrals, abbeys and parish churches. The aristocracy built manors and castles – Germany alone once had ten thousand castles. The merchants, the burghers and the guilds built the towns. The power of these chartered corporations was of tremendous importance. Cloth halls, guild halls, warehouses and big gabled market squares show that long before the Middle Ages came to an end, fine building was not just a function of the Church but also a symbol of worldly success. Moreover, it was in the town that a man could apprentice himself to a guild, and thereby become a craftsman. The independence of the town was as vital to Gothic art as was the wealth of the Church.

134 The Cloth Hall at Bruges, with its overwhelming tower raised in 1482, expresses the secular, mercantile wealth of one of the most prosperous towns of medieval Europe

127

While the bishops built churches, the aristocracy castles and the merchants towns, the peasantry built cottages, mills and barns. The hovels of the twelfth century, without glass or chimneys, have not survived, but by the fifteenth century – as may be seen in many villages and farms – Western Europe had one of the finest vernaculars in history.

This great wealth of building reflected an elaborate system of customs and institutions. The Seven Sacraments and the Seven Deadly Sins covered almost everything from birth to death, and were planned for. There were a thousand local cults, with their holy trees and wishing-wells, which, like the greater heresies, had to be stamped out: the Church became more militant and this, too, was reflected in architecture. There was the institution of the pilgrimage, which, as we have seen, already in Romanesque times seems to have led to a greater specialization of church plans, with aisles, ambulatory and radiating chapels. In Gothic the planning of these eastern chapels was taken to further extremes of ingenuity. The Crusades – six of them in two hundred and fifty years – were an institution momentous for architecture. Apart from such things as Frankish castles in the Holy Land, there was the undoubted feedback of Saracenic influence upon Gothic art, upon mathematics and upon manners.

The institution of the siege – a very formal operation – dictated the progressive development of the castle, while within the castle wall – as we may see it portrayed in the *Romance of the Rose* – the troubadours inspired the 'paradise', the enclosed garden with fountain and trellis, forerunner of the Elizabethan parterre. Chivalry, with its mystique of knighthood and its heraldic emblems, became a basis for decoration, particularly in that last blaze of Gothic that we see in Tudor England.

The emotional appeal of Gothic structure was such that for the carver, broderer or glazier, the representation of architectural elements in miniature became in itself a

135 In this 15th-century stained glass window at Long Melford Church in Suffolk, the knight kneels under a miniature vault complete with capitals and buttresses

decorative motif. In the canopies above saints' heads, for instance, we may see whole vaults, flying buttresses and mullioned windows, all a few inches high – a sure sign that architecture was the dominant art of the age.

Like medieval life, medieval architecture was highly systematized. Every part was dependent upon every other part. Function, structure and decoration were, more than in any other style, an absolute trinity. From a complex plan one can deduce, almost, the smallest cusp; from the carved boss one can deduce the form of the vault, and so back to the system of abutment and to the plan.

What, then, was Gothic architecture? *First:* it was a system whereby a fireproof roof of stone had its outward thrust resisted, not by thick walls as in Romanesque building, but by external buttresses. As the style developed from the twelfth to the sixteenth century, this system was so exploited by putting mass and strength into the buttresses – where it was needed – and by paring away the wall itself, that there was in the end virtually no wall at all, nothing but very big windows between buttresses. Since the many small panels of glass had to be supported, and since such windows had necessarily to be wind-resisting, they were subdivided by mullions and by tracery. This, in turn, gave such scope to the stained-glass worker that his art became as much the concomitant of Gothic as mosaic had been of Byzantine. This last manifestation of Gothic – the lantern church that is all window and buttress – was the goal towards which the Middle Ages moved. *Second:* Gothic was a carved architecture. Although when we look at, say, the west front of Wells (begun *c.*1200) or of Rheims (*c.*1240) we see a building designed, as was a Greek temple, to receive sculptured figures, this is secondary to the fact that almost every stone is carved for its position in the building, carved with mouldings. Every element – rib, mullion, shaft, arch, jamb – thus incorporated the three qualities of architecture: function, structure and decora-tion. The mouldings of each stone added to its efficiency

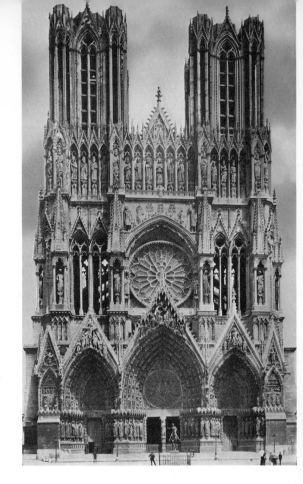

136 In the west front of Rheims Cathedral (c.1240) we see how completely Gothic is a carved architecture. Every stone is moulded to fit into the sculptural scheme, the vertical elements ruthlessly asserting themselves against the horizontal. In this extreme statement of the classic French Gothic façade, the twin towers have become open cages of stone; the nave is lit by rose window whose tracery is like the veins of a flower; and the great portals, filled with statuary and projecting outward under separate gables to get greater depth, stretch upward a third of the way to the tower tops

by reducing its weight, and added to its decorative nature by expressing lines of force – tension, rhythm, thrust – throughout the building. The larger buttress played a similar structural and aesthetic role: it placed weight where it was needed, at right angles to the line of thrust; it divided bay from bay externally as the tall Romanesque vaulting shaft had already done internally.

The key features of Gothic architecture were: *1*, the pointed arch; *2*, the flying buttress; *3*, the vaulting rib; and *4*, the moulding. Each of these had been only tentatively foreshadowed in Romanesque. The pointed arch had, for instance, been used in the third church at Cluny about 1100, but nobody ever dreamt that it might revolutionize the plan. The flying buttress, to carry the thrust of the nave vault across the aisle to the outer wall, was used by Romanesque builders, but was hidden under the lean-to roof of the aisle, never exploited architecturally. The vaulting rib also, of course, existed in Romanesque times, but only in so far as the essential cross-arches and diagonal arches of the square vaulting bay were exposed as heavy ribs below the smooth soffit of the vault; a multiplicity of delicate ribs to form a richly patterned roof was solely a Gothic thing. The Romanesque articulated pier, with squares and roundels corresponding to the concentric rings of the arch above, was in a sense moulded; real mouldings, as an aesthetic treatment of the stone, were, however, something that emerged, as at Chartres and Wells, only around 1200.

Although these were key features of Gothic architecture the thing which truly liberated Gothic, making it technically possible, was the pointed arch. We have seen how the Romans, in the halls of the thermae, built un-ribbed quadripartite vaults over square bays, and did so on a very big scale. We have also seen how there were heavily ribbed Romanesque vaults, but also virtually only over square bays. In fact, in spite of courageous structure and superb art, both Roman and Romanesque

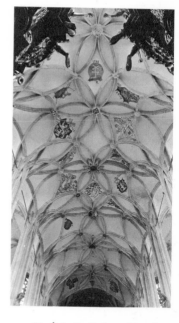

137 Vault in St Barbara, Kuttenberg (1512–47), by Benedikt Ried. Whereas the ribs of most Early and High Gothic buildings were functional, Late Gothic masons so mastered the vault that they could use ribs merely to form delicate or fantastic patterns

138 Beauvais Cathedral choir, begun in 1225 and left unfinished in the 16th century, shows the flying buttress used – in two flights – to the limits of what was possible in stone. Even so, the collapse of the vaults in 1284 was due not to their height but to bad foundations. The transept front shows the lavish late Flamboyant style of decoration

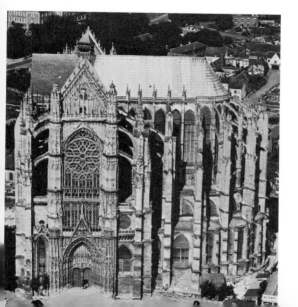

builders were always subject to the tyranny of the square bay. If the ridge of the vault was to run level, then clearly the arches on all four sides of the bay must all rise to the same height and – since neither Roman nor Romanesque builder could conceive of an arch other than the semi-circular – the vaulting bay *must* be square. Both Roman and Romanesque builders occasionally tried to solve this problem by stilting or depressing the semi-circular arch; this must be regarded as a botch.

The pointed arch – since it could be steeply or slightly pointed at will – resolved the situation completely. It was one of the great breakthroughs of architectural history. Once the pointed arch was accepted and understood, then a vaulting bay could be rectangular instead of square, with steeply pointed arches on its short sides, and shallower arches on the long sides. Indeed, by varying the steepness of the various arches and ribs the bay could be almost any shape that was necessary to conform with the function of the plan. Examples are the rhomboidal bays of the ambulatory, the polygonal chapels of the French chevet and the polygonal chapter-houses of England.

The technical advantages of the pointed arch were, therefore, tremendous. Viollet-le-Duc, according to Nikolaus Pevsner, has overestimated them; it would be difficult to do so. The pointed arch, by making possible rectangular and irregularly shaped bays, completely emancipated the plan. The pointed arch made possible a multiplicity of vaulting ribs; all spring from one shaft, all are of different curvature; all could rise to the same height. The ribs of any given vaulting bay did not necessarily all rise to the same height. The ridge, specially in western France, might be slightly curved so as to give each bay a domical appearance. But the important thing is that, with the pointed arch, the height to which each rib would rise was under the absolute control of the designer. By the early fourteenth century, when English Gothic was fully developed, no fewer than eleven ribs

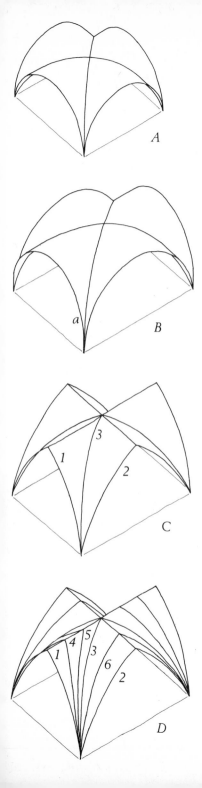

139 *From Romanesque groin vault to Gothic tierceron vault:*

A. *The round arch requires a square vaulting bay*

B. *If a vault with round arches is built over a rectangular bay, then the arches on the shorter side must be stilted (raised on straight sides, as shown at 'a') to rise to the same height*

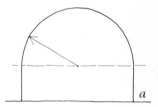

C. *The pointed arch, with its extreme flexibility, solves this problem. The arch over the short side (1) is steeply pointed; the arch over the longer side (2) is less steeply pointed; the arch across the longest span, the diagonal (3) is very obtusely pointed, even semi-circular – and yet all three can rise to the same height, giving a level ridge-line. In the Gothic vault these arches are ribs, forming a stone web to hold the lighter infilling in each cell*

D. *Additional ribs (4, 5, 6) are added, called 'tiercerons'. They simplified construction by reducing the size of each cell of the vault; aesthetically, they opened the way for the Late Gothic vault, a highly decorative ceiling. The awkward junction of ribs at different angles was masked by the use of the boss*

rose from each tiny capital on the vaulting shafts of Exeter nave. By a biological analogy we may say that the ideal of the Roman or Romanesque builder was to make a dome or vault like a turtle shell, with as smooth a soffit as possible, while the ideal of the Gothic builder was to make a vault like a mammalian skeleton, an organic complex of spine and ribs – structural and tense, yet also unified.

The pointed arch also made possible the rectangular as opposed to the square bay, thus causing the total weight of the building to be distributed over twice as many points of support. It made possible the large traceried windows and the slenderer supports of triforium and nave arcade, so that all was brought into organic harmony with the vault above. The pointed arch caused a more precise

140, 141 St-Denis Abbey Church: right, the ambulatory; opposite, above, plan. The narthex (on the left of the plan, in black) and the chevet (on the right) were rebuilt by Abbot Suger from c.1134 onward, and represent the very earliest examples of the Gothic style. The chevet (right) in particular shows what opportunities for lightness and flexibility were provided by the pointed arch and the rib vault. Not only could spans of different widths easily be brought to the same height, but the vaulting-bay itself could be of any plan. The nave and transepts of St-Denis were rebuilt in High Gothic a century after Suger

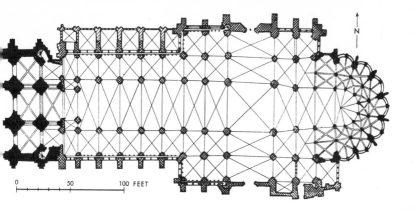

0   50   100 FEET

concentration of thrust at the abutment, with a consequent lightening of the whole structure and the
apparent miracle of the flying buttress. The *aesthetic*
qualities of Gothic were only possible because of the
technical qualities inherent in the pointed arch. Having
stated the nature of Gothic in general we now turn to its
development in specific examples.

One of the greatest of medieval patrons of building was
Abbot Suger of St-Denis. Finding his Carolingian
abbey church inadequate for pilgrims, he built a
narthex, then started to rebuild the choir in 1140. He has
left a book showing the medieval attitude to architecture
– a mixture of daring innovation and mystical symbolism.
That the chevet was the Crown of Thorns was only part
of a system of symbols running through the whole
building. The master mason is not named; this shows
only, perhaps, that good building was taken for granted,
as a technology rather than an art. The chevet at St-
Denis has not only a polygonal chancel with a circumambient aisle but also, in effect, a second outer aisle
running through the chapels. The result is an airy
interior, full of intriguing vistas and perspectives. The
pointed arch is used throughout; it had to be over such
a complex plan, but already this new-found flexibility is
giving us marvellous new spatial possibilities.

142 *Chartres Cathedral façade, of the standard two-tower type, spans the Gothic centuries. The lower part of the centre, including the famous Portail Royal, and the towers belong to the work begun in 1134. The circular window of plate tracery is contemporary with the present church, begun after 1194. The Flamboyant spire on the left was added in 1507, on the eve of the Renaissance*

143 *Opposite: Chartres Cathedral transept (c.1194–1260). Earlier Gothic builders had favoured a four-storey elevation (see Ill. 147). Here the masons returned to the three-storey arrangement, retaining the shallow tri-forium and eliminating the gallery, whose buttressing role was superseded by the external flying buttress. The clerestory lancets were enlarged and crowned by a wheel of plate tracery (visible top left), and filled with stained glass. Shafts running from floor to vault increase the vertical emphasis*

The new choir of St Denis was consecrated in 1144. Throughout the Ile de France and beyond, there was a great wave of emulation. In central France alone Sens, Noyon and Senlis were built between 1140 and 1220. Then came the great cathedrals of Paris (1163–1235), Laon (1163–1225), Bourges (1190–1275), Chartres (1194–1260), Rheims (c.1210–1300), Le Mans (1220–64) and Amiens (1220–88). Chartres had actually been begun simultaneously with St Denis, but only the west front was ever built (an earlier church remained behind it and was burnt in 1194). Its magnificent portals, a marvellous marriage of sculpture and architecture, already belong to the first generation of Gothic. About some of these churches there is still some Romanesque austerity. The famous stained glass at Chartres, for instance, may be likened to a series of glowing banners hung upon the walls; it is set in very large lancet windows, the arches barely pointed and still without tracery. Only by the time the builders had reached the clerestory did they begin to group the lancets in pairs and crown them with a wheel of 'plate-tracery' consisting of patterns cut through the thickness of the wall – hinting at a different kind of window. However with Rheims, barely twenty years later, we have an architecture that is almost like lace, with its fully developed bar-tracery where patterns are made by stone 'bars' in the windows – appearing dark against the light rather than, as was the case with plate-tracery, light in the dark wall – and arcading. This is also an architecture that in its height and lightness had reached the most thrilling extremes of which stone was capable. Within a hundred years of Abbot Suger's achievement at St Denis we may say that we have the High Gothic style of France.

These cathedrals have certain things in common. They all have very broad but cruciform plans – that is, transepts of slight projection. Notre-Dame in Paris, with its double aisles and complete unity throughout its length,

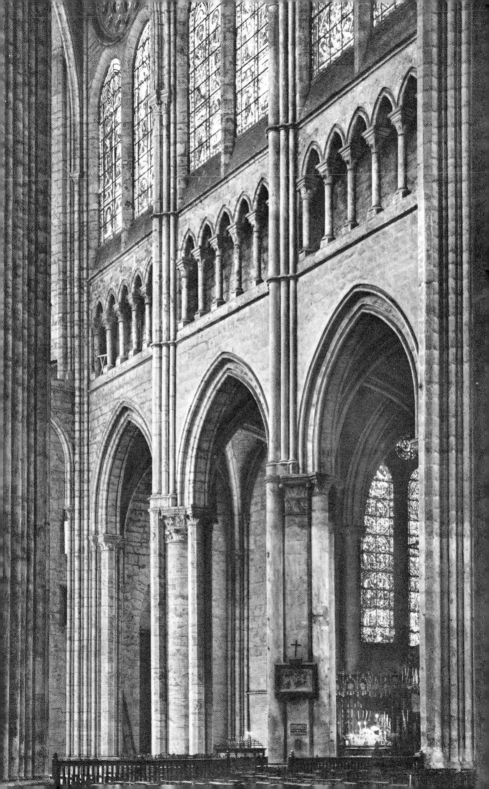

144, 145 English and French Gothic cathedrals differ in their position and in their form (see pp. 142-3). Wells (begun c.1180, below) stands in a grassy close, isolated from the town. Amiens (begun 1220, opposite) dominated its town like a great ship, the small houses pressing in round it. Where Amiens soars, Wells spreads, its two massive towers extending beyond the width of the aisles. At Amiens the ornament is integrated with the structure; at Wells it seems rather to be surface decoration. Finally, the three western portals of Amiens, like those at Rheims (Ill. 136) are overwhelmingly vast and cavernous; those at Wells are insignificant, made unnecessary by a grander entrance in the side of the north tower, at the left

may be thought of as the realization of an ideal. These cathedrals nearly all have cavernous doorways. Not only at Chartres were the doorways a field for sculpture; the portals of Laon, Rheims and Amiens are among the great things of architecture. Most have western towers, or substructures intended to take towers. In fact externally few of these cathedrals were ever completed. The builders of Chartres intended nine towers – two on the west front, two on each transept, two flanking the apse and one central tower at the crossing – with spires rather than the mere conical roofs of the twelfth century. Laon came nearest to the ideal with five completed towers. The sheer height and fragility of French Gothic usually excluded the possibility of a heavy central tower – a flèche was enough.

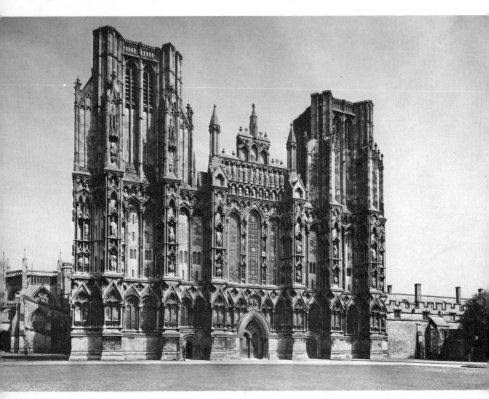

146 *Right: the interior of Bourges Cathedral (1192–1275) has double aisles which are used in a uniquely impressive way. The main arcade rises to a great height and through its arches one sees, as it were, a second interior elevation, complete with arcade – leading through to the second aisle – triforium and clerestory*

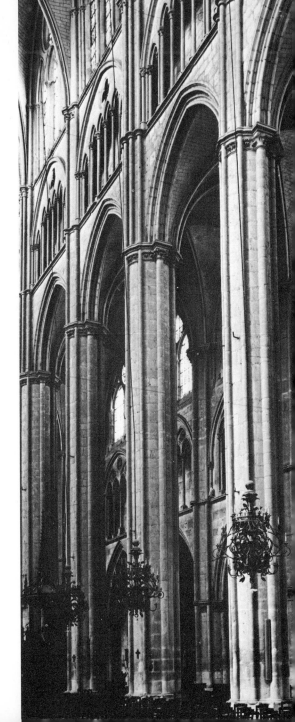

147, 148 *Opposite: the choir of Noyon Cathedral (begun c. 1150, above) shows the Early Gothic four-storey elevation. The choir of Beauvais Cathedral (below), begun in 1225 but altered later after the collapse of the original vault in 1284, attempts a different solution by glazing the triforium; its total height is almost twice as great as that of Noyon*

Internally the great High Gothic cathedrals present a three-storey arrangement. First, there is the nave arcade opening through into the aisles; second, the triforium; and third, the clerestory flooding the nave with light. From clerestory level there springs the ribbed vault. The cross-rib, dividing bay from bay, is no longer much more heavily moulded than the other ribs – as it was in Romanesque – and so what we see here in the vault is not so much a series of bays as a pattern of equal ribs growing organically from the vaulting shafts.

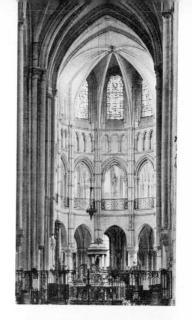

It is mainly in ringing the changes on the relative proportions of arcade, triforium and clerestory that the builders of mature French Gothic made one cathedral differ from another. The triforium which, after all, only screened the aisle roof, tended to disappear or to be glazed like the clerestory; this had happened by the late thirteenth century. At Le Mans and Bourges the pattern is varied by introducing double aisles, each with a complete elevation – three-storeyed at Bourges, two-storeyed at Le Mans. The great increase in height during the thirteenth century is shown by the difference between Noyon, a mere 85 feet from floor to vault, and Beauvais: begun less than a century later, its total height is 157 feet – achieved in three storeys, where Noyon had four.

English Gothic was derived from France, but soon developed a character of its own. Archaeologists of the early nineteenth century divided English Gothic into four main categories, which our greater architectural knowledge can now fill out. First was Early English, the style of plain lancets or simply traceried windows, from c.1175 to c.1275. Decorated was, as its name implies, the style of ornate carving and more inventive tracery, as well as spatial experiments; it flourished from c.1290 to c.1380. Perpendicular originated in the 1330s with the disappearance of the characteristic curves of Decorated; set back by the Black Death, it reappeared in the 1360s and persisted with little variation until the sixteenth century. In every case the dates given do not represent the

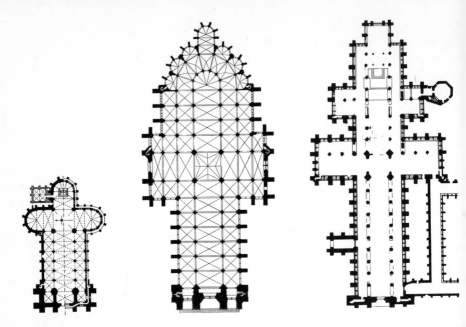

149–151 *Comparative plans, to scale, of St Elisabeth, Marburg (1233–83), Amiens Cathedral (begun 1220) and Salisbury Cathedral (begun 1220). Marburg – only a parish church – has a characteristically German trefoil east end, with apsed transepts and choir of equal length. Amiens is wide and unified, with shallow transepts and an elaborate chevet; the large axial Lady Chapel is exceptional. Salisbury is narrow in rela-tion to its length, and 'compartmented': beyond the nave there are double tran-septs, a square ambulatory around the choir, and a square-ended Lady Chapel; a cloister and chapter-house lie to the south*

absolute beginning and end of a style; as always, old ideas persisted alongside new inventions.

In 1174 there was a disastrous fire at Canterbury. William of Sens, a master mason of ingenuity, was commissioned to design the new choir. Though built by a Frenchman for a Norman archbishop, the new work does have certain English traits: it is, for instance, lower than contemporary French cathedrals. William of Sens incorporated the Cluniac device of double transepts, which in turn became an English feature, reappearing at Salisbury, Lincoln, Worcester, Hereford and – in partial form – at Exeter and York. It was a device which lengthened the whole eastern limb, thus providing for the large choir of monks or canons. Many of the English cathedrals were monastic churches, whereas the French were built for the secular clergy. This is not just an ecclesiastical point; it is of great importance for architec-ture and town planning. The English cathedral was very long from east to west, while the French cathedral remained relatively short, especially in relation to its

reat height (Westminster Abbey, for instance, is 560
eet long and 80 feet high to the springing of the vault;
Rheims is 460 feet long but 124 feet high). The French
athedral, in the middle of the town, dominated the little
ouses like a hen with her chicks. The English cathedral,
1 its 'close', has great groups of towers rising above the
ees; it could afford to be long and low. It is the monastic
rigin of so many English cathedrals which may explain
1e English neglect of the west front: while the west
oors of Salisbury or Wells are mere mouseholes,
specially in comparison with the great portals of Rheims
r Amiens, the builders lavished their attention on
orches and doorways used by the congregation, on the
pposite side from the monastic buildings.

If Canterbury was still rather French, the other classic
1onuments of the Early English style, Wells, Salisbury

152 Canterbury Cathedral choir
(begun 1175), by William of Sens and
William the Englishman. The design
retains some features of English
Romanesque (low proportions, some
round arches, zigzag ornament) combined with others from early French
Gothic (crocket capitals, sexpartite
vaults in the western bays, and coupled
columns – a speciality of Sens). It was
such combinations which, together with
the use of Purbeck marble, were to
characterize the development of English
Gothic

nd Lincoln, are very English. Wells, begun about 1190, s vigorous and fresh. The windows are single lancets, he triforium a series of continuously-moulded lancet penings, the arcade richly and deeply moulded; where n Chartres at the same time there are four attached shafts, t Wells there are twenty-four. The façade is a heavily rnamented screen, made even broader by the device of lacing the west towers beyond the width of the nave. Its ame is due more to the setting and to the main propor-ions than to any excellence of sculpture.

In 1220 Salisbury was founded afresh on a virgin site; : was built in one generation and – except for its great ourteenth-century spire – has been scarcely altered since, o that it stands as a model Early English cathedral. The

153 Opposite: Wells Cathedral nave (early 13th century). The clustered piers, relatively low and thick, still have something of Norman solidity. Note the superb foliage capitals and the continuous triforium, without capitals, just visible through the arches

154 Air view of Salisbury Cathedral from the south-east (top right, in the plan on p. 142). Part is added to part, the design pulled together only by the mid-14th-century spire. Note the 'screen' façade which projects beyond nave and aisles, and the polygonal chapter-house – both English specialities. The cathedral's position may be compared with that of Amiens (Ill. 145)

windows are mostly plain lancets, but in the triforium and in the eastern parts there are punched quatrefoils and foiled circles which correspond to French plate-tracery. The horizontality of the interior is, as we have seen, characteristic of English Gothic. There is no vertical emphasis, such as a vaulting shaft, to tie the three tiers together. Instead, the horizontal is stressed – especially in the triforium – by two other characteristic of the moment: the multiplication of mouldings, and the use of blackish-brown Purbeck marble for decorative shafting. The Lady Chapel is the masterpiece of this somewhat linear style, a tiny hall-church with vaults supported on extremely slender monolithic Purbeck shafts. In its decoration Salisbury is as austere as a Cistercian church: like Wells, it is roofed by a simple quadripartite vault without a ridge rib. Outside, Salisbury also expresses an English ideal: it is low and spreading, clearly articulated in separate parts; there were originally no flying buttresses, and there is little sculpture. The façade, like that of Wells, is a screen with tiny doors. It is often compared with Amiens, built during the same years, but the internal effect of their differences is seldom noted. The French church, with its great height and shallow transepts, tends to be felt as one vast hall because its total space can be grasped instantly. The English building, with its deep transepts, articulated choir, chancel and Lady Chapel, tends to be more a series of compartments. One overwhelms, the other asks to be explored.

In the nave at Lincoln, of *c.*1230, we have the beginning of that English feature, the enriched vault. To the main diagonal ribs of the classic quadripartite vault other ribs, called 'tiercerons', are added that spring from the same point and rise to the same height. Here at Lincoln seven ribs spring from each corbel, giving fourteen compartments to the vault. In addition to these the Lincoln master added a continuous rib running along the ridge, its potentially awkward intersections with the other ribs masked by carved bosses. The ridge rib, which

155, 156 Opposite: the interiors of Salisbury Cathedral (above) and Amiens Cathedral (below), both begun in 1220, epitomize the contrast between English and French Gothic; Amiens is tall, its height emphasized by wall-shafts; Salisbury's length is accentuated by horizontal division. The chevet of Amiens is immediately visible; the square chancel wall of Salisbury lies near the end of a mysterious perspective

157 Lincoln Cathedral nave (c. 1230). In the vault more ribs are used than are structurally necessary. The ridge is emphasized by the use of a ridge rib. With the addition of bosses, the vault is becoming a decoration as well as a roof

158 The Angel Choir at Lincoln Cathedral (begun 1256) is not fundamentally different in structure from the nave, but there is now carved enrichment everywhere. The angels, from which the choir takes its name, appear in the spandrels of the gallery

159 *East window, Carlisle Cathedral (c.1290): the beginnings of Decorated*

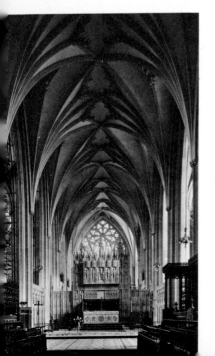

became standard in England, again emphasizes length and minimizes height.

With the Angel Choir at Lincoln, we are nearing the summer of English Gothic. Every capital and corbel is foliated, every spandrel and arch ornamented, and the vault itself is further enriched with additional tierceron ribs and bosses. Both triforium and clerestory are filled with tracery, as is the great east window: this, with its eight lights, is more complex – though smaller – than anything in France at the time.

It is in the development of tracery – the introduction of uneven numbers of lights and eventually the appearance of the double curve, with consequent fantasy in the treatment of the window head (note especially Carlisle, c.1290) – that the Decorated style is most immediately apparent. If, however, we would get at the essence of the style in England, as it governed space and structure, we should look at, say, the nave of Exeter Cathedral. Begun in 1280, only sixty years after Salisbury, here indeed is architectural consistency of a different kind. There is virtually no carved ornament, yet from the clustered bundles of ribs down to the clustered piers there is hardly an inch of plain wall; the vaulting ribs have been multiplied until the nave seems a stone forest. Strong, masculine, even severe, fully moulded throughout, this is indeed the orchestration of stone.

More radical structural innovation appears in the choir of Bristol Cathedral, begun in 1298. Clerestory and triforium have vanished; the aisles are the full height of the choir. Like Exeter nave, it is more dependent upon the play of light and shade on mouldings than it is upon ornament. In its central vault we see introduced 'lierne' ribs, small ribs laid across the vault from one main rib to another to form such patterns as stars – a motif carried to extremes of complexity in the Perpendicular vaults of England and the Late Gothic vaults of Germany. The aisles at Bristol show that desire to play with space which is so characteristic of the moment in England: the vault

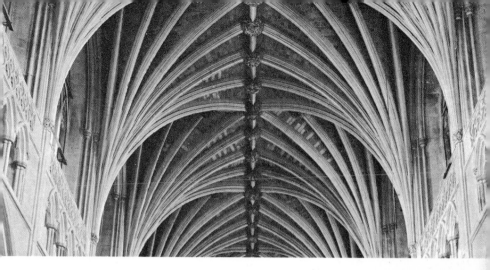

come down in cones on to curious strainer arches, which span from side to side at the springing of the nave vault. Nearly forty years later, in 1338, huge strainer arches were built under the central tower at Wells to strengthen the crossing piers; here the device is in its form almost equally odd, and in fact grossly out of scale with the rest of the building, but the point of departure is the same: the desire to provide a startling – if sometimes dubious – solution to a structural problem.

161 *In the nave vault of Exeter Cathedral (begun 1280) the increasing number of ribs not only achieves an effect of enrichment but almost abolishes the division into bays*

160, 162 *Opposite, below, and left: Bristol Cathedral choir (begun 1298). Here the Decorated style is seen not merely as surface decoration but as a different kind of structure. The aisles are the full height of the choir, like a German hall-church; in the central vault, additional 'lierne' ribs run from one main rib to another. The aisle vaults come down on to bridges, creating a unique vista*

A more daring experiment was the central octagon at Ely, built between 1323 and 1330, probably by the royal master carpenter; it is the spatial triumph of English Gothic. Where the choir and the nave aisles emerge into the crossing they are canted so as to transform that central space into an octagon (a similar arrangement, although in a very different style and less well handled, is the space below the dome of St Paul's, London). From each corner of this octagon the vaulting shaft runs up the full height of the cathedral, the vaults arching over to leave a smaller octagonal aperture, crowned by a timber cupola. The unique top lighting, as well as the novel planning of space – innovation as opposed to development from precedent – surely proclaims this work as one of genius.

Ely Lady Chapel (1321–49) shows another aspect of

163 Detail of wall-arcading in Ely Cathedral Lady Chapel (1321–49). The ripple of oak leaves, the double ogee curves of the arches, and the way in which these 'nod' forward allowing a shaft to pass, as it were, behind them, makes this a triumph of the Decorated style

164 Ely Cathedral Octagon (1322–42). From each corner of the crossing – opened out into an octagon – ribs close in to support a central wooden lantern. The placing of windows at a diagonal to the nave-axis is another bold innovation

150

he Decorated style. It is rich in ornamental arcading round the walls. This arcading has complex three-dimensional ogee arches complete with shafts, pinnacles, crockets and vaults – all in miniature. The carving, a ripple of oak leaves, runs over all; the gilding and colour can only be imagined.

If at first English Gothic had been derivative, by the fourteenth century it had in the ogee curve a unique decorative motif, which was to become the dominant motif on the Continent from about 1375 until well into the sixteenth century. Whereas in England it never became an overriding architectural device, in France whole buildings seemed to be clothed in brittle lace, as the Tour de Beurre (1485–1500) and other parts of Rouen Cathedral; the structure of St Maclou at Rouen

165 *La Trinité, Vendôme (1485–1506). The centre of the façade shows the Flamboyant, flame-like, character of French tracery at a date when English tracery was already assuming the rectilinear character of the Perpendicular style*

166 *Tour de Beurre, Rouen Cathedral (1485–1500). Here the wall surface is practically abolished and the whole tower seems a play of light, shade and filigree tracery – a sculptural rather than an architectural conception*

151

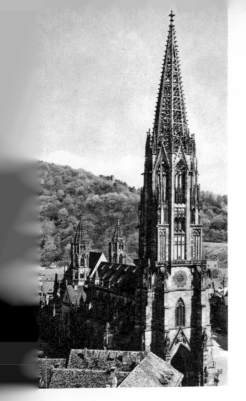

(c.1500) and La Trinité at Vendôme is envel
flickering flames of tracery – hence the French r
the style, 'Flamboyant'.

In Germany a similar stage was reached with
but not Flamboyant, openwork spire of Freiburg
finished about 1340. Like the rest of Europe, (
was at first influenced by the Gothic of the Ile de
the great cathedral at Cologne, begun in 12
finished, to the original design, in the nineteenth
is essentially French, with its extreme height and
emphasis. But as time passed and the style de
German masons evolved a characteristic arch
form in the hall church, with nave and aisles
height. The decoration, as in France and E
became more and more ornate, but for near
hundred years the basic form remained the sar
clerestory and triforium vanish entirely; the ais
consequently the arcade, rise to the full heigh
building. The church has become a columned h

167 *Freiburg-im-Breisgau Minster (c.1340). Germany specialized both in single west towers (as opposed to the two-tower façade popular in England and France) and in lacy openwork spires, of which this one was extremely influential*

168 *Franciscan Church, Salzburg (c.1408). The Gothic choir, added to a dark Romanesque nave, superbly combines the tall slender piers of the traditional hall-church with the star vaults that were becoming a favourite feature with German architects*

169 The choir of Cologne Cathedral (begun 1248) is more French than German; its glazed triforium and its insistent emphasis on high, soaring proportions look back to the most ambitious of the Ile-de-France cathedrals, Beauvais, still under construction at the time. Like Beauvais, it remained unfinished throughout the Middle Ages

153

170 *The final phase in rib-vaulting: in the parish church at Langenstein, near Kassel, probably after 1500, the actual vault is seen through a separate net of ribs without any structural function. The angularity of the rib profiles and of their junctions is typical of the moment*

171 *Choir of St Lorenz, Nuremberg (begun 1434) – a hall-church, with tall piers merging into a spiky vault. The aisle windows have something of the mechanical, angular quality of English Perpendicular tracery*

it is the tall aisle windows sending their shafts of light between the slender piers that illuminate the interior. Again and again, at St Elisabeth, Marburg, begun in 1233, at Schwäbisch Gmund in 1351, Landshut in 1387, and the Franciscan church at Salzburg in 1408, the Germans maintained the drama of height through all the superficial changes of the Gothic style. In the choir of St Lorenz, Nuremberg (begun in 1434) we see some of the qualities that we can also see in English Perpendicular. St Anne, Annaberg, begun in 1499, has ribs which snake across the surface of the vault, weaving fantastic patterns. Nowhere more than in Germany can one find Gothic pushed to extremes, the twisting and tormenting of stone into shapes that are macabre as well as fantastic. Perhaps the most curious feature of this late phase in Germany is the development of skeleton vaults, where the ribs form a net below, and separate from, the surface of the vault itself.

Italian Gothic, for all its beauties of colour and its grand scale, can never, to a northern mind, seem truly medieval. Internal tie-beams were always preferred to external buttresses, and surface decoration – usually in the form of coloured marble panelling – preferred to structural articulation. Siena Cathedral is part of one of the most poetic town plans in the world. It is an essay in zebra-striped marble, without either structural or planning innovation. It was being built, incredibly, at the same time as Amiens. One should note, however, that the cathedral at Florence has a Gothic nave of only four bays and yet is about half as long again as the twelve bays of Westminster Abbey nave! The Italians may have known little of the Ile de France, but between the fall of the Roman Empire and the time of Michelangelo one thing at least was not forgotten – size and scale. We see it again in the Florentine church of Sta Maria Novella (*c.* 1278) and in the vast Venetian church of SS. Giovanni e Paolo, begun in 1246. At S. Francesco, Bologna, in a

172 *SS. Giovanni e Paolo, Venice (begun 1246). This vast church, impressive as it is, brings out the limitations of Italian Gothic. Widely spaced arches, circular piers and large areas of plain wall surface belong to a Romanesque, or even Roman, aesthetic, while the use of tiebeams shows a complete rejection of the Gothic system of abutment and of the effects which that system could achieve*

173 *Siena Cathedral (1245–1380). The west front, designed by Giovanni Pisano, is clearly influenced by the great west fronts of Northern Gothic, but the whole conception is different; the central doorway even has a round arch. The veneer of black and white marble, like the separate bell-tower, is a legacy from Italian Romanesque*

174 The Doge's Palace in Venice (late 14th century – c.1457) adjoins St Mark's Cathedral, at the far end of the Piazzetta to the left

175 Toledo Cathedral (begun 1227), looking across the transept. The style is basically French, though it differs in having only two storeys – arcade and clerestory

city where almost everything is too big, we have a building of which the chief quality is an impressive size, and the same is true of the late Gothic edifice in Milan. It is an intriguing experience for the student of architecture to stand in the Piazza in Venice, to look up at St Mark's and at the Doge's Palace. In the big cusped, traceried and ogival arches of the Palace we discern an outpost of Gothic. An outpost – too remote from the centre to have imbibed anything of the great structural principles of the Ile de France, but Gothic of a kind, all the same. In St Mark's, on the other hand, we see in the golden mosaics of domes and pendentives a western outpost of Byzantium. There, on the frontier between the Latin and the Greek churches, the two styles may be seen butting, quite literally, one against the other.

The other province of the old Empire to cling to the tradition of size was Spain. Seville Cathedral (c.1401–1521) has an area half again as big as Milan and was the largest building in the medieval world. Already in the eleventh century Santiago de Compostela had by its size alone given prestige to Spain as a stronghold of Catholic building. Burgos Cathedral, built between 1220 and 1550, is the first example of Spanish High Gothic. There is German workmanship in the later parts, notably in the Flamboyant vaulting and in the west front with its spires, almost certainly designed by a German from Cologne.

But the cathedral is largely, needless to say, a derivative of French Gothic, mainly through the influence of Coutances. The low, strong thirteenth-century ambulatory aisle, with forbidding iron grilles to the chapels, hints at that grim character which runs through almost all Spanish Gothic. Toledo Cathedral, begun in 1227, is very close to Bourges in its plan; but it is both broader and lower, with a two-storey elevation of arcade and vast glazed clerestory. Characteristically Spanish is the ornate choir enclosure west of the crossing.

178, 179 At Gloucester Cathedral choir (c.1337–57, right) the Perpendicular style is fully established, in the enormous east window, the strong vertical emphasis, the rectilinear arrangement of window lights and wall panels, and the multiplicity of vaulting ribs. At King's College Chapel, Cambridge (finished 1515, below), the window tracery is recognizably of the same type, but the roof is now fan-vaulted, enabling it to be evenly panelled as well

180, 181 Opposite: the ideal of the glass or 'lantern' church was attained in the Sainte-Chapelle, Paris (above), as early as c.1240. The choir of Aachen Minster (below), added to the Palatine Chapel in 1355, shows the development of the Sainte-Chapelle scheme – a single, apsed room, completely glazed – on a very large scale

In England, Gothic died slowly. A century and a half of increasingly stylized Perpendicular died almost imperceptibly into Tudor. It is often held that the richness of Decorated was brought to an end in 1349 by the Black Death, to be succeeded only by the poverty-stricken style of Perpendicular. This is not true, in two ways. While Perpendicular could be arid, it could also blaze with ornament and structural genius. More important, the Perpendicular style was introduced in the south transept of Gloucester Cathedral in 1331-7, more than a decade before the Black Death. It is true that Perpendicular was often economical, with endless vertical stone panelling covering the walls – hence its name. On the other hand this grid of panels was often continued, in the form of mullions and transoms, to form those huge windows which, both as a source of light and for their stained glass, were one of the great things of fifteenth-century England. All through Gothic we find this desire to substitute glass for wall. Beauvais choir, begun in 1235, had been a triumph of clerestory lighting, while the Sainte-Chapelle, begun a few years later, was a tall, aisleless chapel with windows almost from floor to vault; Aachen Minster followed suit in 1355. But it was not until nearly three centuries after Beauvais that this craving for light was consummated in King's College Chapel, Cambridge.

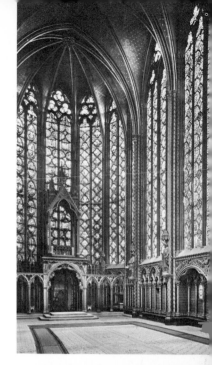

The fifteenth century was also the golden age of the English parish church, the big 'lantern church' with big windows. Built by mercantile rather than ecclesiastical wealth, these churches were all large, all brilliantly lit, rather hard in detail and with very slender piers giving great spaciousness. More elaboration is found in chancel screens, private chapels, splendid towers and, above all, in those carved timber roofs of which Westminster Hall (1394-1402) was merely the largest.

The 'poverty' of Perpendicular is also repudiated by the further enrichment of the vault. The metamorphosis of the English vault from a structural roof to a decorative

182 Canterbury Cathedral nave (1379–1403). Henry Yevele was one of the great English master masons, and among the first whose career we can follow in detail. His work at Canterbury is a fluent exercise in Perpendicular. The emphasis is vertical, the mouldings multiple and thin, the triforium merely panelled. The vault – like that at Gloucester (Ill. 178) – is an ornate ceiling

183 Gloucester Cathedral cloister (begun after 1351). The newly invented fan vault is on a miniature scale, but the pattern of ribs of equal length and equal curvature forming half-circles is clear. The vaulting rib has become merely a moulding

ceiling was a headlong process. The first Perpendicular vault, in the choir of Gloucester, was already an undisciplined tangle of ribs and bosses. Such design needed control. The typical four-centred Tudor arch in time gave the builders a vault with a flattened apex – virtually a flat stone ceiling, heavily ornamented with lierne ribs and bosses, and held up on either side by the clusters of ribs forming the true vault. On a small scale this occurred in church and college porches, in canopies over tombs and in cloisters such as Worcester (c.1372) and Canterbury (1397–1412). On a big scale one recalls that the Norman nave at Winchester was redesigned by William Wynford, between 1394 and 1460, with the heavy eleventh-century piers transformed or replaced by flat angular Perpendicular mouldings; that Henry Yevele's great nave at Canterbury (1391–1403) was one of the masterpieces of English Gothic; that the next generation

began the building of St George's Chapel at Windsor,
and that every one of these had the kind of roof described,
a rich stone ceiling clipped between the two halves of the
vault.

There was to be one more phase of vaulting. Shortly
after 1351 a master mason at Gloucester realized that if
you increase the number of ribs indefinitely the whole
vault becomes, in effect, solid stone. In Gloucester cloisters
the vault is just a series of inverted stone cones with the
simulacrum of ribs carved upon their surface. This has
come to be called 'fan-vaulting' and is the typical roof of
Tudor Gothic.

Architecture not only reflects but also foreshadows
historical changes. Even before the fall of Wolsey in 1530
had transferred patronage from Church to Crown,
English Gothic was blazing forth the piety and power of
burghers and princes. The last phase was secular in

*184 The greatest timber roof of the
Middle Ages, that of Westminster Hall
in London (1394–1402), shows a
master carpenter – Hugh Herland –
working with the daring we have seen in
master masons. Hammer-beams, a yard
thick and nearly 21 feet long, project
from the wall to narrow the span, and
there are arched braces as well. Everywhere one sees delicate Perpendicular
tracery in wood; the hammer-beams end in
carved angels*

161

spirit, royal in fact . . . mainly collegiate chapels which might, in architectural terms, look back to the Sainte-Chapelle but also looked forward to Chambord or to Longleat. Although the great colleges of Oxford and Cambridge were basically ecclesiastical foundations with an almost monastic life, those of the fifteenth and sixteenth centuries form a bridge between the purely sacerdotal colleges of the Middle Ages and the secular schools and colleges of the post-Reformation era. They were founded by kings, statesmen and merchants, as well as by churchmen. Their planning, with blocks of students' cells grouped around a court, dominated by chapel and hall, may have had monastic roots, but was also a rare example of an English contribution to the history of planning.

In 1441 Henry VI started to build Eton College Chapel, and in 1446 King's College Chapel, Cam-

185 Trinity College, Cambridge, in the 17th century. Around the Great Court entered through the gatehouse (foreground), are the chapel (right), Master's lodge and hall (far side), as well as living quarters for teachers and students

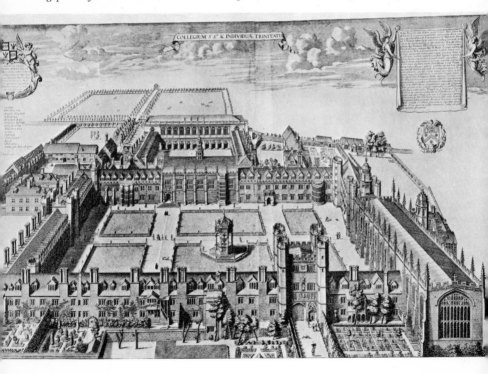

186 Henry VII's Chapel, Westminster Abbey, London (1503–19).
This astonishing roof – with its stone
pendants apparently hanging from a fan
vault – is the last blaze of English
Gothic. The handling of masonry could
go no further, while the spirit of the
building is royal and secular rather than
ecclesiastical: it is the end in more senses
than one

bridge, finished in 1515. St George's, Windsor was
begun in 1481, while Henry VII's great mausoleum at
the east end of Westminster Abbey was built between
1503 and 1519. These buildings are the last flowering of
Perpendicular. In so far as their style is angular, rigid,
matter-of-fact, they really are Perpendicular. Those
qualities are, however, limited to plan and structure.
With absolute logicality the windows stretch from
buttress to buttress, and those buttresses carry the whole
weight and thrust of the vault. The plan of King's
College Chapel is an arid rectangular stone cage filled
with glass, with no hint that the building is in fact a
miracle. It is when we turn from the plan to the decoration, the shields, the heraldic beasts, the emblems, the
glass and the vault itself that we realise that this is a great
our de force of masonic skill. This is even more true in the
case of Henry VII's Chapel at Westminster. The lace-
like stone of the vault, with its astonishing pendants, is
the end of English Gothic. There was nothing more to do.

187 Opposite: in the cloister at Batalha (c.1515) the concept is still basically Gothic, but – as at Tomar – all the ornament is in the fantastic encrusted style known as 'Manueline', after King Manuel of Portugal

188 The octagonal Capilla del Condestable (1482–94) in Burgos Cathedral is crowned with a star vault upholding a central lantern of openwork tracery

189 Window of the chapter-house at Tomar (c.1520). Ingenuity and imagination mark this strange work which can only partially be counted as Gothic. Decorative motifs include vegetation, shells, tree-roots, ropes and navigational instruments

We are a million miles from the arches of Durham, but it is the end of the same story.

If we would find any later Gothic than this we must cross the Pyrenees. At Burgos, in the Capilla del Condestable (1482–94) we have the Spanish version of this marriage between Gothic architecture and heraldry. At Segovia, in 1532 – when Michelangelo was at the height of his career – Gothic still flourished. In Portugal, in the Manueline ornament at Batalha in 1515 and at Tomar c.1520, we see only the last frenzied effort to pretend that the Middle Ages still exist. Christendom was no longer an overriding concept; it had collapsed, to become the secular and sovereign powers of modern Europe.

Chapter Seven

RENAISSANCE, MANNERISM, AND
BAROQUE IN ITALY

The word 'Renaissance' was once used to designate European architecture from the rebirth of the classical tradition in fifteenth-century Florence, through some four hundred years, to the emergence of Romanticism and Industrialism at the end of the eighteenth century. Through all that time, from Naples to Dublin, from Petersburg to Virginia, the architectural vocabulary of Greece and Rome was the basis of design. Modern criticism has subdivided this whole movement into Renaissance proper, Mannerism, Baroque, Neo-Classicism, Greek Revival and so on. These terms must be used, but there can, of course, be no rigid dividing line between them.

It has been said (by Professor Nikolaus Pevsner) that the Gothic style was created for Suger, Abbot of St-Denis, counsellor of the kings of France, the Renaissance for the merchants of Florence, bankers to the kings of Europe'. This statement is illuminating even if it leaves out a good deal. Gothic architecture was born in France and, however many palaces or castles were built, was primarily ecclesiastical. The Renaissance was born in Italy and, however many churches were built, was primarily royal and mercantile – specially north of the Alps. Great architectures, however, such as Gothic and Renaissance, are not 'created' overnight. They have periods of gestation and are the product of functional necessity and of historical forces. They are not invented, they come about. It has often been said that the sack of Constantinople in 1453, and the consequent flight of

190 Lagoon façade of the Libreria Vecchia in Venice, by Jacopo Sansovino (1536; see p. 194). High Renaissance architecture was an attempt to revive the glories of Rome. The basic classical elements appear over and over again and are easy to recognize, e.g. the combination of large Doric and Ionic columns – Doric below, Ionic above, each with its correct base, capital and entablature – with piers carrying arches (cp. the Colosseum, Ill. 54). At the same time the way these elements are handled can be extremely individual. Here, for instance, the use of oval openings in the frieze, the insertion of smaller columns by the upper windows, the precise balance of upper and lower storeys all show the genius of one particular architect

191 The first great monument of the Renaissance, 1420–36: Brunelleschi's dome, raised without centering over the trefoil Gothic east end of Florence Cathedral. Though Gothic in structure, it could never have been built without Brunelleschi's study of Roman brick-work. The drum, the double-skinned dome and the crowning lantern set a pattern for the future

classical scholars to Florence, was the 'cause' of th Renaissance. It had almost nothing to do with it. Th scholars who migrated west taught their hosts Greek bt had no interest in classical architecture. At most the may have stimulated an interest in antiquity. Several c the most exquisite Renaissance buildings were in fa erected thirty years before the fall of Constantinople while the cathedral at Milan was still being built i debased Gothic fifty years later.

The Renaissance was a great awakening and a grea enlightenment. It was born in Italy because Italy ha known so little of the glories of Gothic towers and vault and remembered so vividly the glories of the Roma Empire.

The Florentine banking house of the Medici family ha representatives all over Europe. Several Medicis had bee mayors of Florence in the thirteenth century. Cosim de' Medici and his grandson, Lorenzo the Magnificen were common citizens by rank; by right of culture the were great princes. They made Florence the mo attractive city in Europe. 'The charm which [they exercised over Florence', wrote Burckhardt, 'lay less i their political capacity than in their leadership in th culture of the age.' They were the first great merchai patrons of history. To them we owe not only palace painting, sculpture, literature, but the overwhelming fa that the Renaissance was accepted by the Florentines ; the basis of culture. The first achievements of th Renaissance – until the time of Michelangelo – wei virtually a Roman Revival. In the climate, landscape an historical air of Tuscany, some kind of Roman Reviv. was as natural and inevitable as, four hundred yea later, a Gothic Revival was in the North. And indee the so-called 'Tuscan proto-Renaissance' of the thirteent century provided as persuasive a model for Brunellesci as the remains of ancient Rome.

Like many Renaissance artists Filippo Brunellesci (1377–1446) was a goldsmith by training, and versati

in many crafts. He was chosen by competition in 1420 to build the big dome over the existing cathedral. He was chosen because he alone had devised a method of supporting the centering – erecting it upon a timber platform which he slung by iron chains from the dome's drum. He then built the most graceful of the world's domes. Perched on a drum it lacked all abutment at its base, and was weighed by a lantern at the top. To resist the consequent outward thrust, Brunelleschi chained in the dome, burying in its thickness a series of timber baulks fastened together with iron bands. This dubious device was probably the only solution, pending the scientific use of pre-stressed concrete five hundred years later. All Renaissance and Baroque domes were thus chained in; that of Florence was the first. The silhouette of Brunelleschi's dome is slightly pointed, thus still in a sense part of old Christendom; but to create a new skyline for a princely city by raising the dome on a drum and then to crown it with a lantern, was a Renaissance thing to do. At about the same time Brunelleschi was also building the Foundling Hospital where he again achieved astonishing grace. In this charming arcade are the famous plaques by Andrea della Robbia, and the Corinthian Order used in a deliberately scholarly way. Never, however, do we find Brunelleschi or any other Renaissance architect actually copying a complete Roman model: that had to await the Classical Revival of the eighteenth century.

Grace allied with strength would seem to be the hall-mark of Brunelleschi's work. His S. Lorenzo and Sto Spirito are both basilican churches with a nave arcade of semi-circular arches, and semi-circular vaults over the aisles. In Sto Spirito, each bay of the aisles has its own semi-circular apse or niche for an altar. The result, with each element outlined in grey stone (*pietra serena*) is a wonderful symphony of semi-circles. The grace of the symphony has its counterpoint in the strong simplicity of the columns.

192 One bay of the arcade of the Foundling Hospital, Florence, by Brunelleschi (1421–4)

Brunelleschi also designed but never completed two entralized churches – that is, polygonal churches with entral domes, classical in style, vaguely Byzantine in lan. Again and again Renaissance architects, from runelleschi to Wren, were to hanker after the architec-ural or geometric fascination of this type of plan. It has een suggested that while the medieval or basilican plan d man onwards towards the distant mysteries of God, e centralized plan was typically Renaissance in that it lorified man himself by setting him at the centre of all nings; and that it was this which made the Church ject it. But we know from the writings of that brilliant nd influential Renaissance architect, Leone Battista lberti, that the centralized plan was in fact regarded as *ore* divine, since – according to neo-Platonic theory at e time – the circle is the perfect, divine, form. The bjection of churchmen to the plan was related instead to turgical function. In the Eastern Church, the priest artakes of the bread and wine directly beneath the entral dome. The Western Church, on the other hand, elebrates the entire Eucharist at an altar in a chancel, in

194 Sta Maria della Consolazione, Todi (begun 1508), by Cola da Caprarola: one of the few large central-space churches, built up within a pyramidal outline. Three of the four apses are polygonal; the sanctuary apse – right – is differentiated by being round

full view of a congregation who stand behind the pries facing the altar. Nothing of liturgical significance woul therefore happen beneath the central dome. In th centralized plan which Renaissance architects so longe to build for their patrons, the climax of plan and th climax of function did not coincide. It is significant tha at both St Peter's in Rome and St Paul's in London th architect's first plan was a centralized octagon, but tha both buildings ultimately emerged as glorified basilicas – a victory for the clergy over the architects. The famou church of Sta Maria della Consolazione at Todi – buil by Cola da Caprarola in 1508, perhaps from a desig by Bramante – had an 'ideal' plan, based on a Gree cross with four equal arms; these four identical arms a have different functions.

However, the secular nature of the Renaissance – th triumph of Humanism even in the Catholic South – finds a symbol in the villa and the palace, not least th palaces of Florence. The palaces were built in the middl years of the fifteenth century for such princely an mercantile families as the Medici, the Pitti, the Strozzi the Pandolfini. They vary in detail but conform to type Unlike the villas which were set among the fountain and cypresses of the surrounding hills, these palaces ar fundamentally urban. Each fills a city block and each i built right up to the street frontage, presenting a cliff o masonry to the outer world. Each has an internal court yard of shaded and colonnaded charm. Each relegates t the ground floor such subordinate things as offices stables, kitchens and guard-rooms. These rooms ofte have quite small windows to the street, covered wit heavy grilles. The grilles themsevles, as in the case o the Palazzo Pitti, were often fine works of art, thei metallic quality being a foil to the rusticated stonework Each palace has great suites of state apartments on th first floor – the *piano nobile* – with coved and painte ceilings. Externally this gives a splendid area of blan wall above each range of windows. Each palace has

195, 196 *Palazzo Strozzi, Florence (begun by Benedetto da Maiano in 1489, continued by Cronaca, 1497–1507). The impression of power given by the massive overall rustication is increased by the huge shadow of the overhanging cornice. All the important rooms look inward upon the quiet and cool courtyard*

crowning cornice; that of the Palazzo Strozzi overhang the street by more than seven feet, casting a might shadow. The façades, while having scale and dignity were austere. Often the greatest enrichment was th craggy character of the rusticated masonry or, as in th Alberti's Palazzo Rucellai, very flat pilasters.

What is more important than individual façades is th fact that here had been created a new urban type, which was to be found throughout the centuries in the Georgia square, the Pall Mall clubs, the Wall Street bank. Th wealthy businessman, now neither a churchman nor feudal lord, had found his architectural symbol. More over, the modern street, the 'corridor' of stone frontages had, for better or worse, been invented.

Leone Battista Alberti (1404–72) was, like Brunel leschi, a Florentine. Michelangelo and Bernini wer primarily sculptors; Giotto, Raphael and Leonard were primarily painters. This coloured their view o architecture. Alberti, however, was a dilettante, a write more interested in theory than in practice. He has bee regarded as second only to Leonardo in being th complete and universal 'Renaissance Man'. He excelle as horseman and athlete, as conversationalist, playwright linguist, composer and mathematician. He was for som years a civil servant in Rome, with ample time to stud the ruins of Antiquity. The ancient Greeks had con ceived their temples in mathematical terms; in his *T Books on Architecture* Alberti tried to formulate simila laws. His theories rest upon a number of fallacies suc as: *1*, that man is made in the image of God; *2*, that spread-eagled man fits into a circle; and *3*, that the circl is therefore the basis of a divine harmony in nature. A these things are false. The image of God is not knowr The circle does not exist in Nature. Le Corbusier, i this century and with equal dogmatism, has proclaime quite a different system of proportions derived from ma in quite a different posture. Such systems also ignor function and size. Is an Alberti church, for instanc

197 Sta Maria Novella, Florence. Alberti completed the façade – of which the lower part is medieval – in 1456. His work is based upon a module, represented by each of the dark squares below the round window. Volutes link nave and aisles (see Ills. 224, 233, 275). The marble veneer used throughout was one of ancient Rome's most persistent cultural legacies

equally perfect as architecture if halved in size? Clearly not, although its proportions remain the same and there, fore, presumably, equally divine. All this does not invalidate the fact that Alberti was a marvellous example of the 'Renaissance Man', or the fact that the proportions of his buildings, even if they owe more to his unerring eye than to his theories, are always in themselves superb.

Alberti's sensitivity and puritanical restraint – he thought all churches should be pure white inside – gave us some remarkable buildings. He completed the façade of Sta Maria Novella in Florence (1456), introducing the motif of large volutes to link the heights of nave and aisles – a feature with an enormous progeny through the centuries, from Vignola's Gesù onwards – and re, modelled the Gothic church of S. Francesco at Rimini (1450) as the mausoleum of the Malatesta family. S. Francesco has a west front based upon a Roman

198 Tempio Malatestiano (S. Fran, cesco), Rimini. Alberti began the re, modelling – never finished – in 1447. The façade, with its half-columns and flanking arches, is derived from a Roman arch at Rimini. Note the row of deep niches along the side, in the thickness of the encasing stone wall, intended to hold tombs

175

199, 200 S. Andrea, Mantua (1470–72), by Alberti, is raised on a podium, with an even grander 'triumphal arch' façade than the Tempio Malatestiano. The scale is fully Roman, the central arch emphasized by smaller elements on each side. Internally the east end is treated like a central-space church, with transepts and choir of equal length. The aisles are replaced by alternately large and small chapels, seemingly hollowed out of the thick wall – another Roman device

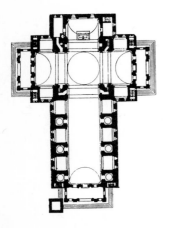

triumphal arch, austere and with every piece of carving perfectly placed, and externally a series of deep arches down the sides for the sarcophaguses of the Malatesta and their court. Alberti also designed two fine churches in Mantua: S. Sebastiano (1460), later much altered, had the centralized plan that Alberti advocated, but based upon a square and not upon a 'divine' circle. S. Sebastiano and Alberti's other Mantuan church, S. Andrea (c.1470), are raised upon high platforms or podiums – another Albertian theory. The most influential aspects of S. Andrea were its use of the pedimented façade, also based on the triumphal arch, and its reduction of the aisles to chapels within the thick buttresses; the internal elevation consists of a series of overlapping triumphal arches.

In Tuscany and Lombardy – mainly Florence, Milan and Mantua – and at Urbino in the Marche, the Renaissance had been born. In Rome it became a great international style, giving Europe an architecture destined

to endure for three centuries, much as Paris had given Europe the Gothic style. The Palazzo della Cancelleria, for instance, begun in 1486 by an unknown architect for a nephew of Sixtus IV, is so much larger than the Florentine palaces that its scale alone marks the arrival of the Renaissance in Rome. And then, at the turn of the century, Bramante arrived in the great city. Bramante (1444–1514) was born in Urbino when Piero della Francesca was painting there, and when Laurana was building one of the most poetic palace-towns in Italy. *En route*, as it were, from Urbino to Rome, Bramante had worked on two churches in Milan. He built Sta Maria presso S. Satiro (1482–6) and the east end of Sta Maria delle Grazie (1492); these had a new and very delicate ornamentation – delicious arabesque fantasies in stone, set against plain Lombardic brickwork. With Raphael, Sangallo and Michelangelo, Bramante must be regarded as one of the four leading architects of the High Renaissance . . . a Renaissance now, in Rome, come of age.

201 Part of the façade of the Palazzo della Cancelleria, Rome (begun 1486). The superimposed pilasters – with, here, the alternating rhythm of a triumphal arch – against a background of flat rustication derive from Alberti's Palazzo Rucellai in Florence (Ill. 209); the window treatment is North Italian; the vast scale is Roman

202 *Tempietto at S. Pietro in Montorio, Rome (1502), by Bramante. Regarded by Palladio as 'classical Roman', its gravity marks the beginning of the High Renaissance. The severe Roman Doric Order is preferred to the more decorative Corinthian, and a straight entablature preferred to an arcade. Note, too, the vertically symmetrical balusters and the niches scooped out of the walls. Bramante meant the dome – now Baroque – to be a pure hemisphere*

Bramante had learnt much from Leonardo da Vinci. Leonardo – most 'universal' of men – was never actually an architect, but in that fertile brain geometric and structural problems were continually stirring. His sketches, for instance, show many permutations of the centralized plan – circles, Greek crosses, polygons. Moreover, if function and liturgy made the centralized plan unpopular with the clergy, it was not ruled out for the smaller chapel or the family mausoleum. From Brunelleschi's charming little Pazzi Chapel (begun in 1429) in the cloister of Sta Croce, Florence, to Michelangelo's great Medici Mausoleum at S. Lorenzo a century later, there were many such monuments. One of the finest was the circular Tempietto of S. Pietro in Montorio. This monument was built by Bramante in 1502, soon after his arrival in Rome, on the supposed site of the crucifixion of St Peter, and was, therefore, a kind of sacred reliquary.

The long, fantastic story of the rebuilding of the old basilica of St Peter's began in 1505. In that year Pope Julius II commissioned Bramante to rebuild the mother church of the Western World. A centralized plan – a Greek cross with four equal arms – was approved by the Pope, and this, for some inscrutable reason, has been called a triumph of Humanism over clerical obscurantism. It was, inevitably, a short-lived triumph – not least because the Pope died in 1513. It did, however, give us the 'Bramante plan', a vast affair with a central spherical dome, four huge apses, four corner towers. Bramante was sixty when the foundation stone was laid. The church then took exactly one hundred years to build, almost every notable Roman architect of the time being involved. Another fifty years passed before Bernini could create his colonnaded Piazza. Bramante's plan was geometrically brilliant, liturgically impossible; in which of four *equal* apses does one put a *high* altar, and if one puts it under the dome – never done in a Byzantine church –

203 Upper level of the Cortile del Belvedere in the Vatican (begun 1503), by Bramante. The rhythm of the walls, based on a triumphal arch, is marked by smooth, 'cut out' elements set in layers against a background of flat rustication. The large niche ('exedra') in the end wall is itself an ancient Roman feature

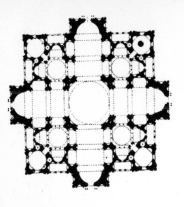

which way does the celebrant face? The church was also monstrous in scale, a quality which always haunted it.

The foundations of Bramante's four central piers still support the dome of St Peter's; little else remains of his scheme. Raphael wanted to transform the Greek cross plan into a Latin cross, by adding a nave, but died before this could be done. Peruzzi reverted to the Greek cross in an even more elaborate form than Bramante but – again fortunately – funds ran out. Sangallo cut down the plan, but could not refrain from suggesting an enormous domed porch or vestibule. Magnificent but useless, it was never built. (This Sangallo plan, with the big porch, is said to have been the inspiration for Christopher Wren's first and abortive project for St Paul's, London.) In 1546 Michelangelo was appointed architect. What is good in St Peter's – the fine scale of some of the detail, for instance, and the silhouette of the dome – is mainly his. The dome, 250 feet above the floor, is tied in by ten chains. Although designed by Michelangelo it was finished after his death by della Porta. Then at the beginning of the seventeenth century, Carlo Maderna built the present nave, transforming the church from a Greek to a Latin cross. Architecturally this was disastrous. Michelangelo had designed a big western portico, intending to tack it on to the Greek cross plan. It was never built, but the scale of the giant order necessarily fixed the scale of Maderna's nave and of his new façade. What, however, was merely large and monumental when combined with the main mass of the building and crowned by the dome, becomes monstrous when isolated as a façade in its own right. Furthermore, the whole of Maderna's façade, with its lateral extensions and so on, is extremely confused. Worse still, of course, is the fact that the forward projection of the nave simply cuts off the view of the dome from the Piazza.

The final plan of the church has an internal length of over 600 feet, and a width across the transepts of 450 feet. The dome is 137 feet in diameter. As a plan it is hopeless,

204, 205 Above: Bramante's plan for St Peter's in Rome (1505/6). Below: Michelangelo's (c.1546). Where Bramante planned a complex web of walls, hollowed out with niches in the ancient Roman manner, Michelangelo yielded to the demands of structure, and laid down enormously thick walls and four single massive piers. The church is oriented – as was Constantine's basilica – to the west rather than to the east

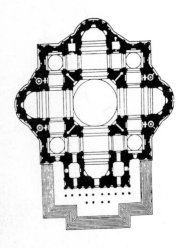

206 Opposite: St Peter's, Rome. Giant pilasters some 80 feet high, grouped in pairs, frame niches and oddly angular windows. An attic, severely plain, leads the eye up to the great dome – intended by Michelangelo as a hemisphere

but fortunately so large that it is seldom used as a whole. The scale of most of the detail is grotesque. The height of the main pilasters is only 7 feet less than Trajan's Column. The inscription on the internal frieze has letters 6 feet high; the entablature is the height of a cottage; the baldacchino over the altar a hundred feet high. Such things were necessary; once the building had been begun on that scale it had to go on. What Julius II and Bramante had sown, Bramante's successors had to reap. St Peter's demonstrates the Renaissance and Baroque architects' ability to handle stone and sculptural detail quite superbly; it also demonstrates that the age was incapable of any sustained co-operative or administrative effort in order to achieve unity.

In Bramante's plan for St Peter's the internal spaces, such as apses and chapels, seem to be as it were hollowed out of the immensely solid mass of the walls and piers.

207 Interior of St Peter's, Rome, from an 18th-century painting. Michelangelo's scheme was continued in Maderna's nave, foreground. The baldacchino over the altar and most of the decoration are due to Bernini (see p. 202)

208, 209 *The Palazzo Vidoni-Caffarelli in Rome (c.1515), by Raphael, shows the palace design invented by Bramante in the 'House of Raphael': a heavily rusticated ground storey, below a 'piano nobile' with windows set between paired columns. The High Renaissance achievement is clearly seen if one compares this richly sculptural façade with the first palace design to make use of the orders, Alberti's Palazzo Rucellai in Florence (below), of 1446–51*

This highly sculptural concept is the first distant glimpse of the Baroque. Elsewhere, however, as in his little Tempietto and in the two Vatican courts – the Belvedere and the Damaso – Bramante firmly retains his High Renaissance mastery of the harmony of parts. In this he was followed by Raphael (1483–1520). Raphael, like Bramante, was born in Urbino, and was buried in the Pantheon – a signal honour to the greatest of painters. In architecture, apart from his advice on the St Peter's problem, his contribution was modest. Nevertheless, his Palazzo Vidoni-Caffarelli in Rome (c.1515), although much altered, shows clearly the difference between the Florentine Renaissance and the Roman High Renaissance. It is strong, solemn, deeply shadowed. It may be contrasted with Alberti's Palazzo Rucellai in Florence where the decoration is little more than a careful surface patina. This contrast shows the road that architecture had travelled in less than a century, the distance between the Early and High Renaissance.

210 Loggia of the Villa Madama, Rome (begun 1516). The elaborate fresco work and stucco arabesques, carried out by Giulio Romano, were based upon newly discovered Roman models. Equally Roman is the intended plan of the Villa, with a circular courtyard and rooms whose curving surfaces seem hollowed out of immensely thick walls

This increasing desire for a 'Roman' quality in architecture led to a greater study and greater understanding of the actual ruins of the Empire . . . and how very much more of the imperial past existed then than now! These remains then included much of the decoration of the Golden House of Nero and of other palaces and villas. In 1515 Raphael became Superintendent of Antiquities, and it was upon the arabesques and paintings of Nero's palace that he based the rich and glowing interior of his Villa Madama (1516). Paradoxically this new interest in the more 'frivolous' or decorative aspects of Roman art may have accounted for many characteristics of the next phase, Mannerism.

Although the sculptural quality of Baroque may be already glimpsed in Bramante's plan for St Peter's, or the Baroque city in Brunelleschi's skyline, neither High Renaissance nor Baroque are adequate terms to designate the architecture of Italy through the sixteenth and seventeenth centuries. Between the Roman strength of Sangallo's Palazzo Farnese, of the High Renaissance, and the full Baroque of Bernini's Piazza, there lies over a century. Much had to be fitted in, and for that purpose the word 'Mannerism' has proved useful.

The Renaissance and the High Renaissance – right up to the time of Raphael, Sangallo and Michelangelo – had balance, harmony and Roman gravity. Mannerism, however, had different ideals. It attained its effects by deliberate discord, by emotional tension, by elegance, scenic effect or decorative fuss. Mannerist architects could flout all the Vitruvian rules and could be more romantic, more individualistic than their immediate predecessors. To compare and contrast, say, the Palazzo Farnese of 1530 and the Palazzo Massimi, of only a few years later, may make the point.

The Palazzo Farnese (1534–50) was designed by Antonio da Sangallo (1485–1546), and completed by Michelangelo. Its 185-foot frontage, together with its sheer strength and fine scale, make it a major achieve-

211 Plan of the palaces in Rome designed by Peruzzi for Angelo (left) and Pietro Massimi, 1535. Opening off a curving road, each has a vestibule (a), grand cortile (b) and minor court (c)

ment of the High Renaissance. Each window is a beautifully proportioned aedicule laid upon an equally well proportioned expanse of plain wall. Michelangelo's central doorway (1546) is a wonderful demonstration of how monumental scale can be created by the build-up of all the subordinate details, the big things looking big because the small things are small. The balustrade of the balcony, the cartouches of arms, the larger cartouche crowning all, the window grilles, and so on, all give scale to the enormous rusticated arch in the centre. When, however, we turn to the Palazzo Massimi, only five years later, we realise that something has happened. This little palace (actually two palaces for two brothers, cleverly arranged to have a single frontage) was designed by Baldassare Peruzzi (1481–1536). Peruzzi was the friend of Bramante, Raphael and Sangallo, but his Palazzo Massimi initiated a new and more original phase of Italian architecture. It was an innovation. It marks the beginning of Mannerism. Apart from its originality and its picturesque courtyard, it has a curious and gently curved façade which ignores all the strong and masculine qualities of the High Renaissance. It is very elegant but much of its detail is thin and rather affected. Its upper windows – quite unclassical – are more like prettily framed easel pictures hung upon the wall than anything which Sangallo would have called a window. They are a whim, if a delightful whim, of Peruzzi. The Farnese is heroic, the Massimi is charming. Classicism is now an attitude, an aesthetic viewpoint, rather than a real submission to Antiquity.

Michelangelo's doorway to the Palazzo Farnese has been maintained as an example of the High Renaissance. If one looks above this, however, to the top storey that he added after Sangallo's death, one can see that in Michelangelo himself the new Mannerist current was running strongly. It was he, in fact, in painting, in sculpture and in architecture, who more than any other man was responsible for leading art in that direction. Qualities

213 *Palazzo Massimi alle Colonne, Rome (1535; at the right in Ill. 211), by Peruzzi. Note its individualism, even its eccentricity – e.g. windows framed like pictures, and the use of flat detail and flat rustication – compared with the masculine directness of the Palazzo Farnese, below*

natural to his temperament – physical strength, violence, tension, suffering – became the ideals of the next generation, who regarded him with almost supernatural reverence.

Michelangelo (1475–1564), born at Settignano near Florence, lived to be ninety. In that long life he gave his genius little rest. He slept with his boots on and took his meals at the work bench. In spite of the wide training of so many Renaissance artists, Michelangelo did in fact move from painting and sculpture to architecture without

212, 214 *Palazzo Farnese, Rome (1534–40), designed by Antonio da Sangallo and completed – with the window over the doorway (opposite, below), and the upper storey where window-frames rest on twin consoles – by Michelangelo. Smaller parts, such as the balcony and cartouches, build up to tell the eye how large the building really is*

any specific schooling. His commission to design and to carve an enormous tomb for Julius II came to nothing, and left us little more than the famous figure of Moses. To house the tomb, however, meant no less than the rebuilding of St Peter's. While Bramante was planning and laying the foundations of the new basilica, Michelangelo's energies were diverted to the painting of the Sistine Chapel. He resented having been, as he thought, ousted by Bramante, and it was only after the death of Bramante and Sangallo that he was able to remodel St Peter's – a task that had by then become little more than a scaling-down operation.

It was in 1520, after his completion of the Sistine and the abandonment of the papal tomb, that Michelangelo came back to Florence to work on the Medici Chapel (the mausoleum of the Medici family) and on the Biblioteca Laurenziana (the Medicean Library) together with its ante-room and staircase. The total scheme may be described as Mannerism at its finest. Not yet have we anything like full Baroque. There is no struggle against

215 *Biblioteca Laurenziana, Florence (1524–57), by Michelangelo. The vestibule is carried out in dead white and sombre grey. The coupled columns, apparently carried on brackets – Mannerist illogicality – give height to a room which had to contrast with the long perspective of the library itself (visible beyond) – another Mannerist trait*

the laws of nature, no deliberate distortion, no anarchy, very little plasticity . . . only a certain arbitrary use of classical elements to fulfil a sublime objective. The spatial quality of the library is purely Mannerist. It is also Michelangelo's first architectural work without the support of sculpture, an astonishing feat for one untrained in architecture, however 'sculptural' the architecture may be. The vestibule, a tall room containing the staircase, goes further. Here he actually recessed his grey marble columns back into the thickness of the wall. As columns they are correct, even austere, but they seem to support nothing (actually they support the roof trusses and their curious position was to a certain extent dictated by the existing buildings) and to stand, inexplicably, upon huge balusters slightly out of alignment with them.

The Medici Chapel, 40 feet square, is a symphony in white marble and black Istrian stone. Unlike the library it was, of course, designed primarily as a setting for sculpture – for those great seated figures of Giulio and Lorenzo de' Medici, and for the semi-recumbent figures

216 *Medici Chapel in S. Lorenzo, Florence (begun 1521), designed by Michelangelo as a marriage of sculpture and architecture. The architectural features – complex niches set above the doors, a frieze with upside-down balusters above the monument, right – are unique. Their strangeness creates a distinctive, disturbing effect, increased by the combination of cold, angular masses and plain surfaces with unusually delicate ornament and mouldings*

189

of Day and Night, Dawn and Evening. Here, as in his Palazzo Farnese doorway, Michelangelo achieves scale by a continual breaking down of the elements from the large pilaster which runs the full height of the chapel, to the smaller pilasters flanking the niches. This chapel, like the Parthenon or the portals of Chartres, is a perfect marriage between sculpture and architecture – the highest architectural ideal, regardless of style, as long as stone remained the material of which buildings were made.

The Capitol, when Michelangelo started work on it in 1538, was a scene of confusion, a planless collection of old buildings on the historic hill above the Forum. From this chaos he welded a masterpiece of town-planning. He seized, as it were, upon one of the main axial lines of Rome, and on that he created the central space around which he then set the Palazzo dei Conservatori (1563–8) the Palazzo del Senatore (1573–1612) and the Capitoline Museum (1544–55). These buildings had to be finished by the next generation, but they demonstrate Michelangelo's mastery over the use of the 'giant order' – the taking of the column or the pilaster through *two* storeys with, perhaps, a smaller column flanking the arcade or the windows on the ground floor. Once again, the smaller column acts as a foil, giving scale to the large one, and thus to the building as a whole, and, indeed to the whole urban complex. Thus is grandeur built up by a relationship of parts. One also notes the skilful placing of the three buildings – not at right angles and not concealing each other but, nevertheless, enclosing three sides of the central space. In the middle of that space – a focal point – is the great equestrian statue of Marcus Aurelius. The broad approach stairway, the pattern of the paving, the whole arrangement of steps and levels is, in the highest sense of the word, sculptural. Michelangelo here created a new node in the plan of Rome. As town-planning it ranks with the piazzas of Venice, Florence, Urbino or Siena, but unlike them it

217 Plan of the Capitol, Rome, laid out by Michelangelo (1538–1612). A monumental staircase leads up the hill into a piazza ingeniously arranged to give a sense of enclosure; in a clockwise direction from the left, the buildings are the Capitoline Museum, Palazzo del Senatore and Palazzo dei Conservatori. The ancient equestrian statue of Marcus Aurelius is the focal point, at the centre of a complex pavement (see Ill. 218)

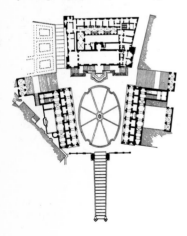

esign was basically the work of one man.

The work of Michelangelo's younger contemporaries, highly individual as it often is, reflects a common urge to scape from the sober monumentality of the Roman enaissance into something more dynamic, expressive r fantastic. In 1544 a pupil of Raphael, Giulio Romano 1492/9–1546) designed himself a house – almost a alace – at Mantua. A typical example of Mannerism, his house combines a rigid basic formality with considerable license in the handling of its detail: a pediment vithout a horizontal member, a smooth string-course ipping, as it were, behind the keystones, and windows et in flat, ornamented frames. Again, one can only ompare the Farnese or even the Palazzo Pitti; this, rchitecturally, is a different world. Some ten years arlier Giulio Romano had built the Palazzo del Te at Mantua; this is typically Mannerist with its rhythms of

218 Palazzo del Senatore on the Capitol, Rome, largely designed by Michelangelo, and built 1573–1612. Standing opposite the steps, it is raised on a basement storey which gives it prominence over the buildings on either side. All the façades are governed by a giant order of pilasters; in the flanking palaces this is enriched by smaller columns on the ground floor, just visible at the left. The statuary is ancient Roman

219 In the Palazzo del Te, Mantua (1525–35), Giulio Romano used exaggerated rustication to create an effect of almost monumental strength, but the details are playful. Pediments are placed directly on to the 'rocky' window-surrounds; in a seemingly symmetrical composition, the bay between columns at the right turns out to be narrower than that at the left

220 The house at Mantua designed by Giulio Romano for himself (c.1544) appears formal in its general composition, but its parts show Mannerist freedom – the string-course which becomes a pediment, the squeezed-in windows, and the varied rustication carried out, as at the Palazzo del Te, above, not in stone but in stucco

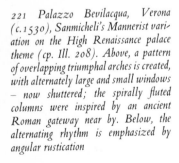

221 Palazzo Bevilacqua, Verona (c.1530), Sanmicheli's Mannerist variation on the High Renaissance palace theme (cp. Ill. 208). Above, a pattern of overlapping triumphal arches is created, with alternately large and small windows – now shuttered; the spirally fluted columns were inspired by an ancient Roman gateway near by. Below, the alternating rhythm is emphasized by angular rustication

unevenly spaced Tuscan columns and its lively use of rustication, but it also has a certain strength as if remembering its High Renaissance forerunners.

Mannerist space also has its own character. Architects could deliberately build perspectives. This, of course, was not an exclusively Mannerist feature, but the long, monotonous perspectives of some Mannerist designs would seem contrived to draw one on towards some unrevealed climax. Vasari's court of the Uffizi in Florence (begun in 1560), the interior of Palladio's S. Giorgio Maggiore in Venice (designed in 1565), or the Biblioteca Laurenziana itself all have this quality, which Nikolaus Pevsner has called the power of 'suction' – the spectator is sucked into the heart of the design.

About this time Michele Sanmicheli (1484–1559) built a number of palaces in Verona, the most notable of which are the Palazzo Pompei (c. 1529) which is conservative for its date and in the Bramantesque tradition, heavily columniated and rusticated; and the Palazzo

222 S. Giorgio Maggiore, Venice, designed by Palladio in 1565. Serene columns and arches, of a purity that is wholly un-Mannerist, create a spacious nave; beyond them the eye is drawn to the mysteriously glimpsed monks' choir, behind the altar

193

223 *In this air view of Venice we see one of the most famous and harmonious urban spaces in the world, developed throughout the centuries. From St Mark's (top right), the long Piazza S. Marco stretches out to the left; linking it with the lagoon, bottom, is the Piazzetta, bordered by the Doge's Palace on the right and Sansovino's Libreria Vecchia on the left. Beyond the library is Sansovino's Zecca (Mint). At the hub of the two squares stands the Campanile of St Mark's, providing the indispensable vertical accent*

Bevilacqua (*c.*1530), which is on the other han distinctly Mannerist with its alternation of wide an narrow bays, triangular and segmental pediments an spirally fluted columns. Sanmicheli was famous for h fortifications – a sideline for many Renaissance architect – and the Porta del Palio at Verona, a town gate begu in 1524, shows a skilful use of plain stone ornamenta tions such as cartouches and columns, set against textural background of rustication.

Jacopo Sansovino (1486–1570) built the Libreri Vecchia in Venice (1536). This building is a displa not merely of a style but of architectural ingenuity Although so wildly different in date and style from th Doge's Palace on the other side of the Piazzetta, i matches it in scale and sculptural richness or chiaroscurc and is therefore a contribution to the unity of th Piazzetta – a contribution in fact to town-planning, s much more important than style. In the design of i façade Sansovino was faced with the old problem of hov to place small openings over larger ones while, at th

224, 225 The Gesù in Rome (begun 1568), by Vignola and della Porta, set a pattern for later façades in Europe (Ills. 233, 275) and even – transmitted by the Jesuits – in the New World. The centre of the façade is treated as a kind of two-storeyed temple-front, which is linked to the lower sides by volutes. The plan, below, tries to get the best of both worlds by having both a long nave and a big central space. The aisles are treated as chapels (cp. Ill. 200)

me time, avoiding too great a mass of wall in the upper orey. He solved it neatly. The windows of the upper orey actually are narrower than the openings below, at they are flanked by colonnettes and it is these olonnettes that reduce or mitigate the apparent wall ass between the windows. Sansovino's last work, the lint (La Zecca) with its wildly exaggerated rustication, ay be seen as yet another variety of Mannerism, com- arable to the garden façade of the Pitti Palace (1558–)) by the leading Florentine architect of the time, artolommeo Ammanati.

Among the most influential of all Mannerist buildings or reasons other than purely architectural) was the esù, the chief church in Rome of the Jesuits and of the ounter-Reformation. Hundreds of churches all over urope have, for some four hundred years, been fluenced by it. The architect was Giacomo Vignola 507–73). The Gesù has been described as an attempt to mbine the centralized and the longitudinal plan. In at the aisles, following the example of Alberti's S.

226 Longhena's Sta Maria della Salute
in Venice (1632) is very rich, very
Venetian, piling up diverse elements and
culminating in the enormous volutes
abutting the dome (a typically Venetian
hemisphere). Primarily, however, its
place is in town-planning: this church
and the Campanile of St Mark's are the
two gateposts at the entrance to the
Grand Canal

Andrea at Mantua, are reduced to merely vestigial
side-chapels, and that there is an explosion of space at
the 'crossing', this may be true. The building was begun
by Vignola in 1568 and continued by della Porta. The
latter followed Alberti in using large scrolls or volutes
to link the two storeys of the façade. This device also
succeeded in hiding the buttresses, features necessary in
a vaulted church but hitherto untranslatable into the
classical vocabulary. Wren concealed his behind false
walls (see pp. 244-5). It was Longhena (1604-75), at
Sta Maria della Salute in Venice, who actually equated
scroll and buttress so that they form part of the silhouette
of his dome, dominating the rich Venetian scene which
can absorb so much.

   To Vignola must also be ascribed the Villa of Pope
Julius (c. 1550), a typical Italian villa with a formal
garden, summer rooms, grotto and fountains, all carefully related to the grand cortile – a great semi-circular
colonnade forming one façade of the villa. The Vill

rnese at Caprarola (1559–73) is a strange pentagonal
tress-like building; Vignola made the most of a high
dium which already existed, and created an impressive
proach of both ramps and steps. In Genoa, strong,
avily designed palaces mainly with courtyards and
ps exploiting the steep sites, were built by Galeazzo
essi (1512–72), a pupil of Michelangelo, or under
essi's influence.

In spite of the almost universal acceptance of Manner-
n in northern and central Italy, the man who was in
any ways the most original architect of the whole
riod stands largely outside it. This was Andrea
lladio (1508–80) of Vicenza. The very word
alladian' – at least for the English-speaking world –
s become almost synonymous with classical architec-
re. Almost any house with a portico may be dubbed
alladian'. Palladio had a style which was personal,
ol, serene and refined. His two major churches in
enice – one has already been mentioned as having a
annerist preoccupation with perspective – S. Giorgio
aggiore (designed in 1565), and Il Redentore (1576–7),
e part of the tourists' familiar scene. It was, however, in
uses inland from Venice, in and around Vicenza, that

*227 In the Villa Farnese at Caprarola
(1559–73) an existing podium with
corner bastions gave Vignola the oppor-
tunity to create a luxurious 'fortress' on a
curious pentagonal plan. The great
double staircase is a version of that
invented by Bramante to link the two
levels of the Belvedere Court*

228–230 The serenity of Palladio's work, which endeared him to 18th-century Englishmen, is here evident. The absolute symmetry of the Villa Rotonda (opposite) is clear on the plan; the view shows an idyllic, almost Arcadian, scene. The Palazzo Chiericati in Vicenza (below) has the same cool elegance, though it is richer; statues decorate the roof (cp. Ill. 190) and pediments. Note, in both buildings, how colonnades are terminated at the sides by arches

Palladio gave his best to the world. Admittedly Palladio *Quattro Libri dell' Architettura* gave added fame to h work, but buildings such as the Palazzo Chierica (c.1550) or the Villa Rotonda (c.1550–1) will alway rank among the most civilized houses ever designed aristocratic without pomposity, symmetrical withou being forced, elegant without effeminacy. In the puri of their design they purged Mannerism of its affectation These buildings are memorable if for no other reaso than that they lifted the architecture of the private hou to a new level of importance. Also, in spite of the gre beauty already attained by the Italian garden, the Palladian villas established a new and more form relationship between house and garden. A house such the Villa Rotonda does not have merely a symmetric façade; it is symmetrical on all fronts, and being al raised on a podium approached by great flights of step

acquires something of the quality of a glorified gazebo
garden temple. The main axis was extended outwards
to the garden and park. It was this marriage of architec-
re and nature which – in spite of the difficulties of
apting an Italian style to the English climate – assured
alladio's popularity with those eighteenth-century
nglish gentry who ventured upon the Grand Tour
ee pp. 265–6).

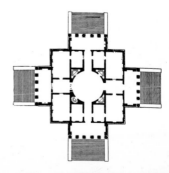

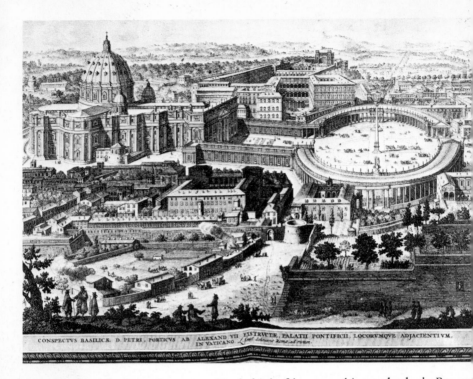

CONSPECTVS BASILICÆ. D. PETRI. PORTICVS AB ALEXAND VII EXISTRVCTÆ. PALATII PONTIFICII. LOCORVMQVE ADJACENTIVM. IN VATICANO

231 St Peter's and the Piazza, Rome, in the 17th century. Bernini's oval colonnade forms a magnificent prelude, contrasting in its fine simplicity with the complexities of the enormous church. One sees here also, however, how Maderna's projecting nave would cut off the view of the dome from below (see p. 180). In the background is the Vatican Palace with, just visible, the Belvedere Court (Ill. 203)

For the birth of the next architectural style, the Baroque we must return to Rome. Rome had always been the city of the grand gesture. We have seen how Michelangelo replanning of the Capitol was part of a new and dramatic understanding of town-planning. Sixtus V, at the end of the sixteenth century, inaugurated an ambitious programme of rebuilding, involving the cutting straight new streets and the creation of new focal points the Piazza del Popolo, the Piazza Navona and, course, the Piazza of St Peter's. None of these project came to fruition until after his death, but they mark the beginning of that proud, confident, rhetorical spirit that differentiates Baroque from the clever sophistication and self-conscious ambiguity of Mannerism.

The Piazza del Popolo – created over the centuries – an enormous urban space, the meeting-point of several streets and, in itself, a link between the gardens on the

Pincian Hill and the Vatican City on the other side of the Tiber. The Piazza Navona is an elongated *place* with fountains down its length – the whole being subtly related to the two Baroque churches on the long side, one of which, S. Agnese, has a façade by Borromini.

The Piazza of St Peter's was at first intended to be completely closed – virtually an outdoor extension of the church itself, thus acquiring real meaning. As things are the open side of the ellipse towards the Via della Conciliazione is distracting and completely destructive of any feeling of enclosure. Bernini's sketch for closing the gap exists but has never been used. Even as it is, however, with the magic curving perspective of those noble and unadorned columns, the marbles and the

232 Detail of the Piazza of St Peter's, Rome, designed by Bernini in 1656. The colossal Tuscan columns are made of travertine, the coarse golden stone used in the temples at Paestum (Ills. 21, 22)

fountains, the Piazza almost redeems St Peter's. The columns are of the Tuscan Order, the plainest and most puritanical of all; adornment lies not in the application of any carving, but rather in the actual shape of the great curves, in the architecture itself – which is true Baroque.

The Piazza was Bernini's masterpiece, and Bernini was the archetype of the Baroque artist. Baroque architecture – as distinct from Baroque planning – cannot really be said to have begun before 1600, when Carlo Maderna (whose front to St Peter's was ultimately a failure) designed the façade of a much smaller church in Rome, Sta Susanna. This has all the qualities of a developed Baroque building. A relatively simple, unified idea is expressed as directly as possible and with the utmost force. Columns, demi-columns, pilasters, pediments and sculpture rise to a single climax. This quality of directness, of emotional certainty, is the hall-mark of all later Baroque, however subtle it may become in detail. Bernini is its most typical exponent because he united the arts of sculpture and architecture. But his two greatest rivals, Francesco Borromini and Pietro da Cortona, were in many ways his superiors in their feeling for volume and material.

In 1624 Bernini had begun the erection of the baldac-chino over the high altar of St Peter's. All Roman and High Renaissance restraint has vanished. This huge affair, a hundred feet high, with its twisted columns and outrageous silhouette, is an extravagance that Michel-angelo would have disliked. It is the austerity of the Piazza that is surprising, not the sensuality of his other work. In the Cornaro Chapel (1645–52), in the church of Sta Maria della Vittoria, he is truly himself. The famous figures of St Teresa and the Angel, dramatic, voluptuous and ecstatic, are beautifully poised in space above the altar, magically lit from above through yellow glass. This is the art of illusion, of the theatre, but is superbly done. Only in Spain perhaps, or Bavaria, can we find such titillation of the passions by artifice.

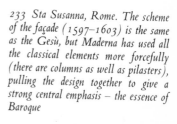

233 *Sta Susanna, Rome. The scheme of the façade (1597–1603) is the same as the Gesù, but Maderna has used all the classical elements more forcefully (there are columns as well as pilasters), pulling the design together to give a strong central emphasis – the essence of Baroque*

234 *Cornaro Chapel, Sta Maria della Vittoria, Rome (1645–52; from an 18th-century painting). Bernini here combines architecture and sculpture in a single dramatic composition. The figures of St Teresa and the Angel above the altar are superbly related – both in lighting and in composition – to each other and to their setting. On either side members of the Cornaro family, carved in marble, watch as though from theatrical boxes*

The Scala Regia (1663–6), that tremendous stairway between the Piazza of St Peter's and the papal apartments, is another Bernini masterpiece. It forms the main entrance to the Vatican Palace, but had to be fitted into a narrow and awkward site between the Galilee Porch and the Palace itself. A brilliant piece of planning overcame the difficulty with dramatic result. Necessarily smaller in scale than the Piazza itself it is richer in ornament and yet manages somehow to be a real continuation of the Piazza into the Palace. It is lined with columns but relies very little upon any specifically Baroque device. The only 'trick' is the false perspective due to the tapering of the plan. This increases the apparent length of the stair – at any rate as you go up – and seems to add something to its processional air.

Bernini also collaborated with Borromini on the Palazzo Barberini. This palace had in fact been begun by Carlo Maderna in 1628 and so represents a collaboration

236 In the Palazzo Barberini, Rome (begun 1628) Maderna opened out the plan: instead of a building round a court, there is a solid central block with wings to left and right; instead of a rusticated ground floor, there is an open loggia. Most of the façade is by Bernini, but the upper windows, with their curious sham-perspective frames, show the hand of Borromini

235 Opposite: Bernini's Scala Regia in the Vatican (1663–6) is made to seem longer by reducing the height and width as it ascends. A landing half-way up is mysteriously lit from the side

237 *S. Andrea al Quirinale, Rome (1658–78): Bernini's essay in the oval plan which, with its plasticity and flexibility, was to appeal to many Baroque architects. Here the oval is placed transversely: the high altar is in the middle of the long side to the left. All the sculpture is by Bernini*

between three major Baroque architects. At first glance the main façade, with its superimposed orders, might be of the High Renaissance; then we notice that the second-storey windows are set in heavily chamfered arches, giving very nearly the illusion of a vaulted corridor. Maderna's plan is fully Baroque with an entrance through a vaulted undercroft leading to a large oval salon carved – as it were – out of the solid. The main stair is also contained within an oval.

The oval plan, which made its appearance in Michelangelo's first project for the tomb of Julius II, was taken up by Vignola and became almost a sign manual of the Baroque. Bernini's S. Andrea al Quirinale, Maderna's S. Giacomo al Corso and Rainaldi's Sta Maria in Monte Santo all have oval plans. The explanation may lie partly in fashion, partly in the flexibility of the oval. It was eagerly copied in the next century in Germany.

Francesco Borromini (1599–1667), was trained as a ason and was over thirty when, in 1633, he began his st major work, the church of S. Carlo alle Quattro ontane. This is a tiny church, so small that it is virtually o more than a chapel, but it is packed with ingenuity d with architectural innovation. Its plan is highly mplex, based on two equilateral triangles with arcs d segments drawn from various points of their inter-ction, but it resolves itself at the level of the dome into oval, and at the lantern into a circle. The whole of chitecture here becomes plastic, almost molten. Beneath the undulating forms there is still, of course, the ghost a classical building – the absolute freedom of Ron-amp is still three centuries away – but subject only this single link with the classical past, Borromini ated architecture as abstract sculpture. Internally, in ite of an exaggerated height in the order, the apses and

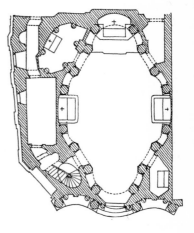

240 S. Ivo della Sapienza, Rome (1642–60). Borromini has here based his plan on a six-pointed star with three lobes and three points, and we see how this is taken upwards to be developed into a fantastic dome

241 The façade of S. Carlo alle Quattro Fontane in Rome (1667), Borromini's last work, has the same qualities as the interior (Ills. 238, 239). Classical elements are used with the utmost freedom, concave plane set against convex. The little 'temple' placed on the upper storey is reminiscent of Petra (Ill. 55), while the larger cupola on the roof resembles the 'Temple of Vesta' at Baalbek

niches flow one into another, while externally the façade is a series of alternating concave and convex surfaces, swaying and swerving. This quality of abstract modelling – even if it is compiled from such things as entablatures, vases, pediments – informs all Borromini's work. The church of S. Ivo della Sapienza uses the six-pointed star (two interlocking triangles) as the basis of its plan, while S. Filippo Neri uses one concave front for a whole building. Borromini's spires for S. Carlo, S. Ivo (a fantastic spiral motif) and S. Andrea delle Fratte, develop their spatial ideas with even more freedom. The same plastic qualities, achieved by the setting of curve against curve, are found in his con-temporaries and immediate followers. Pietro da Cortona

242 The cupola of Borromini's S. Ivo, which again recalls Baalbek, develops out of the six segments of the interior (Ill. 240). It is then surmounted by a fantastic spiral ending in an equally fantastic wrought-iron flourish

243 The façade of Sta Maria della Pace, Rome (1656–7), by Pietro da Cortona, takes the Gesù scheme and makes it fully three-dimensional, bring-ing the upper level forward in a curve and introducing a semi-circular porch below. The tension of these tightly interlocking motifs – especially the seg-mental pediment inside the triangular one – recalls Michelangelo (Ill. 216)

244 *Dome of the chapel of the Santis-sima Sindone, Turin Cathedral (1667–90). Guarini's greatest interest was in vaulting. Here he combines ideas from Gothic and Islamic architecture to produce a unique dome built up by tiers of segmental arches resting on one another. Each is pierced, admitting light*

(1596–1669) gives them an extraordinary feeling of tension in his façade for Sta Maria della Pace, a church whose influence reverberated throughout the next century. Further north, in Piedmont, Guarino Guarini (1624–83) took them to lengths which still seem almost wilfully extravagant. His Chapel of the Holy Shroud (Santissima Sindone), Turin, has a dome made of an ascending series of segmental arches standing on top of one another; the dome of S. Lorenzo, in the same city, consists of an eight-pointed star conceived in terms of flying ribs, the dome itself floating above them and silhouetting them with light from its windows; while the Palazzo Carignano, of brick, projects the concave-convex-concave scheme on to the long horizontal front of a secular palace, as Bernini had wanted to do at the Louvre. All these qualities, however, are shown to perfection in Borromini's S. Agnese in the Piazza Navona in Rome, mainly in the fine modelling of the twin towers,

245 At S. Agnese, in Rome (begun
1652), Borromini not only flanked his
dome with twin towers but devised a
plan which gives those towers independence of the main building – each, as it
were, a sculptural entity. This church,
on the long side of the Piazza Navona,
plays a major town-planning role

246 Palazzo Carignano, Turin (begun
1678). Guarini gives interest to the long
façade by alternating concave and convex
sections, in a way which seems to derive
from Bernini. The texture and ornament,
entirely of brick, is almost Arabic in
character

but especially in the way that they are, as it were, swung
clear of the main building. In the Baroque of southern
Europe Borromini had come as a great liberating
influence; and elsewhere, as far afield as England and
Germany (p. 250), we can detect his influence.

Chapter Eight

RENAISSANCE, MANNERISM, AND BAROQUE OUTSIDE ITALY

The story of Italian architecture has been taken up to the end of the seventeenth century because there is properly speaking no break, and each phase emerges from the one that preceded it. But we must now go back in time and trace the spread of Renaissance ideas outside Italy. This is a complicated subject because development within any one country was neither continuous nor logical. Italian influence came in arbitrary waves, depending largely on political circumstances, and the Netherlands, for instance, could be influenced by Italian Mannerism without ever going through a real Renaissance phase at all. Moreover, in all countries where the Gothic tradition was deeply rooted the new style was at first only applied superficially as a novel form of ornament. The earliest phase of Renaissance architecture in France, England and Germany is thus a hybrid art which is difficult to evaluate in its own terms.

In Spain, although Gothic churches went on being built with undiminished confidence, the pure Italian Renaissance style appears at an extremely early date. The unfinished Palace of Charles V at Granada, by Pedro Machuca, was begun in 1527 and has a circular courtyard with superimposed Doric and Ionic columns. Its austere classicism is taken even further in the vast palace of Philip II outside Madrid, the Escorial, begun by Juan Bautista de Toledo and completed by Juan de Herrera (1563–84). This is a combination of palace, monastery and cathedral, its exterior almost completely plain, its church on a centralized plan, simple and

247 Palace of Charles V, Granada (begun 1526), by Pedro Machuca. Designed with a circular courtyard only ten years after Raphael's Villa Madama, this has an austere classicism which was not achieved in northern Europe until much later

248 *Escorial, near Madrid (1563–84), begun by Juan Bautista de Toledo and finished by Juan de Herrera. In the severest classical style, it housed palace, monastery and school. The big cathedral, whose dome and towers rise here above the range of monastic cells, is the focal point of a vast complex including some fifteen courts and cloisters*

impressive in a way that recalls Bramante. Diego de Siloé in the choir of Granada Cathedral, created an equally monumental effect, with perspective coffered vault between the piers. Early Spanish Renaissance is surprisingly restrained when compared to the Baroque excesses that were to succeed it within a generation.

France gained its first glimpse of the Renaissance in 1494 when the armies of Charles VIII of France crossed the Alps and marched down into the plains of Lombardy. They got as far as Naples but a year later – with all Italy in arms against them – had to fight their way home. Seventeen years later it was François I, the true Renaissance prince, who entered Milan at the head of his troops. Those two expeditions had changed the cultural direction of the Western world.

When the French soldiers invaded Italy, Michelangelo and Bramante were at the height of their powers, Brunelleschi and Alberti already dead. It must have seemed to those medieval Frenchmen as if they were on some expedition to another planet. St Peter's was only

alf built, but the glories of the Early Renaissance were
1 there. The impact of Medicean Florence – palaces,
aintings, furniture, costume – was also immense. And
r the Italians the French Court offered a new outlet, for
though it was still a medieval court it was nevertheless
littering and wealthy. Leonardo da Vinci, for instance,
as among those who returned with the French armies –
e *Mona Lisa* in his baggage; he died in the end at the
tle château of Amboise on a cliff above the Loire.

That France should suddenly start building Italian
alaces was, needless to say, out of the question.
evitably, to begin with, it was in small things – silks,
ramics, jewellery – that the Italian craftsman was
lowed his way. Architects would not have been
elcome to this last generation of French master masons.
heir achievement and indeed their whole world had
en a Gothic world. The Italian, or the Italian pattern
ooks, might be allowed to influence ornament, marble-
ork or the like, but, after all, the French masons were
asters of their craft.

What we find going on, therefore, in this first genera-
on of the French Renaissance, is a curious battle
etween old and new. If we look back at the medieval
stle in, say, the early fifteenth-century illuminations of
e *Très Riches Heures du duc de Berry*, we see it as a highly
mantic affair, white towered and turreted. If we look at
e châteaux of the French courtiers in the first part of
e sixteenth century, we find the same thing. It is in their
ood. The romanticism of the Middle Ages did not
ve to await Victor Hugo; here, in the very first phase
the Renaissance it had begun almost before they were
ad.

And yet the Renaissance château is not a castle.
zay-le-Rideau, Chenonceau, Chambord, Blois – all
tween 1508 and 1520 – were none of them fortified
stles. The life within was civilized, cultivated and
xurious. These palaces of the Loire Valley were not
anned in the high classic manner, as were the Strozzi

*249 Granada Cathedral (c.1529),
designed by Diego de Siloé, is another
example of early Spanish Renaissance
at its grandest. This view shows one of
the monumental coffered arches leading
from the ambulatory into the circular
choir*

250 The staircase tower in the François I wing at Blois (begun 1515) is an extraordinary stylistic mixture. The elements of the early French Renaissance – classical pilasters, 'grottesche' and balustrades – decorate a stair supported upon Gothic arches and vaults

or the Farnese, but they did have big rooms of state, gre hearths and panelling. They had, moreover – unli castles – large windows looking outwards upon law and parterres, and upon a secure world. The battlemei have become a huge crenellated cornice, the moat a l pond, and the donjon – at Chenonceau – a gazebo. Mc superficially, it is around the doors and windows ai fireplaces that we find actual classical detail – Ionic ai Corinthian pilasters with panels of arabesque ornamei These minor fripperies must have come out of Itali pattern books. They are the only outward and stylist sign that Charles and François had ever been to Italy.

It would be a pity if the over-ornamentation ai 'fancy dress' air of these palaces on the Loire were blind us to their real qualities. Blois, the largest, and al a royal house, is a collection of buildings, dating fro the thirteenth to the seventeenth century, around a lai quadrangle. The Early Renaissance portion – c.151 25 – is richly and deeply carved with ornament ai heraldic devices. The most famous feature is the stairc. tower – half inside and half outside the building – fantastic mixture of Gothic and classical, in whi Corinthian pilasters carry ribbed vaulting. It is at Bl(that we can first discern the nature of this château styl(white limestone, small purple-black slates used both f roofing and as inlaid panels, steep roofs and conica roofed turrets with elaborate chimneys and dormers, ai much carving everywhere. The setting was the gre meadows of central France, hunting forests, and t river Loire.

It was from such ingredients that men made fantas like Chenonceau and Chambord. Chambord (151 47) is, at one and the same time, a medieval castle out Mallory, an Italianate palace, a sophisticated pastiche. first glance it is also a fortress. Its plan shows an inner a an outer court, and a disused moat. At all its corner: has enormous circular towers, severely plain. All tl however, is a mere preparation, a platform upon whi

the architect, Pierre Nepveu, could set his *tour de force* –
the roof. It is like no roof in the world. Turrets, towers
and chimneys, pinnacles, belvederes, cupolas, fleurs-de-
lys and minarets all luxuriate upon the lead flats, where
Catherine de Médicis watched the stars with her astro-
loger. From far down the avenue it seems like some fairy
village in the sky. How significant that the architect
should take that non-Italian, that northern and Gothic
thing – a high-pitched roof – and use it as a setting for
his pyrotechnic display of Italianate detail.

Only a little less fantastic is Chenonceau (1515–23)
with scores of conical turrets carefully placed to be seen,
first, as a cluster from the avenue of approach and then,
secondly, all mirrored in still water. In 1556 Chenonceau
was more picturesquely extended – the architect being
Philibert de l'Orme – by means of a ballroom carried on
arches over the river, the sunlit water reflected upwards

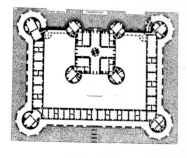

*251, 252 Château de Chambord
(1519–47). The round towers, keep
and moat are medieval, but the plan of the
keep has a new, Italian, symmetry. The
tiers of flat pilasters are characteristic of
the moment, as is the strapwork decoration on the roof; the fantastic skyline is
unique in its scale*

*253 Château de Chenonceau, on the
river Cher. Far left is the old 'donjon'.
Its conical roof is echoed by the main
block (begun 1515), replete with turrets, chimneys and ornate dormers of the
same genre as at Chambord. Beyond this
on the right is Philibert de l'Orme's wing
bridging the river (1556), with an upper
storey added in the late 16th century by
Bullant*

254 *Rood screen at St-Etienne-du-Mont, Paris (c.1545), probably by Philibert de l'Orme*

255 *Detail of Lescot's work in the Cour du Vieux Louvre, Paris (begun 1546). Note the rich carving, the pedimented windows, the segmental pediments and the use of columns rather than pilasters*

on to a plain ceiling. Azay-le-Rideau (1516), summarizes on a small scale the style of the greater Loire châteaux. It is a style which in its day added a slightly idyllic chapter to the history of architecture; it proved a disastrous model for nineteenth-century copyists.

It represented, in fact, only the traditional current of French architecture; the same mixture of the old and the new may be noted in some of the sixteenth-century churches of Paris. St-Eustache (1532–89) and St-Etienne-du-Mont where work went on throughout the sixteenth century, were both planned as five-aisled churches, with irregularly grouped towers, flying buttresses and steep roofs. That such structures should also drip with pilasters, pediments, columns, balustrades and so on, makes them, at best, curiosities. St-Etienne-du-Mont, however, is noteworthy for a truly fantastic rood screen thought to be by Philibert de l'Orme.

The more progressive spirit is seen in de l'Orme's other work and in that of his older contemporary Pierre Lescot. Lescot had been employed by François I to replace the old Gothic castle of the Louvre with something of his own time. Work began in 1546 and continued under various architects for the next century.

indeed, if one counts all the subsequent expansions of the building, for the next three centuries. Lescot's work (approximately a quarter of the Cour du Vieux Louvre) displays some lovely carving by Jean Goujon.

De l'Orme's reputation rests on his château at Anet (of which only the circular chapel, the gateway and the 'frontispiece' survive) and on his influential book the *Premier Livre de l'Architecture* (1569) in which he proposed a new and ornate order, the 'French Order', to go alongside the Doric, Ionic and Corinthian.

The influence of Italian visitors continued to be strong throughout the sixteenth and seventeenth centuries. Serlio built the château of Ancy-le-Franc, and extensions to Fontainebleau are attributed to him; Primaticcio, besides devising the Galerie François I at Fontainebleau (the germ of most subsequent Flemish and English interior decoration), designed a remarkable mausoleum for the Valois family to be built at St-Denis, unfortunately never begun. It was probably these Italian professionals who established the 'artist-architect' in France, whereby the architect might be a superb performer on the drawing-board, but lacking in realism (a curious position which still haunts the studios of the Ecole des Beaux-Arts).

256 Galerie François I, Fontainebleau (1533–7), by Rosso and Primaticcio. One of the first long galleries; the first use of strapwork; elegant Mannerist forms in stucco and paint

257 The circular chapel at Anet (1549–52), by de l'Orme, shows an unusually mature and subtle handling of pure classical forms

Something like this was happening in England too, but with the inevitable time-lag. When Henry VIII and François embraced each other on the Field of the Cloth of Gold in 1520, the glittering châteaux of the Loire Valley were already built. In England there was no architectural sign that the Renaissance existed. Torrigiano had, between 1512 and 1518, introduced the Italian High Renaissance style in his tomb of Henry VII at Westminster Abbey – a work of the greatest purity and brilliance, but hardly architecture. In 1515 Chambord was building, but in England Cardinal Wolsey was only just beginning to build himself a house at Hampton Court. Moreover, when the house was finished its debt to Italy and to Antiquity was no more than a few busts of Roman emperors on the gatehouse, a few putti in the spandrels of the hall roof. With its gatehouse, its quad-rangles and its great hall, Hampton Court was a glorified Oxford or Cambridge college. Neither a Medici nor a Valois would have called it a palace. In 1525, Wolsey, sensing his own downfall, gave it to his king. Henry's own most ambitious palace, Nonsuch, began in 1538, was even more of a hybrid. Its decoration, nearly all by foreign craftsmen, introduced a wealth of Renaissance motifs. Its structure was an undisciplined amalgam of traditional elements. With large circular corner towers, a crenellated cornice and conical roofs, Nonsuch deliberately emulated Chambord. It was the first Renaissance building in England. No trace of it remains.

Between the building of Nonsuch and the first of the great Elizabethan houses lies an arid generation in English architecture. Here and there, as at Barrington Court in Somerset and Hengrave Hall in Suffolk, both about 1530, a more than usually elaborate house might be built. In the main, however, in those years the English having never learnt Renaissance manners, were content with non-Renaissance houses. In a hundred manor houses or semi-fortified farms medieval life went on, a

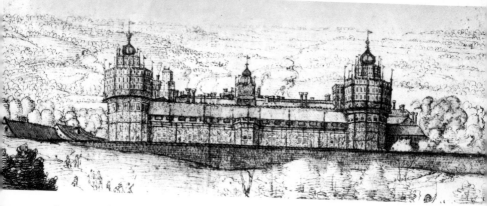

unaware of palaces in Rome or Florence as of the mountains on the moon. In any case those arid years had been filled by the Reformation with all its repercussions – the Dissolution of the Monasteries, the consequent agrarian and educational revolutions, the Marian persecutions, the wars with France. There had been no time or reason for building.

The only exception to this rule concerns the group of buildings initiated during the reign of Edward VI by

258, 259 Wolsey's Hampton Court (begun 1515, top) has two Italian terracotta roundels on the crenellated gate. Nonsuch (1538–58, above) – both grander and later – had towers like Chambord, while its traditional half-timber structure was covered with Italian stucco decoration

260 Old Somerset House, London (1547–52), from a drawing by John Thorpe. Here we see a real attempt to create a genuinely 'Italian' building. The centre is treated like a triumphal arch, the wings are made into unified compositions (topped by open strapwork); well-spaced classical windows are set in rusticated masonry, and there is a balustrade along the roof

the Protector Somerset and his circle. These were men of wide intellectual sympathies and European education. Somerset's own London palace, Old Somerset House, now completely disappeared, marks the beginning – a premature beginning as it transpired – of true Renaissance architecture in England. It had a symmetrical façade using the three orders, a triumphal arch motif for the entrance, pedimented windows and a crowning balustrade. Inside was a courtyard of semi-circular arches on Tuscan columns. The influence of this building is reflected (with diminishing strength) in such later houses as Longleat, the Wiltshire home of Somerset's friend John Thynne. Longleat, begun in 1553, is a stroke of genius. It abandons the use of the orders, but is symmetrical on both axes. Although built around a large court the important rooms all look outwards upon the park, and indeed the house is a composition of square bay windows. It has one thing in common with the Loire châteaux – the desire to exploit joy in a secure and sunlit world. It avoids, however, the French nostalgia for a dressed-up castle. Longleat is also in another respect more Italian than French; as it stands, it suppresses the roof. It has leaded flats. This is not only non-French it is a most radical departure from the whole English tradition. Longleat, therefore, is simply a rich and elaborate essay in fenestration; as such it is a brilliant *tour de force*.

The 1560s contain several pointers to the future. One
' the men working at Longleat (his share is unknown
ut must have been a minor one) was Robert Smythson,
on to emerge as the leader of English architecture. And
1563 the first English literary introduction to classical
chitecture was published, John Shute's *First and Chief*
rounds of Architecture.

Longleat belongs to a period of transition, the uneasy
ars of Mary Tudor and the early part of the reign of
lizabeth. Then quite suddenly the Elizabethan Age is
oon us. England became not only a European power
ut also – with the circumnavigation of the globe, the
efeat of Spain and the founding of Virginia – a world
ower of a new kind, mercantile, secular, cultured,
oullient and self-confident. This found its expression
 architecture. Antiquity and Italian fashions were
 cidental; the basis of Elizabethan architecture lay in
atriotism and splendour. Elizabeth herself built very
ttle – England never had its Louvre or its Escorial – but
ne cult of sovereignty, the desire to entertain and honour
ne Queen, as well as the desire to display wealth and
ower, were the mainspring of a new kind of art,
nanifest in clothes, coaches, drama, ships, gardens and
ouses.

*261, 262 Longleat (begun 1553), the
Elizabethan ideal of a great mansion.
Some features were inspired by Somerset
House, such as the balustraded roof and
the way in which the projecting bays are
unified; but the windows are greatly
enlarged, creating glittering façades – as
in a Late Gothic church. The house is
symmetrical on both axes, and completely rectilinear. The important rooms
now look outward upon a safe world*

These huge mansions – the homes not of royalty but of noblemen and merchants – were built between 158 and 1620. They have all the spaciousness, glitter and novelty of the Loire châteaux. But they are quite different. In their craftsmanship – their leaded lights mullions and panelling – they are a last chapter of medievalism; in the columns and entablature around door or fireplace they are Italianate; in their grotesque strapwork and curved gables they are Flemish; in actual fact they are unique. They are very English, very splendid and rather vulgar. It was only in detail that these houses really owed much to Italy – to Italian writers such as Serlio, and to the fact that 'Italianism' was so much in the English air. John Summerson has called them 'prodigy houses' and it is an apt description.

Apart from the scale and richness of decoration displayed by these houses, significant changes were also taking place in planning. A desire for symmetry impressive rooms and ordered sequences led to the transformation of the hall, which, with its screens passage 'high table' and oriel window, had been the centre of the house where all its inhabitants could gather for meals and warmth, into something more like a grand vestibule. This had already happened at Hardwick by the end of the sixteenth century. Elsewhere, the needs of symmetry were ingeniously combined with the old arrangement in disguise, for instance at Wollaton. By the turn of the century, however, the hall had become secondary to the 'presence chamber', the dining-hall and numerous other chambers, whole wings of 'lodgings' for the guests, and not least the 'long gallery'. This latter – over 150 feet long at Hatfield – was an English contribution to the history of planning. With one long wall for pictures and furniture, the other for great windows looking on to the garden, the long gallery was one of the most charming rooms ever designed.

Wollaton (finished in 1588), like Longleat and the Loire châteaux, is yet another outward-looking house

263 Long gallery at Hatfield House (begun 1607). A typical arrangement, if grander than most, with windows along one side (compare Fontainebleau, Ill. 256). The Jacobean decoration is abstract and on the whole flat, except for the big stone fireplaces; the motifs are panels, strapwork and the classical orders

taking a positive pleasure in the world outside its own windows. The design, as we know from his tombstone in the nearby parish church, was by Robert Smythson – the first genius in English architecture since the close of the Middle Ages. It is difficult now to realize this revolutionary moment, the moment when, in security, one could forget the arrow-slit window and when – thanks to centuries of effort by church builders, masons and glaziers – it was technically possible to build *big* mullioned windows and fill them with leaded lights. The windows of these Renaissance mansions were the application to secular use of the methods used in glazing Perpendicular churches, the adaptation to rich men's homes of the windows of, say, Gloucester choir or King's College Chapel, symbolic in themselves of the shift of patronage from Church to laity.

264 Wollaton Hall (finished 1588), by Robert Smythson. Its stylistic features come from an odd assortment of sources – Italian Renaissance, Flemish pattern-books, Gothic and even – in the tourelles – fantastic castle architecture. The plan is extremely novel (while based on Serlio): the hall rises through the centre, lit by a clerestory just above the roof, and is in turn surmounted by a 'great chamber'

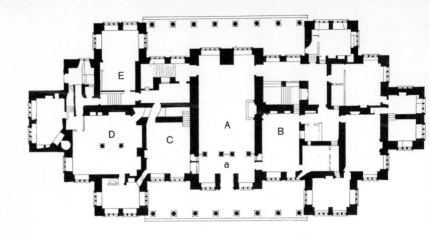

265, 266 Hardwick Hall (1590–7), probably by Smythson. The plan, above, is compact and symmetrical. For the first time the hall (A) is treated as an impressive vestibule – though originally it still fulfilled its traditional role as dining-room, with the 'screens passage' (a) flanked by pantry (B), buttery (C) and kitchen (D). The chapel (E) is at the back of the house.

Outside (opposite, above), note the corners heightened to form mock 'towers', the big grid-like windows, and the initials of the proud builder, Elizabeth Shrewsbury, displayed in strapwork on the skyline

The great leaded windows of Wollaton look outward, indeed, more than those of Longleat. Where Longleat had an inner court, Wollaton has a huge central hall, towering up like a turreted fairy castle from the middle of the house, to be brilliantly lit by windows above the surrounding roof level. There are also fantastic square corner towers, almost detached from the main building. Wollaton may, through Serlio's books, have been derived from the Poggio Reale in Naples; in fact it was something quite new.

Hardwick Hall (1590–7) is almost certainly to be attributed to Smythson. The phrase 'Hardwick Hall, more glass than wall' explains the excitement it must have caused in a world where still – at least for the peasant – glass was an extravagance. The plan, compared with Longleat and Wollaton, has contracted; the whole house is more compact. In compensation the six big bay windows – rooms in themselves – are carried up above roof level so that there is a silhouette of square towers . . . romantic and beautiful, an English version of the idealized castle of a dream-like Middle Ages.

The glamour of Elizabeth's reign is such that it is sometimes forgotten how much that is called 'Eliza-bethan' – the Bible and some of Shakespeare – actually

belongs to the time of James I. This is also true of architecture. In the sphere of the great house, and of a hundred smaller houses, there is a whole Jacobean sequel to the 'prodigy houses'. Renaissance grandeur, for instance, had already spread to simpler dwellings such as Montacute in Somerset and Condover Hall in Shropshire, both finished in the last years of the Queen's reign. In the really big houses, such as Hatfield or Bolsover, there was an increasing richness, a grotesque ornamentation. It is linked with Italian Mannerism – via Flanders – but is altogether more outrageous, with banded columns, marble inlay, carved tassels, arabesques, bulbous balusters, masks and eroticism. We can detect the beginnings a generation earlier in houses like Kirby Hall and Burghley, both in Northamptonshire – the latter with a 'roofscape' that almost rivals Chambord. At Bramshill in Hampshire (1605–12) the grotesque entrance and oriel are set between severely plain wings, but the full Jacobean flavour is to be found in the great staircase at Hatfield (c.1611). This stair is notable both because it was one of the first grand staircases in England and also as a display of the ornate Jacobean style.

We have spoken about Flemish influence without describing developments in Flanders, and to this we

267 *Great Stair, Hatfield House (c.1611). The monumental open staircase, an Italian invention, is here translated into terms of Jacobean carpentry – complete with carved figures, strapwork, and lattice gates to keep the dogs from straying upstairs*

268 Antwerp Town Hall (1561–5), by Cornelis Floris. A crowded and rather gauche though grand exercise in a style which, clearly, was not yet understood. The central feature is really a Gothic gable-front, disguised with columns, pilasters, obelisks, huge statues, and a pedimented aedicule

269 Mauritshuis, The Hague (1633–35), by Jacob van Campen. This square palace shows a complete command of the new style. A giant order in stone – from its base storey through pilasters to entablature and pediment – is set against brick walls to create an original piece of classicism, influential in England as well as in Holland

must belatedly turn. It is significant that the most important item to be mentioned is not a building but a book – Vredeman de Vries' *Architectura*, published in 1563. This contributed an inexhaustible fund of models for ornamental details (including strapwork, invented by Primaticcio at Fontainebleau) and was extensively used in all the northern countries for many years. It provided less guidance on architecture proper. Antwerp Town Hall (1561–5) by Cornelis Floris, the first major work in the new style, is still an awkward exercise. Later architects, such as Lieven de Key and Hendrik de Keyser, learned to handle it with more finesse. By the time of the Mauritshuis at The Hague (1633) Holland was as up to date as France and England, and was evolving a national Protestant style that was to keep her relatively immune to Baroque and to provide one of the chief models for Sir Christopher Wren after 1660. Development in Germany, which had begun promisingly with such buildings as the Ottheinrichsbau at Heidelberg (1556–63) and Augsburg Town Hall by the Italian-trained Elias Holl, was to be stifled by the tragedy of the Thirty Years War (1618–48). During the first half of the seventeenth century the centre of architectural interest north of the Alps was Italy's nearest neighbour, France.

The flow of Italian visitors continued. Vignola and Bernini paid prolonged visits, but men such as Salomon de Brosse (1541–1626), Jacques Lemercier (1585–1654), François Mansart (1598–1666) and Louis Le Vau

270 Pavillon de l'Horloge in the Louvre, Paris (begun 1624). Lemercier by this accent joined Lescot's wing, on the left (see Ill. 255), with his own replica of it on the right. In the upper part of the pavilion there is a new freedom: note the trebled pediment, 'caryatid order'; and domed pavilion roof

(1612–70) were establishing a true native classical style. The Louvre, begun by Lescot, provides us with a representative catalogue of the work of most of them. Lemercier, in 1624, began the enlargement of the inner court of the Louvre to its present 400 feet square. He adorned it with the splendid Pavillon de l'Horloge. Between 1650 and 1664 Le Vau completed the court under the direction of Cardinal Mazarin. Ten years later, for Colbert, Claude Perrault built the eastern façade; this consists of a magnificent colonnade of coupled columns topped by a flat entablature with a central pediment. It must owe its roof-line to Bernini, who provided three designs for this front.

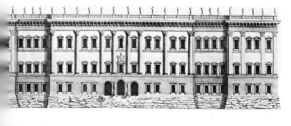

271, 272 East front of the Louvre, Paris. Bernini's third design (1665, left), monumental but the least Baroque of his three projects, was actually begun. Work stopped when he left, however, and the façade was built to the designs of Claude Perrault and Le Vau (below). With its flat roofline, monumental coupled columns, and boldly simple organization, this was the most accomplished classical building of its date north of the Alps

273 *Palais du Luxembourg, Paris (begun 1615), built by Salomon de Brosse for Catherine de Médicis. The heavy rustication deliberately recalls the garden front of the great Florentine palace of the Medici, the Pitti*

274 *Orléans wing, Blois (1635). Mansart's classicism is subtler and more sophisticated than that of any of his predecessors. Blois is especially notable for the quality of the stonework and decorative carving*

Except for this eastern façade all the Louvre work is typically French, typically seventeenth century – richly carved with classical motifs, professional rather than inspiring. The northern spirit persists in the high-pitched roofs, elaborate chimneys and, above all, the large corner *pavillons*, a feature in direct descent from the circular towers of the Loire château and, therefore, from the medieval castle. The separate roofing, and consequent emphasis upon these projecting blocks, runs through the whole French Renaissance. In Italy the roof is suppressed;

in England a continuous roof-line runs round the whole building, unifying rather than emphasizing the parts.

De Brosse had a remarkable feeling for masonry and he expressed it by the lavish, often exaggerated, use of rustication. His châteaux at Coulommiers and Bléran-court, and his town palace of the Luxembourg all bear this stamp of his personality. His successor as *premier architecte* was Jacques Lemercier, whom we have already met at the Louvre. De Brosse had been alive to Italian Mannerism; Lemercier was young enough to respond to Baroque. His church of the Sorbonne (begun 1635) has a dome, a two-tier façade on the familiar model of the Gesù and an interesting three-part plan in which the chancel is equal in length to the nave.

With François Mansart the French Renaissance reaches its most interesting phase. In 1635 Gaston d'Orléans decided to add a wing to the vast château of Blois; Mansart's design is, in its rather cold way, an accomplished masterpiece, and exposes the naïve classicism of the earlier work. The curved colonnades joining Mansart's building to those on either side have something of the quality of Italian Baroque. At Maisons-Lafitte, a great country house, the system of linked but apparently separate *pavillons* is taken to extremes with great skill.

The Val-de-Grâce (1645-65), begun by Mansart, continues the line of Lemercier's Sorbonne. It has a typical two-storeyed west front – one pediment unit on top of another. The slopes of the lean-to aisle roofs are screened with large scrolls. This is a familiar Baroque dodge fully justified, perhaps, only when used on the uninhibited scale of, say, Sta Maria della Salute in Venice. The seventeenth-century church of St-Gervais Paris (1616–21) by Clément Métézeau is another example.

After Blérancourt and Maisons-Lafitte came the greatest of all seventeenth-century mansions, Vaux-le-Vicomte, designed by Louis Le Vau in 1657. It achieves

275 Church of the Val-de-Grâce, Paris (1645–65). Another member of the family of the Gesù and Sta Susanna (Ills. 224, 233), but with the addition of a dome on a very high drum. The lower part of the façade has a severely monumental portico, showing a development in Mansart's style since Blois. The upper parts were built by Lemercier, after Mansart had been dismissed

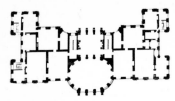

276, 277 *Vaux-le-Vicomte (1657),*
by Louis Le Vau, is one of the greatest
houses of the century. Both the general
economy of its plan, above, and the use of
the oval for the most important room
point to Italian influence. But the house,
in its setting as well as its big pavilion
roofs, is unmistakably French. Note the
'false moat' and the highly formal
relationship of house to garden

the difficult feat of incorporating a central oval salon into
the plan without awkwardness. On the entrance side a
false moat, like an orchestra pit, separates the approach
avenue from the forecourt, giving additional drama to a
house already raised on steps. On the garden side Le
Nôtre laid out vast formal gardens on the axis of the oval
salon. These gardens were famous as the setting for the
illuminated 'Nights of Vaux-le-Vicomte', and as the
prototype of even grander work at Versailles. Le Nôtre
created a law in the planning of palace grounds –
everything on one side is road, gates, gravel, horses and
coaches, everything on the other side is grass, avenues,
parterres, fountains and canals and a far line of forest.

Le Vau was responsible for several other buildings of
interest, in particular the Collège des Quatre Nations, in
Paris, now the Institut de France, with its church of 166
– a Greek cross plan with an oval centre and a dome high
on a drum.

The climax of these French domed churches was
reached in 1679 when Mansart's nephew, Jules Hardouin
Mansart, designed the church of the Invalides; it is
truly Parisian achievement – grand, but just on the righ

278 *Church of the Invalides, Paris (1679), by Jules Hardouin Mansart. In this very assured and successful design, the Baroque dome and façade are retained; but by giving up the volutes and imposing a more sober rhythm on the coupled columns, the architect achieved an effect midway between Baroque and Neo-Classicism*

ide of pomposity. The use of the space, in three dimensions, is dramatic and truly Baroque. One looks upwards through an aperture in a lower dome to perceive a richly painted upper dome, lit by concealed windows. Now that the tomb of the Emperor Napoleon is beneath the dome (with a hole cut in the floor to reveal it) the total effect is awe-inspiring in a totally French manner . . . a mixture of *gloire* and God.

The Invalides may be the best work of the second Mansart, but his most famous was undoubtedly the enormous final version of the palace of Versailles – a building that stands at the end of one phase of French architecture (the Baroque) and the beginning of another (the Neo-Classical). Like the Louvre, it offers us a microcosm of French architectural history. In 1624

279 *Garden front, Versailles (see Ill. 280). The side pavilions of the central block (the seven windows at each end) belong to Le Vau's encasing of the original hunting-lodge, in 1669. The centre – in which the design of the ends is repeated – and the wings in the background were added by Hardouin Mansart from 1678 onward. The scale of Le Vau's work, maintained throughout, was not really strong enough for the eventual size of the building*

Salomon de Brosse had built a hunting château fo Louis XIII. In 1669 Le Vau, working for Louis XIV turned this château into a palace. From 1678 on this wa concealed and extended north and south by Jule Hardouin Mansart. That superb Neo-Classical designe Jacques-Ange Gabriel, made further additions in th 1760s: the lovely wings of the courtyard, so reminiscen of his work in the Place de la Concorde. In the end th megalomaniac palace was over a third of a mile long one of the largest houses in Europe. Internally the state rooms are planned on one long axis, one opening int another – the *enfilade*.

Versailles reveals the merits and defects of Frenc architecture. The two finest things about it are, as it wer

280 *Versailles from the air. Le Vau's building is in the centre, around three sides of a courtyard. In an attempt to give it emphasis, Hardouin Mansart set back his vast lateral ranges. From the two corners where these ranges meet the central block, Gabriel extended wings towards the town, beyond. For the complete plan of garden and town, see Ill. 283*

t opposite ends of the architectural scale. We have already noted how, with the first generation of Italian immigrants, the 'artist-architect' as opposed to the true builder dominated the French scene. At Versailles, both in the palace itself and in the Trianons, it is the interiors that create delight. These include not only the famous Galerie des Glaces (1680), with its green marble, its mirrors and painted panels by Lebrun, but also a hundred other rooms. Those of the Petit Trianon (1762–8), created through half a century for the Dubarry, Marie Antoinette and then for Pauline Bonaparte, are among the more sophisticated confections of history. At the other end of the scale we have something almost exclusively French – the vast layout. The poetic water gardens of

281 The Galerie des Glaces at Ver-sailles (1680) takes up practically the whole of the main storey of the central block, seen above. To set a wall of mirrors opposite a wall of windows was a bold and typically Baroque coup-de-théâtre

235

villas in the Italian hills, the dream-like gardens of
English manor-houses all have their charms, but it is
Versailles that gives us – for the first time since the fall of
the Roman Empire – the grand manner. We find it
again in Paris, at Nancy, at Vaux-le-Vicomte and in
L'Enfant's Washington. In Rome it came about
gradually, generation by generation; in France it was a
deliberate creation, an art. It was not, of course, wholly
an architectural thing. A highly centralized monarchy
in France, as opposed to 'city states' in Italy, petty
monarchies in Germany and squirearchies in England,
is a sufficient social explanation for those royal avenues
leading to infinity.

Le Nôtre's scheme at Versailles started on the west side
of the palace, with the beautifully planned town of
Versailles, and the great approach roads from Paris and
St-Cloud converging upon the palace forecourt, upon
the equestrian statue of the King. On the other side of
the palace – the royal bedroom being the centre of everything – the avenue and the grand canal led for two miles
through trimmed woods to the forest. Among the trees
are innumerable walks, parterres, water-gardens and
conceits of all kinds, the most important being the Grand

*282 Petit Trianon, Versailles (1763–
69). The façade shows the absolutely
pure classicism, beautiful proportions, and
fine sensitivity of Jacques-Ange Gabriel,
a century after Le Vau. Note the effect
of differentiating the storey heights, and
the value of spreading the terrace
outwards to form a wide base*

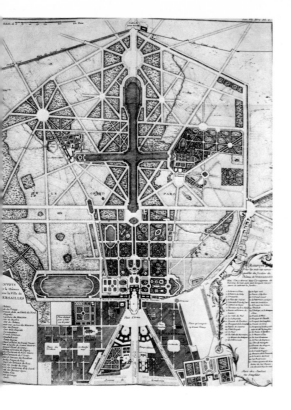

283 *Plan of Versailles in the 18th century. In Baroque fashion, the vast layout stamps itself upon the landscape. It is very logical. On one side of the palace (bottom) are the stables and courts and the town, laid out on a grid with open squares and crossed by three broad avenues. On the other side, all is formal garden around the vast canal. The asymmetrical garden plan, where walks converge on 'ronds-points', played a part in later town-planning*

Trianon and Petit Trianon added by Gabriel in 1763–9. The sheer size of the layout does, now and again, lead to boredom – deserts of gravel – but the scheme has its supreme moments. There are the huge flights of steps. There is the austere Orangery, acting as a big retaining wall or platform above which rises the rich orchestration of Mansart's façade. And one or two of the water-gardens are idyllic scenes for Watteau's brush. Except, however, for Gabriel's courtyard wings and his delightful little cube of the Petit Trianon, those moments are never purely architectural.

France was on the threshold of Neo-Classicism, and at various times and by various processes the other nations of Europe were to reach the same spot. The story is one of some complexity and much overlapping. In England,

perhaps, it can be followed at its simplest. A reaction
against the excesses of the Jacobean prodigy houses, in
favour of purity and restraint, was bound to come. That
reaction, in fact, is found mainly in the work of one man.

Inigo Jones (1573–1652) was an Italian-trained
draughtsman from whose drawings other men erected
buildings. As a youth he paid a visit to Italy, of which
we know nothing. From 1605 to 1611 he served James'
queen, designing costumes and scenery for the palace
masques – those short dramas, fashionable at the court
of the Medici, compounded of satire, mythology, music,
choreography and scenic effects. For these masques
Inigo Jones did some 450 designs. In favour at Court
he became tutor to a prince and then, in 1613, visited
Italy again in the train of the Duke of Arundel. He
returned a year later with full sketch-books, to be
appointed Surveyor to the King's Works – a post of the
highest architectural responsibility.

In this post Jones established his claim to have both
understood and purified the Renaissance. He exorcized
it of a mass of barbarous Jacobean ornament. He gave it
restraint and fine proportions. Elizabethan houses were
medieval buildings with Renaissance ornament; Inigo
Jones designed Renaissance buildings. He believed that
architecture should be disciplined, masculine and un-
affected. He had no use for splendours or romantic
fantasies, nor those excesses of Mannerism which he had
seen in Italy. With the works of Vitruvius, Palladio and
Scamozzi at his elbow, he practised a quiet, serene
classicism, making the very word 'Palladian' as English
as it is Italian. Let the reader contrast, say, Hardwick
Hall with the Queen's House at Greenwich – and there
is less than twenty years between them – and he will see
the point. Both are secular, but otherwise the division
between them is greater than the division between Hardwick and the last Gothic churches.

It was in 1616 that Inigo Jones began building the
Queen's House. It may be slightly provincial while also

ing too Italian for the climate, but all the same it is a assic jewel. It was the nucleus from which grew the hole Greenwich Palace complex during the ensuing ntury – Wren, Vanbrugh, Hawksmoor. In this large roque group the little Queen's House holds its own. is derived from the Medici villa at Poggio a Caiano tside Florence, but it seems to come to us directly from e sunlit meadows of the Veneto.

More famous than the Queen's House – partly because is in Whitehall, partly for the fortuitous reason that it as the scene of Charles I's execution – is the Banqueting ouse. It was begun in 1619; years later it might have

been incorporated in Jones's design for that Engli
Escorial, the vast Palace of Whitehall, that was plann
but never built. The Banqueting House is now part
a busy street. Internally it is a large double cube wi
ceiling panels for which Peter Paul Rubens was pa
£3,000. Externally the Banqueting House is a m
harmonious and Palladian design . . . so harmonio
that, in the modern town, it is not very noticeable. It
less serene, less elegant than the Queen's House, b
stronger and more masculine.

In 1625, by proclamation, London was given its fi
piece of conscious and deliberate town-planning – t
arcaded piazza of Covent Garden. The arcades ha
gone, except for fragmentary nineteenth-century repr
ductions, but we still have Inigo Jones's church,
Paul's, essentially as it was. It is based on Vitruviu
Tuscan temple, of brick with the simplest possible ord
for the portico, and wide timber eaves. Extremely simp
almost domestic in detail – it would pass for a Quak
meeting-house – this is the least pretentious, most char
ing of Jones's works. Attributed to him is Linds
House, Lincoln's Inn Fields of c. 1638; it is a town hou
with rusticated ground floor, tall *piano nobile* windo
with classically framed windows, and balustrated parap
which may be considered the prototype of a thousa
'Georgian' houses on both sides of the Atlantic.

In the last years of his life, we find Inigo Jones advisi
Isaac de Caux on the building of Wilton, for the Earl

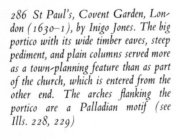

*286 St Paul's, Covent Garden, Lon-
don (1630–1), by Inigo Jones. The big
portico with its wide timber eaves, steep
pediment, and plain columns served more
as a town-planning feature than as part
of the church, which is entered from the
other end. The arches flanking the
portico are a Palladian motif (see
Ills. 228, 229)*

287 *'Double-cube' room, Wilton House (c.1649), by Inigo Jones and John Webb. The panelled walls are only about half the height of the room, giving it a domestic scale; at the same time, the enormous coved ceiling creates grandeur through sheer height. The room was from the beginning conceived as a setting for the Van Dyck portraits*

embroke. There, from 1633 onwards, he created the orious garden front in all its Scamozzi-like simplicity nd elegance. Behind the deceptive plainness of that çade are two of the most richly decorated rooms in ngland; the 'double-cube' and 'single-cube' rooms, :ry French, are decked with heavy swags and clusters of uit and flowers, framing the Van Dyck portraits. ʾilton was a fitting end to the architect's career.

In 1666, fourteen years after Inigo Jones's death, the eater part of the old City of London was consumed by e. The fire raged for nine days; 13,200 houses and ʾ parish churches were destroyed, as was the old edieval cathedral of St Paul's. An incomparable norama of Gothic towers vanished forever. The erchants, so determined to continue trading that they t up tents among the warm ashes, were prepared to

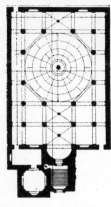

288, 289 *St Stephen, Walbrook, London (1672–87), by Sir Christopher Wren, the most complex of the City churches. The plaster dome is carried over an octagon, with a circumambient aisle doubled at the west end, combining the merits of centralized and longitudinal plans. In the view below, we are looking diagonally across the octagon – from lower right to top left in the plan*

obstruct any planning that might delay rebuilding. Within two weeks Christopher Wren had submitted to the King his plan for a new City. It was a grand, rather Michelangelesque scheme of radiating avenues, with street vistas closed by church steeples. It was accepted by the King and – gradually – sabotaged by the merchants. The pattern of lanes and alleys is still with us.

Christopher Wren (1631–1723) had already dabbled in architecture. He had been Professor of Astronomy at Oxford, and was a fine geometrician. Any Renaissance 'philosopher' was, however – like Leonardo – apt to be considered a man of universal knowledge, as fit for one profession as another. In 1662 Wren had already designed a geometrically brilliant roof for the Sheldonian Theatre at Oxford and, at the same time, a chapel for Pembroke College at Cambridge. In 1665 he visited France where he met Bernini, at work on the Louvre. Wren came home loaded with books and sketches and never left England again.

By proclamation, the City of London was to be rebuilt in brick and stone. All the work was to pass through the hands of six surveyors of whom Wren was one. The churches were never built within the framework of his abortive plan; they were built on the old sites and Wren was the architect.

It is important to realize the true nature of Wren's contribution. It was not the beauty of this church or that, or even of St Paul's, that mattered most. It was the creation of a London that no longer exists. True, Wren's plan was never carried out. That plan, however, was a three-dimensional design; it took account of the height of buildings as well as the alignments of streets. In two dimensions – length and breadth – that plan was lost. In the third dimension it was fully realized. Wren's City churches, for all their incidental charms, are usually just plain halls of brick and plaster, fitted on to cramped sites. Even the towers are usually plain until they have risen above what was once the roof-line of the houses

en and then only, clear of the chimney-pots, did they
blossom into the full-blooded and elaborate steeples with
which Wren's name will always be associated. Seen
from the bridges or from across the green and busy tide of
the river, London at the end of the seventeenth century
must have seemed not less fair than Venice. Above the
ocean of little brown houses the steeples sailed like big
white galleons . . . and yet all paid court to the great
dome. This wonderful scene lasted for rather more than
a hundred years, then the Victorian banks and offices
began the process of corrosion now almost complete.

Although Wren's churches had to be built cheaply,
he was fortunate in being spared liturgical complications
he ran into them at St Paul's – and in having only to
give ecclesiastical dignity to a congregational hall with
the altar set against its eastern wall. Some fine plaster work
in the ceiling, some carved woodwork – possibly by
Grinling Gibbons – on stalls, reredos and pulpit . . . that
is the sum total of a Wren church. In St Stephen,
Walbrook we have a more ingenious plan – a pendentive
dome on columns, with a surrounding aisle, makes an
enchanting use of space. The geometrician and the artist
are here combined. Of the few towers that survive only
St Mary-le-Bow and St Bride's, Fleet Street, give us some
faint idea of that forest of steeples that was once London.

290 *London as Wren left it: a host of
steeples rising above the brick houses, all
subordinate to the dome of St Paul's*

291 *St Bride's, London (spire 1702),
by Wren. The steeple is a medieval
spire restated in classical terms; one of
the tallest in London, it appears second
from the left in the view above*

292 *Wren's Great Model for St Paul's shows that, like so many of the Italians, he would have preferred a centralized plan. It is a domed octagon with alternately straight and concave sides, linked to a large portico (left) by a domed vestibule. The design shows daring Baroque elements which seldom appear in Wren's executed work*

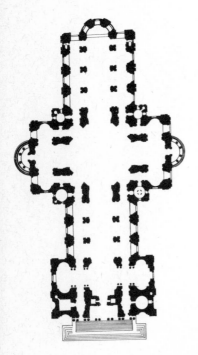

Wren had already been consulted about the parlous state of Old St Paul's, even before the Great Fire. When, after the Fire, it was decided that the ruins could not be restored, Wren prepared a whole series of plans and models. The most notable was the Great Model, sometimes called 'Wren's favourite design'. This model (preserved in the cathedral) takes us straight back to the old Italian controversy of the centralized plan. The Great Model was an elaborate domed octagon with a large vestibule – not a nave – to the west. In a world of Anglican divines less than a generation removed from Puritan persecution this exercise in a Continental, Catholic idiom never stood a chance. St Paul's, as finally built, was – like the City itself – a hopeless compromise. It was a compromise between the clergy's desire for a medieval plan, with long nave, long chancel and aisles, and Wren's yearning for a dominant central dome in emulation of the Italian Baroque.

In the end the clergy got their plan, the architect got his dome, but the scars of battle are everywhere. A tall vaulted nave with side aisles needs flying buttresses. In the Baroque vocabulary there is no such thing as a flying buttress. Wren's buttresses are shameful little things, just emerging above the aisle roofs, so that the outer walls of the aisles – complete with sham windows – have to be taken up the full height of the nave to screen the buttresses, a shift only too obvious when viewed from the dome gallery or from the air. Pugin's gibe that 'one half of

St Paul's was built to hide the other half' was an exaggeration; it was not a gross exaggeration. The dome itself is one of the finest things in all European Baroque. Inevitably the projecting nave, like that of St Peter's, cuts off the view of the dome from the west. Nevertheless, Wren did design a dome which, in its day, dominated all London. He did this, first, by building a very high drum – better handled than any in France or Italy – and then by surmounting the dome with a soaring lantern, 180 tons of stone, which he perched ingeniously upon a cone of brick. This he concealed within the dome, itself of wood and lead. Two iron chains were also necessary. St Paul's is a Baroque building; the pure Palladian serenity of Inigo Jones's Queen's House is now half a

293, 294 Plan (opposite) and air view of St Paul's Cathedral, London (1675–1710), by Wren. The plan shows the final compromise – a central space beneath the dome, but a long and high nave and choir. The air view shows the consequences – the 'pits' behind the sham walls which conceal embryonic flying buttresses. Yet it shows, too, the magnificent ingenuity with which Wren lifted his dome above the City, upon a drum whose open colonnade is reinforced (structurally and visually) at intervals by solid bays with niches

century behind us. St Paul's, like most Baroque build
ings, is splendid permanent scenery. When all the shif
and devices have been examined, it must still be grante
that the silhouette, the proportions, the detail, th
carving – not least Grinling Gibbons's woodwork an
Tijou's ironwork – make this cathedral the greate
monument of its generation.

Wren's palace at Hampton Court – designed in 168
and incongruously tacked on to Wolsey's Tudor pile
was never completed and was never what Wren wante
The white stone dressings in red brickwork, the ta
windows, the dark yews and the fountains make
scintillating scene when the sun shines, but it was nev
the English Versailles which Wren had hoped to buil
in his declining years. At Greenwich Hospital, Wren
beautiful twin domes frame Inigo Jones's Queen
House, as one sees it from the river.

It was in 1704, on the Danube and near the village
Blenheim, that the French armies were broken by th
combined forces of Prince Eugene and the Duke
Marlborough. The wars in Europe were virtually at a
end. Marlborough was rewarded by the gift of a palace
Blenheim Palace, one of the largest houses in Englan
He could choose his own architect, but his choice wa
really limited to the triumvirate in the service of th
Crown – Wren, Hawksmoor and Vanbrugh. Wre
was over seventy, Nicholas Hawksmoor little more tha
a loyal assistant. Sir John Vanbrugh (1664–1726) wa
a man about town, on easy terms with the dukes,
dramatist of genius. Five years earlier he had made
startling entry into architecture. For his friend, the Ea
of Carlisle, he had designed Castle Howard in York
shire. Marlborough chose Vanbrugh.

Wren's genius was mathematical, Vanbrugh's wa
dramatic and romantic, almost impressionistic. Certain
he needed Hawksmoor to turn his impressionisti
sketches into reality. It was he who brought the Baroqu
style in England to its maturity. His mansions we

295 *Castle Howard (designed 1699),
by Sir John Vanburgh. Bold in planning (note the vista of another arch
behind the fireplace), grandiose in scale,
and crowned by a dome, the entrance
hall is one of England's few successful
Baroque interiors*

omantic castles, clothed in robust Roman detail – we
ote the Roman obsession with the round arch – and
marvellously placed in the English landscape.

In Castle Howard, designed in 1699, Vanbrugh
reated the first of those huge lordly mansions which
ymbolize so well the Roman pomp and circumstance of
Queen Anne's England. It is an immense house,
deliberately made to look more immense by the deploy-
ment of far-flung wings and courtyards. The stable
ourt and the kitchen court each cover as much ground
s the house itself, to which they are linked by curved
olonnades. The main central block has a dome; the
iant pilasters run the full height of the building – like
Michelangelo's on the Capitol – and are emphasized by

296 Blenheim Palace (1705–24), by
Vanbrugh and Hawksmoor. The union
of Vanbrugh's brilliance with Hawksmoor's technical knowledge and feeling
for dignity produced a unique and un-
repeatable style. One of the two subordinate wings is seen on the right,
showing how the great building is spread
out on its plateau

297 Radcliffe Camera, Oxford
(1739–49), by James Gibbs. Clear
articulation by means of rustication,
giant coupled columns and alternating
windows and niches emphasizes the
library's monumental rotundity

the rustication of the wall between them. The forecou
is approached through triumphal arches, while othe
arches, obelisks, pyramids, and Hawksmoor's dome
Mausoleum, all serve to emphasize the system of radiatin
avenues and devised vistas that constitute an artificial an
Baroque landscape. The entrance hall at Castle Howar
– with perhaps the dining-hall at Greenwich – i
England's best Baroque interior.

Blenheim is not, and was never meant to be, a home
or even a house. It is a military monument. It is
development of the Castle Howard theme, but wherea
at Castle Howard a landscape was created around th
house, at Blenheim the stroke of genius lay in the sitin
of the house within the landscape. It is set at the very edg
of a plateau. From the south it is seen across level sunli
lawns; from the north, from the lake, it is seen from
below, a dark, dramatic and broken silhouette agains
the sky. The huge pinnacles of the corner towers
designed by Grinling Gibbons in the likeness of
fleur-de-lys being crushed by a ducal coronet, are see
from far off in the park; they add to the romanti
illusion of a castle from the days of chivalry. Blenheim'
other great moment lies in the stepping down of th
terraced gardens from the long library front to the shore
of the lake.

Vanbrugh was to achieve romantic drama once mor
in the rusticated mass of Seaton Delaval (c. 1720–8) o

he bleak Northumberland moors, a strange and ghostly
aroque ruin.

Vanbrugh depended much upon Hawksmoor for the
racticalities of building, but Hawksmoor in his own
ight was the designer of some remarkable Baroque
hurches in London – St Anne, Limehouse (1714–24),
t George, Bloomsbury (1716–31) and Christ Church,
pitalfields (1714–29) among them. James Gibbs (1682–
754) might have built more had he not been suspected
rightly) of both Catholicism and Jacobitism; even so
e owe to him St Martin-in-the-Fields, London (1722–
), the gracious Fellows' Building at King's College,
Cambridge (1724–49) and the magnificent rotundity of
he Radcliffe Camera at Oxford (1739–49).

English Baroque, such as it was, had come full circle.
he next generation, as we shall see, adopted a style that
nay be seen as a parallel to Continental Neo-Classicism,
ut which was largely a return to the ideals of Inigo
ones, and, through him, to those of Palladio. In other
arts of Europe, however, the Baroque style still had a
ast fantastic course to run. In Spain and in central
Europe the reaction against it did not take place until the
niddle of the eighteenth century, and we must therefore
nclude these years in this chapter, even at the cost of
listurbing the chronology.

To the northern mind this sort of Baroque architecture
as often seemed immoral, both because it served a
eligion of austerity and humility with every kind of
ensuality, luxury and sensation, and also because it used
very artifice and fake to achieve its ends. Painting,
culpture, music and architecture merged into a single
iotous glory. If to inflame the mind is to increase faith,
hen every trick in the Baroque game was justified . . . or
uch was the conviction of southern Europe and southern
America for two centuries.

The Baroque of the Austrian Empire or of Bavaria
as at first comparatively moderate. By the early
ighteenth century such men as Johann Lukas von

298 Christ Church, Spitalfields, London (1714–29). Perhaps the most impressive of Hawksmoor's highly original London churches, this uses the vocabulary of late Roman architecture (the central motif, for instance, comes from Diocletian's Palace at Spalato), building up to what is in essence a medieval spire

299 The Schönbrunn Palace at Vienna,
by Fischer von Erlach (begun 1695), is
modelled on Versailles, as the Habsburg
monarchs modelled themselves on Louis
XIV; but the emphatic central feature
(in its present form somewhat altered)
and Fischer's use of the giant order give
greater unity than Hardouin Mansart
had achieved

300 Karlskirche, Vienna (begun 1716).
Fischer von Erlach, a scholar as well as
an architect, here combined elements from
a wide variety of sources, ranging from
ancient Rome (the Pantheon and Trajan's Column) to Borromini (Ill. 245)

Hildebrandt (1668–1745), the more famous Johann
Bernhard Fischer von Erlach (1656–1723) and Hildebrandt's great follower Balthasar Neumann (1687–
1753) had all visited Rome. Fischer, in fact, had travelled
widely in Italy, Germany and Holland, and his buildings
(as well as his scholarly work on architecture published
in 1721) show the fruits of these studies. The Schönbrunn
Palace at Vienna is an attempt to rival Versailles, and in
spite of its size displays an ability to organize a façade
with more variety and charm than Hardouin Mansart.
Fischer's churches reflect the influence of both Classical
and Baroque Rome; his Karlskirche at Vienna, for
instance, with its concave wings and dome, is based
primarily on Borromini's S. Agnese, with the addition
of a double version of Trajan's Column.

In 1714 Hildebrandt had begun to build the palace of
the Upper Belvedere in Vienna. For all its exuberance
this palace is really restrained as Baroque goes, the
exuberance showing itself mainly in low relief surface
decoration. The Upper Belvedere's finest moment is the
great staircase. The lowest level of this stair – the low,
vaulted garden-room – is almost ponderous, while the
stair itself leads upwards to a landing which, by contrast,
is high, light and airy. Regardless of style or decoration
this is the sort of thing from which real architecture is
made – structure, space, light.

301 Staircase in the Upper Belvedere, Vienna (1721-3), by Lukas von Hildebrandt. From this light and airy entrance landing one flight leads down, into the dark and deliberately heavy garden-room; two other flights sweep upwards in the light, to the entrance of the great hall. Note the exquisite plasterwork

These Viennese palaces were the first of many such charming buildings in the capitals of the petty states of Germany or the Holy Roman Empire, at their worst mere confections of Ruritanian opera, at their best the homes of a cultivated aristocracy. Perhaps the most fantastic of these summer palaces, with its own theatre and ballroom, was the Zwinger at Dresden (1711-22) by Matthäus Pöppelmann, a fairy palace with all its glass galleries looking in upon a courtyard.

302 The Zwinger at Dresden (1711-22) is festival architecture at its most free and gayest. The 'Wallpavillon', flanked by one-storeyed galleries, closes one end of a large open courtyard; it owes almost as much to the sculptor Permoser as to Matthäus Pöppelmann, the architect

François Cuvilliés, who built first the Reiche
Zimmer and then (1734-9) the Amalienburg, in th
region of Munich, is of special importance since it wa
he – a French architect trained in Paris – who was chiefl
responsible for transmuting German Baroque int
Rococo. The colours become lighter (white, gold, pal
yellow, blue and pink) and the decoration tends to dis
solve into endless arabesque curves, the interplay of space
taking on an existence independent of the structur
behind them.

Outstanding also are Balthasar Neumann's staircas
hall at Brühl (1740), his bishop's palace at Würzbur
(1734) with a splendid ceiling by Tiepolo, and th
unique stair at Bruchsal, where work was taken over b
Neumann in 1730, of which Dr Pevsner has written
'Words can hardly re-evoke the enchanting sensatio
experienced by anybody who has had the good fortun
to walk up one of its two arms, when it still existe
undamaged by war.' The lowest hall is sombre, th
staircase growing lighter and lighter as one ascends – '
spatial rapture'. Balthasar Neumann's truly immorta
work, however, is the great pilgrimage church o
Vierzehnheiligen (1743-62). While the peasant kneel
in adoration before the white and gold and coral o

303 Amalienburg, Munich (1734-9), by François Cuvilliés. The stucco decoration – here, a detail from the ceiling in the central saloon – is as gay and carefree in its themes as in its arabesque curves

304 Staircase at Bruchsal (begun 1731), by Balthasar Neumann. The central arch leads into a dark oval room; those on either side contain the two arms of the staircase, open on both sides, which curve round the central oval and emerge above it on to a brightly lit landing – a wonderful manipulation of space, light and volume

305, 306 *Vierzehnheiligen Pilgrimage Church (1743–62). The plan – here reproduced with west at the top, so it can be more easily related to the view – gives some idea of how Neumann's masterpiece achieves its extraordinary effects of spaces flowing into one another. It is built up of intersecting circles and ovals. The altar is placed in the centre like an island, a highly unusual stroke*

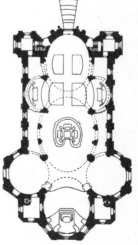

ceramic altars the architect is lost in admiration at the complexity of the structure and of the geometry: ovals and octagons, interweaving arches, balconies and floating domes perform an incomprehensible architectural ballet; it is an arabesque of structure overlaid with flowers, putti, clouds and the hosts of heaven.

From Munich the two Asam brothers (Cosmas Damian, 1686–1739, and Egid Quirin, 1692–1750) also visited Rome. What they saw and learnt there they transmuted into an astonishing series of churches, mainly in a circle of towns and villages around Munich. Both brothers worked on the abbey church at Weltenburg

307 Rohr Abbey Church (1717–25). The high altar, by Egid Quirin Asam, is a tableau vivant of the Assumption – the Virgin soaring aloft upheld by angels, the Disciples starting back in amazement round the empty tomb. This is Baroque drama at its most explicit (cp. the Cornaro Chapel, Ill. 234)

308 Einsiedeln Abbey Church, by Caspar Moosbrugger (begun 1717). After a relatively narrow choir, the nave opens out into vast octagon with a single, complex central pier, far right, which has at its base a shrine. The whole interior is covered by a fantastic garment of decoration, swirling and ecstatic

c.1721. The altar is flanked by pairs of twisted columns; the reredos is a sheet of blazing light from hidden windows. Silhouetted against this great glow, a silver St George prances towards us; the princess and the dragon are dark gold shadows at his horse's feet. The abbey church at Rohr (1717–25), designed by Egid Quirin Asam, is even more dramatic. The reredos, which soars above the altar into the shadows of the high vault, owes much to Bernini's St Teresa Altar in the Cornaro Chapel. It develops Bernini's idea in an un-inhibited manner: life-size figures of the Apostles stand in exclamatory postures around the empty sarcophagus from which an ecstatic Virgin is ascending to Heaven.

Every one of these churches has its vaults and domes painted with tremendous verve – verve in the handling of anatomy, perspective and movement, as well as in the sugary sweetness of the colour.

Among other such Baroque churches one must mention that of Neresheim Abbey, completed according to Balthasar Neumann's designs after his death, and the pilgrimage church of Die Wies by Domenikus Zimmermann. The abbeys of Ottobeuren (1744–67) and Zwiefalten (c.1758; 1740–65), are both by Johann Michael Fischer. Above all, there is that great essay in spatial geometry, the abbey of Einsiedeln (c.1720) by Caspar Moosbrugger, possibly second only to Vierzehn-heiligen or to the abbey library at St Gallen as the crowning achievement of central European Baroque.

In Spain, after the pronounced austerity of the early Renaissance, Baroque was adopted with a passion and violence that has caused it to be compared, not without reason, to the Aztec art which was just becoming known to the West. Certainly it was in Mexico that Spanish Baroque reached its most bizarre and barbaric extremes, but even in Europe its effects were startling enough. In Toledo, in 1732, Narciso Tomé finished the Trasparente in the cathedral – a fantastic reredos devised so that the Sacrament, surrounded by columns, angels and prophets,

309 *Trasparente, Toledo Cathedral (1732), by Narciso Tomé. This is the side facing the ambulatory, carved with figures of angels, swirling clouds and (at the top) the Last Supper. The Host is displayed in the centre, surrounded by sculpted rays (cp. Ill. 234). Imagination must add the yellow light shining from a concealed source above the vault*

could be seen both from the chancel and from the ambulatory. The panels of one of the vaults were filled with golden glass instead of stone, thus casting a weird light upon the sacramental tabernacle. This was mild compared with the work of José de Churriguera and his followers, one of whom, Luis de Arévalo, built the sacristy of the Charterhouse in Granada (1727–64) where a complete fantasy of plate-like decoration covered every surface of the building. Only the faintest ghost of classical form shows through the ornament. This was dubbed the 'Churrigueresque style'.

To return, finally, to Italy. It had been in Piedmont, in the hands of Guarini, that Baroque had been most fully explored and taken as far – at least on Italian soil – as it was to go. It was in Piedmont, too, that the next great Italian architect, Filippo Juvarra (1678–1736), was to provide the last paragraph to that chapter, and the beginning of the next. In both his churches (e.g. the Superga, outside Turin) and his palaces (the Villa Reale at Stupinigi) he used the elements of Baroque with a coolness and clarity that look forward to Neo-Classicism. The pendulum, in fact, was moving swiftly in that direction all over Europe. Even in Rome the two major architectural projects of the 1730s and 1740s, the new façade of St John Lateran and Sta Maria Maggiore, are formally in the Neo-Classical style. It was to dominate the rest of the eighteenth and the beginning of the nineteenth centuries.

311 Superga, Turin (1717–31). Juvarra takes an eclectic collection of elements and makes them into a completely original composition. A central-space church is set into one end of a convent quadrangle, and rises in a dome almost as big as itself (compare the design of walls and dome with St Peter's, Ill. 206). The wilfully large – almost independent – portico is balanced by the convent wings, crowned with towers (cp. Ill. 245)

257

Chapter Nine

THE RETURN TO CLASSICISM

To explain the rise of Neo-Classicism and its adoption in virtually identical form all over Europe would involve a consideration of many factors at greater length than can be attempted here. There was, firstly, the fact that Baroque had reached an impasse, where only greater and greater elaboration of the same ideas seemed possible. But the swing towards restraint was not only a swing of the pendulum of taste; it corresponded with similar changes in other areas – the development of rationalism in philosophy and of regularity in music and poetry, with the elevation of the Greek and Latin classics as models in literature and with the general tendency towards clear rules and principles in all the arts. Classical architecture was at once the most rational, the most Roman and the most clearly defined of all styles. The mid-eighteenth century is significantly also the period of the first serious classical archaeology. The ruins of Rome, Athens, Split, Palmyra, Baalbek and other sites were published in careful and erudite works, and exercised immense influence. Closely linked with the aesthetic appeal was one of ideology. To revive the architecture of Rome was to revive the idea of the Roman Empire. The reign of Louis XIV ushered in an age of despotism, of which Classicism became to a large extent the outward and visible expression.

The influence of Versailles was widespread. All over Europe, whether on a large or small scale, this formality, this subordination of nature to art, was the inspiration of the palace garden. As far afield as the later Hampton

312 Napoleon's Arc de Triomphe (begun 1806), designed by Chalgrin, is one of the most emphatic monuments of Neo-Classical Paris – a return to Rome, but on a scale larger than Rome had dreamed. To hold its own in the vast setting of the 'Etoile' bulk was everything; the central arch is flanked not by niches but by massive groups of sculpture

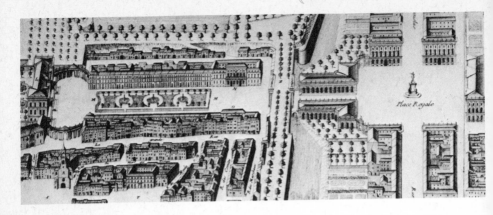

Place Royale

313 Nancy in 1754, in course of construction: the formal linking of variously
designed urban spaces – en suite as it
were – is here seen at its best. The urban
square on the right, the long tree-lined
Place de la Carrière in the centre, and
the forecourt of the palace with its
curved colonnades make a single entity

Court in England, the Schönbrunn in Vienna, or
Williamsburg in Virginia, we can detect the ghost of
Versailles. In France itself the 'grand manner' is as
evident in the city as in the great garden. Apart from
Paris there are a hundred French towns with their own
mite of grandeur . . . the avenue, the place, the hôtel de ville.
When we look at, say, the Italian hill town or the
English market town – utterly charming though they
may be – we appreciate the hallmark which, for better or
worse, France has set upon the towns of Europe.

Neo-Classical town-planning subordinates the part
to the whole in a way that Baroque planning did not.
Instead of the series of dramatic surprises provided, for
instance, by seventeenth-century Rome, Versailles and
its progeny make a single, coherent, satisfying and
expected statement. Outside Paris the finest example is
the eighteenth-century portion of Nancy. Stanislas,
exiled King of Poland and Duke of Lorraine, drove a
new north–south street through the old town of Nancy,
and off this lies the little planning complex which links
the new street to the palace: the Place Royale, the Place
de la Carrière and, at the culmination of the scheme, the
small palace and its forecourt. The Place Royale was
originally a complete enclosure, the entrances being
ingeniously screened by a triumphal arch and large
Rococo grilles, all black and gold. The Place de la

arrière is an elongated rectangle, domestic in scale and with pleached limes down the centre. The whole theme is highly classical and architectural, yet intimate.

Some of the buildings themselves, however, must be given their due. Jacques-Germain Soufflot (1713-80) – superb designer – designed the church of Ste-Geneviève 1756. It was renamed after the Revolution, and has been known ever since as the Panthéon. The dome owes something to Wren; it is less successful than St Paul's the handling of the colonnade around the drum, the columns appearing too detached; it is more successful in the relationship of the body of the building to the dome. The dome rises high above a splendidly plain wall originally in fact pierced with windows, which were filled in after 1791 by Quatremère de Quincy) and, thanks to the centralized plan, is better seen than is the dome of St Paul's from Ludgate Hill. The internal lighting of the Panthéon is beautiful and subdued (due again to Quatremère de Quincy), as is the design of the pendentives and the arches; it is a fitting mausoleum for great Frenchmen.

The Revolution interrupted but did not fundamentally change the architectural ideals of the Age of Absolutism. Indeed with the rise of Napoleon these values were reasserted with the extra panache given them by Romanticism. Leaving out of account such fashions in

314, 315 Panthéon, Paris (1755–c.1792). The relationship of Soufflot's dome (based upon that of St Paul's, Ill. 294) to the body of the building is superb, accentuated by the plain wall – more Neo-Classical in its severity than Soufflot intended. Inside a series of domes rests on piers and columns, creating a most effective perspective of arches lit only from above.

316 *Part of the highly classical composition of central Paris; the Madeleine, Vignon's Roman temple begun in 1807 (top), stands at the end of the Rue Royale, closing the north axis of the pre-Revolutionary Place de la Concorde with its colonnaded frontages by Gabriel*

Court décor as the Pompeian and the Egyptian ephemeral reflections of the Emperor's campaigns Napoleonic Paris strove for highly Romantic effect it was taken for granted and was *de rigueur* that they should always be in the classical style. The relationship for instance, of the Madeleine (begun by Vignon 1807 but finished only under Louis-Philippe) Gabriel's Place de la Concorde, to the Chambre de Députés and to the slight incline of the Rue Royale, far more important than the dull reality – that it is a fair handsome imitation of a Roman temple.

Again, the fact that the long arcaded rhythms of the Rue de Rivoli (begun by Percier and Fontaine in 1802 are primarily a backcloth to the 'carpet' of the Tuileries Gardens, is far more important than their actual architecture which is no more than adequate. We may note in London that Carlton House Terrace (1827) bears much the same relationship – that of a town-planning backcloth – to St James's Park, as does the Rue de Rivoli the Tuileries Gardens.

The Arc de Triomphe (by Chalgrin, begun 1806) on the other hand, is a splendid monument – the greatest all triumphal arches – betrayed by the inadequacy of it setting. True, it is part of the Romantic Classicism of Napoleon's Paris in that it really does manage dominate the long axis of the Champs-Elysées, and that it makes *gloire* almost credible. Its immediate setting however – the Etoile – consists of so many radiating avenues that no continuity of the circumambient façade no enclosure of space, is possible.

Elsewhere in Europe, Classicism had been the accepted embodiment of the ideals of autocracy. Frederic the Great's palace of Sans-Souci at Potsdam (1745–7) still retains many of the light-hearted features of Rococo but the Neues Palais, built towards the end of his reign and the Brandenburg Gate at Berlin both aim at monumentality rather than charm. In Russia, the supreme autocracy, classical severity was tempered by

317 *Rue de Rivoli, Paris, by Percier and Fontaine (begun 1802). A handsome and uniform street, the arcaded shops being as functional as they are elegant; all the more effective because it is seen across the Tuileries Gardens – an excellent example of the one-sided street*

318 *Carlton House Terrace, London (1827–33). The culmination of Nash's plan (see p. 269), these two stuccoed white ranges of houses are, like the Rue de Rivoli, a magnificent backcloth to a park. The podium, made necessary by a change in ground level, has Doric columns of cast iron*

e personal tastes of successive tsars and tsarinas. Peter e Great had founded St Petersburg in 1700 as a liberately austere capital, planned and built almost tirely by foreigners from or under the influence of ance. His daughter Elizabeth turned to Italy, and artolommeo Rastrelli built for her the two last great ow-pieces of the Rococo spirit – the Winter Palace and

319 *Brandenburg Gate, Berlin (1789), by K. G. Langhans. A colonnaded gateway rather than a triumphal arch, based on the Athenian Propylaea (Ill. 26)*

320 Theatre Street, Leningrad, by Rossi (1827-32). Flanking blocks with twin giant columns on an arcaded plinth lead to the theatre. The combination of white and coloured stucco is characteristic of Leningrad

Tsarskoe Seloe. Under Catherine Classicism becam[e] the accepted style, Italians (e.g. Quarenghi), Scot[s] (Cameron) and Russians (Rossi) uniting to produc[e] an 'international' blend that still makes Leningra[d] a unique city. Such an achievement was the pre[-]rogative of power and prosperity. The only souther[n] court to approach it was that of Naples, where th[e] Bourbon kings built their enormous palace of Casert[a] designed by Luigi Vanvitelli, between 1751 and 177[.] It rivals Versailles in scale and surpasses it in monoton[y.]

It is something of a relief to turn from such vast an[d] forbidding exercises to the less ambitious but mo[re] relaxed environments being created in England. Engli[sh] informality may be attributed partly to the political an[d] social structure, with its equal balance of monarch[y,] nobility and middle class, and partly to the vitality of t[he] English domestic tradition in building. The goo[d] vernacular of village and farm still went on almost u[n]changed, but we now find a number of men who we[re] real, if provincial, architects, designing in the classic[al] tradition. Such men were Henry Bell of Lynn who i[n] 1683 designed the Customs House in King's Lynn, [or] the Bastard Brothers of Blandford who, after a disastro[us] fire, rebuilt that little Dorset town in robust Georgia[n] or, above all, the Woods, father and son, of Bath. In t[he] spa and pleasure city of Bath, between 1727 and 178[0] the Woods did two things. First, they developed t[he] English 'terrace' house, prototype of streets and squar[es]

321 Air view of the section of Bath planned by the Woods, father and son, 1727-80. The scheme began with Queen Square (bottom right, tree-filled); from it Gay Street leads up to the Royal Circus, in turn linked with the Royal Crescent (top left)

in Britain and New England for more than another century. Second, in Queen Square, Gay Street, the Circus and the Royal Crescent, the Woods created a progression of harmonious but contrasted urban spaces which, as a piece of town-planning, belong to history.

The whole relationship of architect-patron-builder, however, was rapidly changing. With the new stress on elegance, purity and correctness, architecture was becoming more than ever a matter for scholars rather than artisan builders. This fact lies behind the next important development in English architecture, and England's chief contribution to Neo-Classicism, the Palladian movement. Its chief exponents – the 'Palladians' and their successors – were William Kent (1685–1748), Lord Burlington (1694–1753), Colen Campbell (d. 1729), William Chambers (1723–96) and Robert Adam (1728–92), the last being a link with the pure Romanticism, Classic and Gothic, which would take us into the nineteenth century.

Lord Burlington, because he himself wielded the T-square, was said by Lord Chesterfield to have betrayed the aristocratic principle. Burlington, however, was not the only peer thus to demean himself; the fact shows the curious status of architecture. It was in danger of becoming a polite accomplishment with the Grand Tour as little more than sight-seeing. Chiswick House (c.1725), Lord Burlington's villa, is now beautifully restored. Symmetrically placed on a high platform, with elaborate

322 Royal Crescent, Bath (1764–74), by John Wood the Younger. The sweep of the hemicycle – entirely open to the landscape to the south – makes this one of the most magnificent pieces of urban domesticity anywhere. The use of a giant order, running through two storeys, gives it a scale appropriate to the open setting

323 Chiswick House, London (c.1725), designed by Lord Burlington for himself. Based upon the Villa Rotonda at Vicenza (Ill. 229), this tiny but completely symmetrical house may be regarded as the manifesto of the English Palladians. Chimneys, required by the climate, are disguised as obelisks

steps and portico, it has great charm in so far as
simulates the Villa Rotonda at Vicenza; as a dwellir
north of latitude 51° it is an absurdity. The same man
design for the Assembly Rooms at York (1731–2)
much praised but is in fact ill-proportioned – th
entablature virtually dividing the interior in two. Willia
Kent's great design for Holkham Hall in Norfolk w
begun in 1734. Like Vanbrugh's houses it has far-flur
wings, corner towers and pavilions; each section of th
complex house is a self-contained essay in the pur
Palladian classical. Holkham is an austere masterpiec
Kent's Horse Guards Building (1750–8) has many
the elements of Holkham but also somehow manages
be the very epitome of the toy barracks – almost a piece
Ruritania in the heart of London.

Burlington employed Colen Campbell to remod
Burlington House in London. Campbell is best know
for his large book, *Vitruvius Britannicus*, which is a
account of great English houses, including sever
designed by himself. His almost cringing regard f
Palladio is to be seen at Mereworth in Kent (c. 1722–9
a completely symmetrical house with porticoes on a
sides, based – like Chiswick House – on the Vil
Rotonda.

If Burlington and Campbell could sometimes l
affected, William Chambers is a much greater figure. H
had travelled in the East and among his minor works
the decorative Chinese Pagoda in Kew Gardens. H

*324 Holkham Hall (begun 1734),
William Kent's noble attempt to design
a wide-spreading English country mansion in pure Palladian Classical. The
portico, the pavilions with their tripartite 'Palladian' windows, the wings –
each is a separate study in the style.
Strong horizontal lines hold these dis-
parate elements together*

...udied in Paris and Italy. He started to build Somerset House, a large block of government offices in 1776; until ...e embankment of the Thames in the nineteenth century, ...had one of the great river frontages of the world, with ...rusticated basement storey rising straight out of the ...ater.

...Robert Adam, with his two brothers, had offices in ...oth London and Edinburgh. In one sense he was a ...rerunner of the nineteenth century in that he had a ...rge professional organization with a long list of ...ealthy clients. Some eight thousand drawings remain. ...e had studied and travelled far beyond the normal ...mits of the Grand Tour, making careful studies of the ...alace of Diocletian at Spalato. He was a true Palladian, ...s one can see at, say, Kedleston or Osterley, yet he ...eated the Vitruvian rules with liberality. He extracted

326 The façade of Kedleston in Derby-shire (1761–5) shows Robert Adam combining Palladianism with a new archaeological approach. The sides are Renaissance, the centre – with its Pantheon-type dome – Roman, and more ornate than anything the earlier Palladians would have accepted

267

327 The Library in Kenwood House, London (1767–8) shows Adam in his pre-eminent role as decorator. The elements are almost wholly derived from ancient Rome – in form the segmental ceiling and the exedra screened by columns (cp. Ill. 91), in ornament the delicate stucco 'grottesche' which had also inspired Raphael (Ill. 210) – but they are handled with a lightness that gave a new elegance to English life

the essence of a classical order or cornice but mo
to suit his own purpose. From France he learnt
the matter of planning. A series of rooms *en su*
Versailles, was nothing new, but from the Frenc
learnt to place adjoining rooms so that they sh
contrasted both in size and shape – the oval ar
leading to the great library, and so on. From Fra
as from the later Italian Renaissance, he learn
about arabesques and the *grottesche* of the Vatica
Italy, Dalmatia, Syria and Greece were wi
knowledge, while from others he learnt of Palm
Baalbek. The Chinoiserie and the Pompeian in
his decoration.

Robert Adam has a long list of great country
his credit. By 1761 he was working at Harev
Yorkshire, Croome Court in Worcestershire,
in Wiltshire, and at Osterley and Kenwood near I
It is as a superior decorator that Adam sh
remembered – for furniture, carpets, marble
and plaster ceilings. It was an age conscious of
discovered refinement. In all this Adam played
As Beau Nash had inculcated good manner
fashionable society of Bath, and as Beau Brum
shortly to make cleanliness fashionable, so
brought refinement into the furnishing of th
Without his magic touch the 'Adam style' can
ordinarily insipid, but he worked for an ar
clientele who were almost the last generation
about classical elegance. The swan song of this
'good taste' in England was to be the Regency,
great achievement of the Regency was to lie not
in the sphere of individual buildings as in a new
of urban existence.

While Napoleon's architects were trying to t
Paris into a city worthy of a Caesar, London w
transformed from a rather provincial and northe
another Copenhagen or Oslo – into a great capit
was not, and never could be, anything in Lond

assical expertise of the French or of the grand scale of
aris, but in its way – that of a cultured and comfortable
iddle class – it made its contribution. The Prince
egent, as extravagant as he was eccentric, discovered
hn Nash (1752–1835), an architect as ingenious as he
as plausible. Nash's achievement, in the last analysis,
as that of a town-planner rather than of an architect.
etween 1812 and 1827 he laid out a great complex of
irks, streets, terraces, squares and churches across the
Vest End of London, from Regent's Park in the north
 St James's Park in the south. He thus made London
to a cosmopolitan city, shifting its centre of gravity
om the old maze of alleys and lanes of the City or Soho,
 the more fashionable districts of St James's and
layfair. His scheme consisted mainly of the ten
erraces' – rows of 'genteel' and even aristocratic houses
 around Regent's Park, the incorporation of Robert
dam's finely proportioned Portland Place, an entirely
w 'Royal Mile' consisting of Upper and Lower
egent Street (rebuilt at the beginning of this century),
iccadilly Circus, Waterloo Place, Carlton House
errace and St James's Park, as well as numerous side
reets and subsidiary areas. In this large area Nash was
chitect for all but a very few of the buildings. The best
 these, not designed by Nash himself, is probably the
thenaeum Club, built by Decimus Burton in 1827–30.
he greatest merit of Nash's scheme lay in the planting
 the parks. Informal glades, sloping swards and rich
liage patterns, in both parks, embraced a winding lake.
 was through this foliage that one glimpsed the white-
iinted stucco of the Neo-Greek houses. Stucco,
though used primarily as an economy, was exploited
 as to give the fine, flat, elegant detail which is somehow
 much more Greek than Roman. Nash's architecture
as can still be seen in the terraces along Regent's Park –
gay, versatile and careless. His street design – as can be
en in old prints of Regent Street – was good; the
raights and curves were carefully demarcated by such

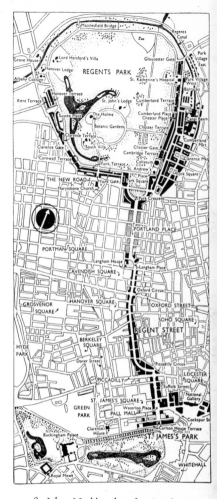

328 John Nash's plan for London
(1812–27) – marked in black – linking
Regent's Park to St James's Park, had
to be laid across the existing town. It is
therefore more irregular than, say, Nancy
or Bath. Also, the new cult of the Picturesque explains a quite deliberate
informality in the design of the parks
themselves and the terraces

329 *The Quadrant, Regent Street, London (1819–20), by John Nash. The County Fire Office on the right closed the vista as one came up Lower Regent Street. Colonnaded footwalks, whose columns would appear in diminishing perspective, emphasized the curve of Regent Street itself*

devices as corner turrets, while the original colonnaded Quadrant linking Regent Street with Piccadilly Circus was as good as anything of its kind in Europe. The whole Nash scheme combined a real classical elegance with that highly Romantic quality that is so mysteriously born when formal architecture is given an informal setting. To compare the Regent's Park terraces with the equivalent streets in Bath, of an earlier generation, is to sense immediately the change that had come over architecture.

At this point, the second decade of the nineteenth century, a new aspect of architecture is about to make itself felt: America. The full impact of American dynamism and technological boldness will not be apparent until later, but we must pause here to trace its independent growth and assess its contribution.

All colonial architecture, all over the world – even in defiance of custom and climate – bears the stamp of the colonizing power. This was true of Roman architecture in Britain, of British architecture in India and North America. Moreover, since the eastern seaboard of North America had a climate not too violently different from that of England, and virtually no indigenous culture, for centuries its architecture was a very precise reflection of the mother country. The main difference was a wide use of timber, in the form of clapboard, instead of or as well as brick. That the Colonial architecture of the United States should, even at an early date, have real distinction is not surprising. The proud, enterprising and lively mind of a first- or second-generation colonial would make its mark, in his determination not to be a squatter but, rather, to establish a civilization.

While New England was first colonized largely from Puritan East Anglia, with an infusion of Cambridge intellectuals, Virginia and the South were colonized with the wealth of London merchants, and with an Oxford outlook. The charm of New England lies in the clean, simple integrity of the Puritan outlook, as we see it in Concord, Salem, on Lexington Green, in Nantucket or the older parts of Boston. The charm of Virginia lies in the courtly and ancestral mansions, in the fine houses along the James River, in the old state capitals of Williamsburg and Richmond . . . a background to a transatlantic version of the aristocratic England that was a colonial's birthright. The ruthlessness of a new land found no direct expression in architecture.

The earliest houses in the United States that can be called architecture owe much of their quality to a rather naïve combination of sincerity and ignorance. They were being built in Massachusetts before the middle of the seventeenth century – a few at least surviving from before 1640. These were heavily timbered structures such as might have been built in seventeenth-century English villages; they established the New England tradition of planning all the rooms around a huge central chimney-stack. Within a few years brickfields had been opened and houses were being built of brick as well as timber. A freak survival is to be found in Isle of Wight County, Virginia, where St Luke's is an 'English' Gothic church, pure and simple.

Through the first eighty years of the eighteenth century
North American architecture – virtually limited in any
case to the Tidewater states – was still colonial; just as
Spain, Portugal and France had had their effect on Latin
America and the Deep South, so Virginia and New
England remained almost wholly 'Georgian'. Side by
side with modern architecture this tradition still persists.
The use of wood may account for livelier colour schemes,
more slender columns in the porticoes, but by and large
many a Colonial house could be transplanted almost
unnoticed to any English market town or cathedral close.
The extent to which design and workmanship actually
were English must remain debatable. The plans for a
Harvard church were drawn in England, and the
original buildings of William and Mary College in
Williamsburg, Virginia, are popularly attributed to
Christopher Wren; he may indeed have made a sketch
for the college which was a royal foundation.

Williamsburg was established as the capital of
Virginia in 1699. It was simply but beautifully laid out,
a fine piece of town planning by any standards. A three-
quarter-mile axis linked the College with the Capitol;
the cross-axis was a tree-lined Mall terminating in the
Governor's House – also, but more dubiously, attributed
to Wren. The church steeple marked the junction of the
Mall with the main axis. The modern tourist, however,
must beware; he must distinguish old from new, and so
meticulous are the restorations that this is not easy. Much
of Williamsburg was destroyed by the British in 1781.
The College is the most intact of all the buildings, and
the others were so carefully restored from documentary
evidence, thirty years ago, that we see Williamsburg
much as it was in its great days. It deserves its fame as the
greatest single monument of the Colonial era.

It is not until well into the eighteenth century that
named architects begin to appear; they were mainly self-
taught amateurs. One of the first was Richard Taliaferro;
he built the beautiful Byrd house, Westover (c.1730).

330 *The Governor's House, Williams-burg (1705, rebuilt 1932): a 'brick box' of tall and narrow proportions, with a high dormered roof crowned by a gallery and cupola, it is typical of English domestic architecture of the time of William and Mary, but marked the appearance of this style in America*

331 *Westover (c.1730), by Richard Taliaferro, one of the first known American architects, shows how 'Georgian' was the best architecture of Virginia. The brickwork, the sashes, the dormers and the big chimney stacks are all very English, and of the highest quality. Only the plan – with the entrance hall running through from front to back – marked a new departure*

a typical classical mansion of the Virginian tobacco lands. This was only one of several splendid houses by Taliaferro, but it is unique in the grouping of its masses, and in the fact that the fine ironwork and carved fire-places were imported from England, although at this date many reasonably good craftsmen – plasterers, joiners, cabinet-makers – must surely have been established locally.

The name of John Ariss appears when he advertises himself as a designer in the manner of Gibbs. He may have built Mount Airy, near Richmond, a house with

273

332 King's Chapel, Boston (1749–58): designed by Peter Harrison, under the influence of Gibbs, this church is important as being the first in New England to depart from the tradition of the absolutely plain and austere meeting house

outlying pavilions linked by curved corridors to the central block – in fact the first piece of true American Palladianism. Little else is known of Ariss.

The real Palladian, however, was Peter Harrison (1716–75) who, in 1749, built the Redwood Library, Newport, with a fine Roman Doric portico, and in the same year began the King's Chapel in Boston, a first departure from the plain and severe Puritan meeting house, with the first of a whole series of steeples, derived from Wren, Hawksmoor or Gibbs. Both the King's Chapel and the same architect's Christ Church, at Cambridge, Mass., have unusually graceful interiors with fine ceilings. In spite of the charm of so much Colonial work, Harrison may be described as the only real scholar of his generation. There can be no doubt, however, about the scholarship of his successor.

Thomas Jefferson (1743–1826) was a Virginian. He achieved fame as one of the authors of the Declaration of Independence, as a Secretary of State to George Washington, as a legislator, as a free-thinker and – rather oddly – as an architect. He had a profound faith in Roman law and, by deduction, in Roman architecture. He was a Palladian, not in the sense that he admired the English Palladians whom, in fact, he despised as effete, but in the real sense that he shared Palladio's own inspiration, that of Rome. In 1769, on a romantic hill, he built himself the villa of Monticello which, after many changes, emerged as a fine intellectual essay in austere classicism.

When the capital of Virginia was moved from Williamsburg to Richmond, Jefferson designed the State Capitol. He was in Europe at the time and sent home a sketch much influenced by the genuinely Roman Maison Carrée in Nîmes, although his building was much more elaborate in its general layout. Even more classical and more formal in its plan was his design for the University of Virginia at Charlottesville (1817–26). By this time, however, Jefferson was deeply immersed in affairs of state, and was making arrangements for the building of a federal capital at Georgetown, renamed Washington. He therefore enlisted the aid of Benjamin Henry Latrobe – to be referred to below.

In the immediate post-Colonial period we find the name of Samuel McIntyre (1757–1811) as a designer of good houses and of the ambitious Salem Court House with superimposed orders and a cupola – now demolished. More famous is Charles Bulfinch (1763–1844), the architect who presided over the growth of Boston. Between 1793 and 1800 he built the Massachusetts State

333, 334 Thomas Jefferson's designs for his own house, Monticello (above, 1769), and for the University of Virginia at Charlottesville (below, carried out in 1817–26 by Latrobe), mark the arrival in America of a new classicism, more formal and self-conscious. The house is, like Chiswick House (Ill. 324) derived mainly from the designs of Palladio. In the larger end block of the university – foreground – Jefferson went beyond secondary sources, returning to the Pantheon for inspiration. Along the sides of the 'campus' are teachers' houses and students' rooms

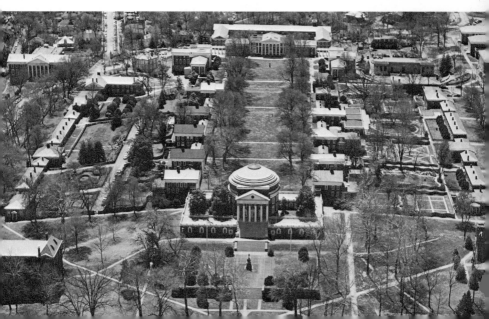

335 *The grandeur of the Capitol in Washington, D.C., lies mainly in the dome and the great flights of steps. To Thornton and Bulfinch (1792–1827) is due the centre, with its colonnade flanked by flat pilastered walls. The wings – heavier versions of the central feature – and the dome are the work of Thomas U. Walter, after 1851*

House, somewhat inspired by Chambers's Somerset House. The golden dome is still a landmark on Beacon Hill. Bulfinch supervised the building of the Capitol in Washington – to other men's designs (see below) – and then returned to his vast Bostonian practice.

Meanwhile in Washington Pierre Charles L'Enfant had, under the spell of Versailles, planned the centre of the splendid, if rather grandiose, city that we know. L'Enfant, however, was arrogant and difficult; he was dismissed in 1792, and the designs of both the Capitol itself and of the White House were entrusted to other hands. The White House was designed by an Irishman, James Hoban. The Capitol, after a rather dubious competition, was designed by an English amateur, William Thornton, and completed by Bulfinch in 1827. (The resulting building was itself virtually submerged by the additions of Thomas U. Walter, after 1851.)

Subsequent developments in American architecture take their place in the continuing story of Europe and indeed of the world. Before proceeding to the age of industrialism, beginning with Victoria and the Second Empire, we must briefly follow the classical tradition until it merges with and is finally engulfed by the new currents.

The most interesting architects of the late eighteenth and early nineteenth centuries were those who tried to evolve beyond the pedantry of archaeological correctness towards a new kind of Classicism, in which the virtues of proportion, harmony and restraint would be preserved but the old vocabulary of ornament modified or abandoned. This 'abstract' style goes back to such an architect as Etienne-Louis Boullée (1728–99) whose executed works were fairly conventional but whose projects on paper show a far bolder imagination – buildings conceived as geometrical forms, hemispheres, cylinders and cubes. His ideas were taken up by the brilliant Claude-Nicolas Ledoux (1736–1806). Again it is his unexecuted designs that constitute his best work, but what was built of his 'ideal city' at Chaux and his Paris tollhouses (i.e. the Barrière de la Villette) show that his failure was not due to lack of practicality. In the barrières (1784–9) he used a massive and austere Doric idiom, but his most original designs are purely geometrical, such as his project for an 'ideal' cemetery (1806), where the central chapel was to be a huge sphere lit by a central 'eye'.

Ledoux was regarded as an eccentric and had few admirers until modern times. Some parallels, however, may be drawn between his work and that of the more successful English architect, Sir John Soane. Soane (1753–1837) was suspicious and autocratic, in contrast with the optimistic and extroverted Nash. He was also a superb and original designer. In 1788 Soane, after visiting Rome, was appointed architect to the Bank of England. His Grecian Romanticism was in fact extremely individualistic, as well as delicate and austere. Walls flow smoothly into vaults – which are themselves

336 Boullée's design for a cenotaph to Newton (c.1784) combines the globe – symbolizing Newton's discoveries – with a Roman mausoleum, ringed by cypresses. The conceit and the form are equally Neo-Classical

337, 338 In Ledoux's Barrière de la Villette, Paris (1789, above), classical elements are reduced to their simplest and most massive. His ideal cemetery (section below), as abstract as Boullée, remained unbuilt.

339, 340 Soane: above, the breakfast parlour in his house in London (1812); below, the Consols Office of the Bank of England (1794). The arches are segmental, not round. The plasterwork has a flat Grecian delicacy. Above, light enters indirectly and gleams in convex mirrors. Below, the flat surfaces are piquantly contrasted with the fully modelled caryatids in the cupola

usually of a flat segmental curve – while arches seem barely to touch the supporting piers. Mouldings, except for the occasional incised line, are almost non-existent. One may say that whereas Robert Adam had exploited plasterwork to achieve ornament, Soane exploited it to achieve the smooth unbroken surface. In his own house in Lincoln's Inn Fields (now his museum), he devised several original methods of using mirrors and of letting in daylight at unexpected places. This, together with the lightly constructed domes which he used over the various offices of the Bank of England – specially the Consols Office of 1794 – suggest that Soane would have delighted in the freedom given to the designer by modern prestressed concrete.

Soane founded no school, but his influence can be seen in several of the more sensitive architects of the next generation. Benjamin Henry Latrobe (1764–1820) was the first man appointed to the post of United States Surveyor of Public Buildings. Born in England, Latrobe emigrated to America in 1796. He worked with Jefferson on the completion of the Virginia State Capitol and then, in 1798, began the Bank of Pennsylvania at Philadelphia, a piece of full-blooded Romantic Classicism. In 1805 he began the cathedral at Baltimore in Maryland. The second design, as built, owed much to the Paris Panthéon, and, with the segmental arches of the interior, to Soane's Bank of England.

By the third decade of the century the clear-cut geometry of a Ledoux or a Soane was gone. Here and there, as in Munich or Edinburgh, in an aura of scholarship and philosophy, the flame was never quite extinguished. There was in Munich, for instance, Leo von Klenze's Glyptothek (1815–34) and his Propylaea across the square, begun in 1846. As late as the fifties there were the Athenian essays of Alexander Thomson (1817–75) in Glasgow and Thomas Hamilton (1785–1858) in Edinburgh. Thomson gave us his fine Free Churches, while Hamilton, in the Edinburgh High

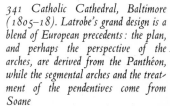

341 *Catholic Cathedral, Baltimore (1805–18). Latrobe's grand design is a blend of European precedents: the plan, and perhaps the perspective of the arches, are derived from the Panthéon, while the segmental arches and the treatment of the pendentives come from Soane*

342 *Glyptothek, Munich (1815–34). Leo von Klenze was, like Schinkel, an exponent of Romantic Classicism. This building, with central Grecian portico and side walls relieved by Renaissance aedicules – the three parts perhaps too nearly equal in width – was built to house the Duke of Bavaria's magnificent collection of antique sculpture*

343 *The Royal High School (begun 1825) is Thomas Hamilton's greatest contribution to Edinburgh's Hellenic revival: a fine Athenian essay in massing, with colonnades and porticoes raised on an extensive podium, it surveys Edinburgh from its own 'acropolis', Calton Hill*

344 *Merchants' Exchange, Philadelphia (1832–4), designed by the city's Greek Revival architect, William Strickland. An elegant Corinthian Order rounds the corner, below a cupola reminiscent of the Choragic Monument of Lysicrates at Athens*

School, gave us a Doric composition worthy of the Greek intellectualism of his city. What Hamilton was to Edinburgh, William Strickland (1788–1854) was to Philadelphia. There he followed Latrobe's lead, and made his name with a bank in the form of a Doric temple (the Branch Bank of the United States, designed in 1818), and an elegant essay in the Corinthian order, the Merchants' Exchange of 1832–4. In his last major work, the Tennessee State Capitol (1845–9), this Grecian purity has been lost in elaboration: the Victorian Age was dawning.

The change was fundamental and all-inclusive, and will be described more fully in the next chapter. One of the features common to both periods, however, was Romanticism and an account of this – not the least powerful agent in the formation of nineteenth-century taste – may conveniently be included here. Among the many elements that go to make up Romanticism is the 'divine discontent' of the artist, the flight from reality to something distant and strange. Whether amidst the last blowsy snobberies of the eighteenth century or the first black onslaught of industrialism, that flight was inevitable. All Classical architecture is to some extent no less Romantic than is Gothic, in that it represents a kind of nostalgia for antiquity, for the world of Greece and Rome. But now, with the Enlightenment, the French Revolution and the Romantic Movement behind them, men's nostalgia, their dreams, were heightened. They had to express their nostalgia, whether in poetry, the novel, painting or architecture. Good design – such qualities as proportion, scale, symmetry, harmony – was no longer enough. Other, more *romantic* qualities had become necessary – charm, novelty, light, escape, the picturesque and, above all, historical association.

As early as the middle of the eighteenth century, on the gentle slopes of Hagley Park in Worcestershire, an English nobleman had built two 'follies': one, a sham Gothic ruin, was designed by Sanderson Miller in 174

345 *Detail of the Royal Pavilion, Brighton. Nash's transformations (1815–21), which included domes of stucco on cast iron, turned a conventional house into a full-scale 'folly' fit for the gaiety of the Regent and for a seaside town*

the other, a Doric temple, was designed ten years later, by James Stuart who, with Nicholas Revett, was among the first to study the Athenian ruins. Neither of these 'follies' had any intrinsic merit; both were redolent with sentiment, straws in the wind. Hermits' cells, Rococo grottoes, broken aqueducts, Gothic dairies – even the 'jardin anglais' of the Trianon with its 'Temple d'Amour', or Walpole's Gothic mansion at Strawberry Hill, or the Regent's 'Hindu' Pavilion at Brighton, or the Pagoda at Kew – all existed for reasons which might be valid, but were certainly literary or romantic rather than purely architectural.

In the 'folly' or the *jeu d'esprit*, when the patron was both rich and eccentric – and eccentricity itself was part of the Romantic pattern – then Romantic qualities were easy to come by. In the more serious architecture of great public or metropolitan buildings there was necessarily more tradition, more restraint. But Romanticism emerged all the same, and its greatest exponent (indeed its only exponent of genius) was Karl Friedrich Schinkel. Schinkel (1781–1841) may perhaps be regarded as

346 Strawberry Hill, Twickenham (begun 1748), Horace Walpole's famous house. Revived for romantic reasons, Gothic was yet scarcely understood. The library, by John Chute, shows a rather naive application of detail in the new style to an otherwise Georgian room – a kind of Gothic rococo

281

347, 348 *Karl Friedrich Schinkel: right, the Schauspielhaus, Berlin (1819–21); below, the Altes Museum, Berlin (1824–8)*

Soane's 'opposite number' in Germany – a master both of the Grecian phase of Romantic Classicism and of the more eclectic phase which followed it. His approach was highly architectonic, that is to say he was – for all his use of stylistic elements – a pure geometrician like Ledoux. He constantly subordinated such elements as the classical orders to his overriding conception. His first large work was the Berlin Schauspielhaus (1819–21) where the complicated masses of an auditorium building detract from the unity so essential to the work of a Schinkel, Ledoux or a Soane. It was in the Altes Museum (1824–8) in Berlin that Schinkel was able to realize his genius and his purism with one splendidly simple Ionic colonnade running the full length of the façade – a design comparable to Smirke's British Museum façade designed about the same time, but more superbly detailed. In the picture-galleries and sculpture-halls Schinkel anticipated the lighting and the display arrangements of good modern museums.

Chapter Ten

THE NINETEENTH CENTURY

When the first factory-made brick was first taken across England by train, the old vernacular craft-building of Europe was doomed. For a hundred and fifty years architecture has now been in the hands of either the speculative builder or of the professional architect – the latter so trained that he could draw upon any of the styles of history, but seeming never to know that buildings are where life is lived. During that century and a half the world saw so many portentous changes – political, social, religious, technical – that the actual function and purpose of architecture also changed beyond recognition. During that time aristocratic patronage vanished; places like Chicago, Essen and Manchester became huge cities overnight; most people began to live in slums; iron was shown to be more efficient than stone. The architect, agonizing about style, seldom admitted these things were true, and seldom responded to them. He lost the battle of life and art to the engineer. It was the engineer, not the architect, who was on the band-wagon of his time.

During the first quarter of the nineteenth century these changes were working underground. That iron bridges, macadam roads, sewage disposal, street lighting, canal systems, steamboats, cheap Irish labour, limited liability companies and even universal franchise should alter the whole nature of cities, and so also of architecture, was unthinkable. In the capitals of Europe, and across the Atlantic, professional architects were, after all, still building in the classical style and, according to their lights, building well.

349 *Palais de Justice, Brussels (1866–83). Poelaert's enormous, even monstrous, building is at least impressive – a great piling up of the heaviest classical elements. But this very heavy-handedness is a sign of that 'collapse of taste' attributed – often unjustly – to the 19th century*

350 *In the Opera House, Paris (begun 1862), Charles Garnier showed that a large auditorium building of great complexity can, in fact, be given unity, and that it can, moreover, be an integral part of a great town plan. The façade is a free, festive build-up of Renaissance elements encrusted with sculpture, culminating in Apollo with his lyre atop the curved roof of the auditorium*

As one moves towards the mid-century, into the Second Empire and the High Victorian style of England, the phrase 'collapse of taste' acquires meaning. All over Europe one can find architecture possessed of flair, vigour and originality. Architecture of refinement, elegance or real beauty becomes ever more rare. The point is made by such obvious mediocrities as S. Francesco di Paola, Naples (1817), the Piazza Vittorio Veneto in Turin (1852), the Opera House in Hanover (1845–52), the extensions to the Louvre in Paris (1852 onwards), the Palais de Justice in Brussels (1866–83), the Opera House in Cologne (1870–2), and so on. The list could be multiplied many times.

351 *Grand staircase of the Paris Opera House: an architecture of 'occasion', richly – if heavily – decorated, gleaming with marble and gilt*

Yet the nineteenth century had standards of its own, ften very demanding standards, and to appreciate its architecture we must as far as possible look for those merits which it strove to make its own. The most sumptuous product of the Second Empire was the Paris Opera House. It was designed by Charles Garnier (1825–98) and was begun in 1862. It has two great virtues: its sense of urbanism and its sense of occasion.

The plan, on a diamond-shaped site at the point where three boulevards converge, presented difficulties. There was no 'back': every façade was of architectural importance. The solution shows the tradition of the École des Beaux-Arts at its best and most brilliant:

352 *Reform Club, London (1837).*
Charles Barry's design for one of the
greater Pall Mall clubs shows his
interpretation, in English terms, of the
Italian High Renaissance – classical
windows well spaced on a plain wall in
the manner of the Palazzo Farnese
(Ill. 214)

every axis is developed to give the utmost value to eve[r]
part of the plan. The massing of the building gives it t[h]
utmost value in the landscape of Paris. Internally t[h]
great staircase, the rich marbles, the chandeliers, the lo[n]
vistas down foyers and promenades, all combine [to]
create a setting for an occasion, for a particular momen[t]
This is one facet of the genius of France.

Side by side with that odd and, to start with, almo[st]
wholly English phenomenon, the Gothic Revival, [a]
number of English architects used the classical sty[le]
until the end of the century. As elsewhere in Europe t[he]
Romanticism faded and the architecture of antiquity w[as]
made to serve the needs of officialdom and of sol[id]
provincial magnates. Perhaps the last English essay [in]
Romantic Classicism was at Downing College, Cam[-]
bridge (1807–20) by William Wilkins. It was nev[er]
finished but was intended to be 'the ideal Grecia[n]
college'. Even as it stands it is both more 'Grecian' an[d]
much better than some of Wilkins' other large buildin[gs]
such as University College, London (1827) or t[he]
National Gallery (1834–8).

Sir Charles Barry (1795–1860), more famous as t[he]
'Gothic' architect of the Houses of Parliament, designe[d]
two buildings in the thirties which – at least in quality [of]
design – lie somewhere between the pure Romanticis[m]
of the Soane epoch and the over-ornamented work of t[he]
mid-century. To this later work Barry contributed h[is]
share, with several large houses for a vulgarized aristocrac[y.]
In 1829 and 1837, however, side by side with Decim[us]
Burton's Athenaeum, Barry built two clubs in Pall Ma[ll,]
London: the Travellers' and the Reform. An Italia[n]
palazzo with a glass roof over the *cortile* may be gre[at]
nonsense amidst the London fogs, but Barry's restraine[d]
astylar façades – with the Reform Club reminiscent [of]
the Palazzo Farnese – are very fine pieces of work.

One of Barry's contemporaries who could also st[ill]
show something of the scholarship of the Augustan A[ge]
was C. R. Cockerell (1788–1863), a sensitive and cul[t]

ted intellectual, far removed from the crude realities
his time. The Taylorian Institute in Oxford (1841–5)
his most 'intellectual' work, while his Bank of
igland in Liverpool (1845) shows his great skill in
ndling complex classical detail.

A building which, in its enormous emphasis upon the
nic colonnade, still presumably retained some scintilla
the Hellenic ideal, was the British Museum. It was
signed by Robert Smirke (1780–1867) and was under
nstruction for over twenty years, from 1823 to 1847.
he obvious comparison is with Schinkel's Altes
useum in Berlin, but the vast London museum is too
g to have the unity of Schinkel's work. It is impressive,
t suffers from column-mania – forty-eight gigantic
nic columns serving no purpose except to overawe the
mmon man and to darken the galleries within.

Another much columned building, but a very fine one,
St George's Hall in Liverpool, designed by H. L.
mes (1814–47) in 1840. Its merit lies partly in its
pressive simplicity, but mainly perhaps in the way the
chitect provided a big stepped stylobate or platform
hich would raise his 'temple' clear of its sloping site.

England is a small island. From the end of the
apoleonic Wars to the start of the First World War –

353 British Museum, London (1823–47), by Robert Smirke. An over-whelmingly single-minded exterior, made tremendously impressive by the sheer scale of the Ionic colonnade

almost exactly a hundred years – she was the richest a
most powerful country in the world, also the m
complex, most romantic, most philistine and m
squalid. Three distinct and, indeed, antagonistic scho
of architectural thought existed side by side. First w
the survival of the classical tradition; second was t
fervour of the Gothic Revival; third was the utilitari
work of the engineers in iron, glass and steel. T
Classicists and the Gothicists waged the 'Battle of t
Styles' – of very little interest to anyone except the co
testants. Each upheld his own stylistic convictions
reasons which might be literary, moral or even aesthet
but were seldom architectural in the sense that archite
should use structure to serve the needs of life. These tv
schools of professional architects agreed only that t
work of the engineers – the great viaducts and railw
stations – was not architecture at all.

This complicated situation was made more so by su
stark facts as the rapidity of technical invention a
manufacturing processes, the consequent growth of t
great black cities, religious revivals and sentimentali
liberalism and philanthropy, bigotry and *laissez-fai*
and the general domination of bourgeois taste.

A Gothic Revival in nineteenth-century England w
almost as inevitable as a Roman Revival in fourteen
century Florence. The English Renaissance and Baroq
had always been, if more than a fashion, no more thar
class taste. The vernacular of village and market tov
had lived on, and Gothic itself had never quite die
Through the centuries – like a golden thread in a da
tapestry or, perhaps, more like what Kenneth Clark ca
'the brackish stream' – one finds these instances of Goth
survival. The Gothic tower of St Mary's, Warwick, w
built in 1698 when Vanbrugh was already designi
Castle Howard. Wren, Adam and Soane could all,
put to it, turn out a piece of 'Gothick' while Na
virtually organized his office with a Gothic 'departmen
and built himself a fine 'castle' in the Isle of Wight. T

oets, even more than the architects, had kept the Gothic pirit alive. From the time when Milton wrote of studious cloisters pale' and 'storied windows richly ight', on to Tennyson's *Idylls of the King*, it was a constant theme.

Horace Walpole had begun to 'gothicize' Strawberry Hill as early as 1750, with fireplaces and bookcases copied meticulously from the tombs of Westminster or Tewkesbury. At Fonthill in Wiltshire, in 1795, James Wyatt built a vast and gimcrack sham 'abbey' for that gimcrack eccentric, William Beckford. Fonthill was filled with lovely things and, moreover, was picturesquely massed – an advance on the idea that 'Gothick' was merely a matter of pointing the arches. By the turn of the century many aristocrats felt such pride in their ancient lineage – the Gothic Revival is perhaps a facet of nationalism – that they were all building themselves 'castles' with moats and battlements. Robert Adam's Culzean (1777–90), Porden's Eaton Hall (1804–12), Smirke's Eastnor (*c.* 1810–16), Wyatt's Ashridge (1808–13), as well as the drastic restoration of Windsor by Sir Jeffry Wyatville, are all in this category.

In 1834 the greater part of the Palace of Westminster – containing the old Houses of Parliament – was

354 St George's Hall, Liverpool (1841–54), by Harvey Lonsdale Elmes, is one of the finest Early Victorian monuments. Much of its merit lies in the advantage taken of a sloping site to build up a great platform – podium, steps and stylobate – upon which the 'temple' is then placed

355 *Houses of Parliament, London (1840-65): the rich Gothic skyline of towers and pinnacles, combined with the very formal river façade, shows both the conflict in Barry's mind between Gothic and Classical, and the importance of Pugin as a Gothic collaborator*

356 *The Royal Gallery in the Houses of Parliament, part of the processional suite in the House of Lords, again reflects the dichotomy of the whole build-ing: it is a four-square 19th-century room encrusted with medieval detail*

destroyed by fire. Gothic was now so much in the a[...] that a Parliamentary Committee of men classical[...] educated, but in Gothic colleges, decreed that the ne[...] Houses of Parliament should be in the Gothic o[...] Elizabethan style. Barry, who worked in Gothic as we[...] as Italianate, won the competition. His plan was brillia[...] axial, logical, well-lit and efficient – a perfect machin[...] for bi-cameral government. It had a long and completel[...] symmetrical façade to the Thames. A few towers – tha[...] of Big Ben among them – were placed at odd corners t[...]

give the whole a spurious Gothic irregularity. The detail – carving, thrones, pinnacles and vaults – has the quintessence of the dead Middle Ages, while being also Victorian. That detail was quite beyond Barry's powers. He knew it, and called to his aid the young A. W. N. Pugin, a fiery and fanatical creative genius. The building that resulted established Gothic as the national style, took it away from the eccentrics and made it official.

If Barry's Houses of Parliament symbolize the recognition of the Gothic Revival as the national style, the work of Augustus Welby Pugin (1812–52) symbolizes its recognition as the Christian style. While Pugin's fanaticism made him a difficult problem for most clients, he did find among the old Catholic families a few wealthy patrons prepared to build Catholic churches. It was said that Pugin 'starved his roof to gild his altar'. The body of the typical Pugin church, such as St Chad's, Birmingham (1839) or St Giles's, Cheadle (1841–6), like most Gothic of the forties, tends to be hard and mean. It is only in the chancel – in the rood screen, reredos and altar – that we find the same magic touch as in the House of Lords library or the central lobby at Westminster. We find it again in the lavish apartments of Scarisbrick House (1837–52) or Alton Castle (1840).

The work of William Butterfield (1814–1900) carries the Gothic Revival a stage further. Butterfield, a stern, puritanical Anglican, was the darling of the High Church clergy and yet, in an odd sense, was hardly a medievalist at all. He was concerned primarily with structural integrity, with his belief that the spirit of medieval craftsmanship should apply equally to drains and altars. He accepted Gothic as a matter of course, but was less intent upon archaeological accuracy than upon making Gothic into a 'modern' style, using sound construction and washable, durable materials such as glazed bricks, Minton tiles and inlaid marble, to achieve his ends. The bizarre but impressive result is to be seen in All Saints', Margaret Street, London (1849–59) and

357, 358 Above: the rich screen of St Chad's, Birmingham (1839), by Pugin. Below: part of the nave of All Saints', Margaret Street, London (1849–59), by Butterfield

in Keble College Chapel, Oxford (1873–6). It is surely significant that John Summerson's excellent essay on Butterfield is entitled 'The Glory of Ugliness'.

Sir George Gilbert Scott (1811–78) shares with Barry and Alfred Waterhouse the dubious honour of being among the first to have large organized offices, with many contracts. Scott's Albert Memorial, begun in 1863, was the secular obverse of the Butterfield medal. In it he too was determined to make Gothic 'modern'. The use of mosaic, marble, pink granite, gilded bronze – as well as a hidden iron frame – are some of its 'modern' aspects. Its excesses and pathos, as well as its iconography and literal representation of virtue and sentiment, also make it a complete symbol of High Victorianism. It is, however, Scott's enormous building for St Pancras station (containing a hotel and the booking-offices) in London, of 1865, that is the culminating masterpiece of its epoch. It combines all the qualities of the sixties – stylistic display and solid philistinism. With its tremendous pinnacled skyline, its emplacement upon a plinth of ramps and terraces, it is in its own right a great piece of uninhibited design.

359 Albert Memorial, London (begun 1863). Prince Albert sits in a Gothic shrine 175 feet high; below him are personifications of agriculture, commerce, manufacture and engineering, and a frieze of great artists. Like Butterfield, Gilbert Scott used every decorative material he could find, and every sort of literal and symbolic carving. This is Victorian 'association' art taken to its limit

360 Scott's St Pancras Station Hotel (1865) was the supreme monument of the Gothic Revival, pride of its generation. The relationship of the hotel to the trainshed behind it (Ill. 364) – visible far left – was nil. Cabs carried passengers up a ramp to the level of the platforms behind

When the old Houses of Parliament were burnt, a
number of miscellaneous courts of law were also lost.
The ultimate consequence was the new Royal Courts of
Justice in the Strand. George Edmund Street (1824–81)
won this commission in a competition in 1866. The
building is disliked by lawyers for its gloom and its
poor acoustics. It has a huge vaulted hall, perhaps the
finest interior of the Victorian Age. Its exterior – though
lacking the verve of St Pancras – is cleverly broken up
into a series of vignettes, as it were, in honest recognition
of the fact that a long façade cannot otherwise be
appreciated in a narrow street.

Alfred Waterhouse (1830–1905) handled millions of
pounds' worth of work with a professional expertise that
makes him the link between a romantic Gothic Revival
and the commercialism of our own day. He could
organize a plan and get it built. Among his larger commissions were Manchester Assize Court (1859), Eaton
Hall (1867), Manchester Town Hall (1869), in London
the City and Guilds College and the Natural History
Museum, South Kensington (1873–81), while St Paul's
School, Hammersmith, and the Prudential Building,

*361 Town Hall, Manchester (1869):
Alfred Waterhouse adapted the current
Gothic style to the elaborate requirements of new commercial and civic
buildings with great ingenuity. The
massive Gothic skyline of the Town
Hall did not prevent it being – in its own
day – an extremely efficient building*

*362 In the Royal Courts of Justice,
London (designed 1866), G.E. Street
showed his genius for grouping and for
breaking up a long façade without loss of
unity. The street-level arcade ties the
composition together*

Holborn (begun 1879) are souvenirs of a fashion for building in terracotta of a loathsome red tint.

The mind of Victorian England was divided between its ideals and its materialism. The attempt to reconcile them – to boss one's factory hands during the day, and to read Tennyson or Carlyle in the evening – has exposed the age to the charge of hypocrisy. This schizophrenia is most marked in architecture; the railways, docks, viaducts and new machinery were looked upon with pride as well as financial satisfaction; 'architecture', Classical or Gothic, was only High Art – possibly desirable, never practicable. Nothing could reveal this dichotomy more clearly than the two cases of the St Pancras Hotel in London and the Oxford Museum. St Pancras towers up from the street – a great medieval pile screening the railway station. At the back, towards the trains, the façade is almost as ornate, but the curve of the magnificent iron and glass roof, designed by W. H. Barlow two years before the hotel, cuts quite ruthlessly across the Venetian windows. There is no evidence that it ever occurred to anyone that a station and a hotel might be designed by one man.

Ruskin's *Stones of Venice* had been published in 1851. The Oxford Museum (1855–9) was an essay in Venetian Gothic directly inspired by Ruskin's magic prose. (Another was P. B. Wight's extraordinary 'Doge's Palace' for the Academy of Design in New York.) Ruskin was in fact consultant to the architects of the Oxford Museum, Deane and Woodward. At a late stage he discovered that in order to give good top lighting to the galleries a cast-iron roof was to be used. He instantly withdrew. The roof still serves, all its Gothic cusps and foliations beautifully cast, the lighting excellent.

The whole controversy about the use of iron – virtually the prehistory of modern architecture – was brought to a head in 1851 by the building of the Crystal Palace to house the Great Exhibition in Hyde Park, London.

363 *The interior of the Oxford Museum (1855–9), by Deane and Woodward, demonstrates in succinct form the conflict of the age. The iron-and-glass roof on the brick-and-stone Gothic structure brings together two kinds of architecture which most Victorians thought should never meet. Its functionalism is mitigated by wrought-iron foliage on capitals and spandrels*

364 *The iron roof by W.H. Barlow which spans the 243 feet of St Pancras Station in London (1864) is one of the finest engineering achievements of the 19th century. Note how the great curve of the girders dwarfs the little Gothic windows of the hotel building, joined on at the end*

365 *Crystal Palace in Hyde Park, London (1851). This contemporary photograph of Paxton's prefabricated exhibition building shows how, although it was made of iron sections, it still retained a touch of Regency elegance*

The story has been told many times. In essence it was simply that Joseph Paxton (1803–65), who had been building very large conservatories for the Duke of Devonshire, was now able to solve the problem of an even larger and equally well-lit exhibition building, a third of a mile long, by designing a prefabricated structure in iron and glass; this was to be made in factories and finished in six months. It was a most remarkable achievement technically. In its marriage of garden-party elegance and railway engineering it also made clear – to all but the most bigoted – that iron and architecture were not incompatible. Nothing was quite the same again.

295

It was all very disturbing. Ruskin's antipathy to iron and its implications was clear. *The Stones of Venice* had opened with a definition of what 'separates architecture from a rat hole or a railway station'. Viollet-le-Duc had also spoken of iron-roofed markets and stations as being 'only sheds'. They had to think again. Viollet-le-Duc in his *Entretiens* of 1862–72, conceived the idea of a complete iron-framed building, and Ruskin thought that 'there might come a time when there would be new architectural laws'. Even before the Crystal Palace, in 1843–50, Henri Labrouste in Paris used slender cast iron for the columns and vault of the Bibliothèque Ste Geneviève; the exterior is a conventional masonry structure. In 1846, J. B. Bunning designed the London Coal Exchange (now destroyed) with magnificent and

366 The interior of the Coal Exchange, London (1846), shows J. B. Bunning's acceptance of cast iron, not only as a structural convenience – allowing a vast glass roof – but as a legitimate field for the richest ornament

much ornamented ironwork – again within a masonry shell. In 1854 L./A. Boileau, at St/Eugène in Paris, built a large 'Gothic' church in iron, and in 1862 Labrouste repeated his triumph with the reading/room of the Bibliothèque Nationale – a delicate fantasy of thin iron columns and airy domes, once again within masonry shells.

It was Gilbert Scott, speaking of the Crystal Palace, who said that 'this triumph . . . opens up a perfectly new field for architectural development'. That development, however, had to be left to another generation and another continent. Iron – like the arch – was one of the few real revolutions in the long story of architecture. It was not a matter of an occasional *jeu d'esprit* such as the Oxford Museum or the Eiffel Tower. Iron and steel changed the nature of building and, therefore, of cities. It was, however, not until the Chicago architects of the 1880s and 1890s that the breakthrough came to the first steel/framed skyscrapers of urban America . . . to another age. As Waterhouse's career came to a close in the nineties, Louis Sullivan was also building large office

367 Bibliothèque Ste/Geneviève, in Paris (1843–50). Henri Labrouste designed an elegant interior with slender columns and vault of iron – the first interior to be governed by the aesthetic of metal construction

blocks in Chicago; and yet Waterhouse and Sullivan belong to different worlds.

If the English railway station, the Paris markets and the Crystal Palace brought home to the professional architects – bogged down in 'style' – the potentialities of metallic architecture, that was only one consequence of the Great Exhibition. In the *exhibits*, as opposed to the 'Palace' housing them, civilization had reached a nadir in design. Excessive ornament, gross sentimentality and a crass misunderstanding of the processes of mass production were all blatant. It was against all this that the young William Morris (1834–96), and his disciples, reacted so violently. Just as the Gothic Revival had been a romantic reaction against all that the Industrial Revolution stood for – technically and socially – so now, in the second half of the century, the 'cash nexus' of capitalism with all that it implied aroused once again the divine discontent of the artist, caused his flight into the dream-world of the medieval craftsman: Pre-Raphaelite paintings, Rossetti's sonnets, the Kelmscott Press, wonderful textiles, oak furniture, the 'discovery' of the English village, the week-end cottage, the first garden cities and country mansions like medieval farms – but with all the apparatus of luxurious house-parties. The English Arts and Crafts movement, from William Morris to Lutyens, from 1850 to 1914, was a swan-song, a nostalgic postscript to five hundred years of country-house building.

When William Morris came to Oxford in 1853 he revelled in its 'dreaming spires'. His mind, sparked off by the horrors of the 1851 Exhibition, determined to lead England back to an idealized Middle Ages, seen through a golden haze. In the event he succeeded only in printing beautiful books and in producing textiles for that very small minority which had both money and taste. In 1859, however, he commissioned Philip Webb (1831–1915) to build him the Red House at Bexley Heath in Kent. This house is now considered to be an

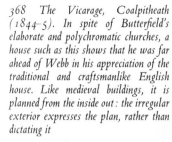

368 The Vicarage, Coalpitheath (1844–5). In spite of Butterfield's elaborate and polychromatic churches, a house such as this shows that he was far ahead of Webb in his appreciation of the traditional and craftsmanlike English house. Like medieval buildings, it is planned from the inside out: the irregular exterior expresses the plan, rather than dictating it

369 Philip Webb's Red House at Bexley Heath (1859–61), built for William Morris, shows a picturesque and romantic grouping of roof and chimneys around the focal point of a well-head. There is practically no ornament or stylistic detail; what there is comes equally from Gothic and from the 17th century

historical landmark. At a time when the West End of London, as well as many country houses, were still being built in debased Palladian stucco, Philip Webb followed the path explored in Butterfield's country vicarages, and used brick, tiles and oak. The house had a few manner-isms – French and Gothic touches – but its justification was its revival of the simple vernacular, the tall chimneys and long ridge lines of the old English farm or manor, with a corresponding integrity of craftsmanship.

Morris and Webb were on the verge of a discovery. With their emphasis upon basic form, sound material and good craftsmanship they might have spotted that stylistic shapes and ornament were the least part of Gothic architecture, just as they might have spotted that iron was beautiful. In the event they did neither, and the modern movement was postponed for half a century.

It was the vernacular theme of the Red House – not its 'functionalism' – that was to assume so many forms in the fifty years that followed. Architects such as Norman Shaw (1831–1912), C. F. A. Voysey (1857–1941) and Sir Edwin Lutyens (1869–1944) handled that theme each in his own manner. These men – together with many others – created a poetic, if not very momentous phase of European architecture. Significantly it is dealt with most fully by Paul Sédille in *L'Architecture moderne en Angleterre* (1890), and by Hermann Muthesius in *Das englische Haus* (1904–5). At least it received European recognition.

Norman Shaw was successful and fashionable. He was no modernist. The nearest he came to it was when he abandoned the literal stylism and High Victorian pomp for something rather more charming, more original. Even so, he ran through the whole gamut of the history books. At Cragside, Northumberland, as early as 1870, he built a fantasia of gables and chimneystacks; at Bryanston in Dorset, in 1889, he produced a megalo-maniac mansion in the style of the age of Wren, splendidly sited on a wooded hill. Towards the end of a prolific career, with public buildings such as the Gaiety Theatre (now demolished) and the Piccadilly Hotel (1905), he gave us a kind of Genoese Baroque pastiche. He was the complete eclectic. His work shows versatility rather than any very sincere architectural conviction.

Sir Edwin Lutyens, with such vast and somewhat arid enterprises as New Delhi to his name, was destined to become something of an 'architect laureate' in England. At the turn of the century, however, he was building for

370 Piccadilly Hotel, London (1905): Norman Shaw's last major work, in which he gave us a powerful – if stylistically mixed – façade, combining Genoese Baroque with Northern Renaissance gables and William-and-Mary windows. The rusticated arches hold their own in the street, while the bedrooms are wisely set back behind the Ionic colonnade

371 *Cragside (1870) is a fantastic pastiche. Shaw here uses every romantic element – gable, half-timber, mullion and so on – to create what is virtually the English equivalent of a Rhine castle on the Northumberland moors*

372 *Bryanston, Blandford (1889), a startling shift in Shaw's style from Cragside. The site is a dramatic one – a wooded hill, now mature. The general mood is pseudo-Queen Anne, with a rather dubious clash in style between the centre and the wings. The banded chimneys are virtually a Shaw trademark*

he aesthetic rich a few dream-like country houses set in wonderful gardens. Among the more famous are Munstead Wood in Surrey (1896), the Deanery Garden at Sonning in Berkshire (1901) and Marshcourt in Hampshire (1901–4). This brief dream was the world of Bernard Shaw's *Heartbreak House*: 'cultured leisured Europe before the [first] war'. It all died, as it should have died, in August 1914.

373 *Deanery Garden, Sonning (1901), one of the most serene of Lutyens's earlier houses. This is the architectural fruit of Morris's revival of craftsmanship, with its impeccably handled brickwork and wooden window-mullions, and also the perfect marriage of house and garden*

C. F. A. Voysey was in a different category. As with Butterfield a generation earlier, integrity and austerity governed all. There was a delightful freshness about his designs for textiles and furniture. He was no prophet of modernism. He shared Morris's respect for tradition, but his frank acceptance of the fact that neither Gothic richness nor Gothic craftsmanship were any longer obtainable gave a curiously functional flavour to his gabled and mullioned houses such as Broadleys on Lake Windermere (1898) or, a few years later, his own house at Chorley Wood in Buckinghamshire. Plain painted woodwork, bright tiles, unpolished oak, square-cut mullions all came as something of a shock in the nineties, while the Belgian designer Henry Van de Velde said of Voysey's wallpapers that 'it was as if Spring had come all of a sudden'.

This curious phase of the vernacular revival in England – and Shaw, Lutyens and Voysey are only a few of those involved – had served only the rich. At the other end of the social scale such architecture was all too easily debased by the speculative builder into that sham Tudor which dominated English suburbia until at least the Second World War. The Victorian Age had seen the building of various tenement blocks – such as those of the Peabody Trust – under philanthropic auspices, but the first systematic municipal attempt to make architecture serve 'the people' came with the found-

374 *Broadleys, Lake Windermere (1898): one of Voysey's best houses, where the low-roofed cosiness of English domesticity is combined with an austerity of detail foreshadowing a more functional style*

ing of the London County Council in 1896, when some municipal housing and, close to the Tate Gallery, some good working-class flats were built under the guidance of W. R. Lethaby. In 1903 the first 'garden city' – Letchworth in Hertfordshire – was founded by Ebenezer Howard and designed by Raymond Unwin and Barry Parker. However, these examples of how planning and 'housing' became more important than great houses belong to another century and to another chapter.

This whole story of English domestic architecture in the half-century that lay between Red House and the first garden city is a curiously interesting interlude. It was compounded, on the one hand, of an almost dream-like conception of the old manor-house and the belief of a wealthy class that that kind of house could be resurrected and refashioned to suit not only the dream but their comforts; on the other hand there was a philanthropic, Fabian and even socialist determination to use archi-tecture as an instrument of social welfare. Neither of these concepts had more than a slight influence upon architecture as we know it in the world today.

The later nineteenth century in America saw the growth of two trends in architecture. On the one hand there was the exploration of new forms and techniques of building, led by the Chicago School; and on the other there was academicism, led by such firms as McKim, Mead and White. Behind both there loomed the giant figure of Henry Hobson Richardson (1838–86), one of the outstanding geniuses of American architecture. Trained at the Ecole des Beaux-Arts in Paris – the main source of American academicism – he is perhaps most famous for the 'Romanesque Revival' initiated by his enthusiasm for the Romanesque of southern France; but whereas few of the architects who joined him in the 'Revival' could dominate the style, Richardson emphatic-ally could. In 1872 he won the competition for Trinity Church, Boston, a fashionable and prominent building that made his reputation. Like all his best work, it show his bold and skillful handling of rugged masonry (I preferred granite), and his powerful sense of compositio His awareness of contemporary English developments shown by the fact that Trinity Church contains stain glass by William Morris's firm. Richardson designed number of buildings in Chicago, including two high original private houses and the Marshall Field Wholes Store (see below p. 308). His genius lay in his ability use historical knowledge in a 'modern' way, by strippi a building of detail in favour of a dominant compo tional theme. It was this that inspired the two m brilliant architects of the Chicago School, Sullivan a Root: they found in Richardson an aesthetic for t modern movement.

Both C. F. McKim and Stanford White, of McKi Mead and White, were trained in Richardson's offi but their role might almost be regarded as that of 'a pioneers'. Stanford White, who had worked w Richardson on Trinity Church, did go further than a English architect of the time towards abandoni historicism in domestic building: there can be precedent for such a design as the low, spreadir enormous-roofed W. G. Low House in Rhode Isla

375 The Great Hall of Pennsylvania Station, New York (1906–10), a major work by the successful firm of McKim, Mead and White: an unabashed reproduction of the main hall of the Thermae of Caracalla (cp. Ill. 40), combined however with an efficient railway station plan

376 *Trinity Church, Boston (1873–77), shows H.H. Richardson's rugged style of masonry – here pink granite trimmed with brownstone – and also his ability to control masses, the almost detached blocks building up to the climax of the tower. The inspiration is clearly Romanesque*

377 *In the Boston Public Library (1888–92) McKim, Mead and White – like Barry in the Reform Club – offer us a most accomplished version of an Italian façade: the range of deep arches owes something to Alberti's Tempio Malatestiano (Ill. 198)*

1887). As Norman Shaw was doing in England, McKim, Mead and White turned increasingly to 'Queen Anne', and to its American equivalent, 'Colonial' architecture of the eighteenth century; gradually they abandoned the picturesque in favour of formality and deliberate imitation of the past. Their commissions included large clubs, the Pierpont Morgan Library (built of solid marble), Pennsylvania Station – as we have seen, a reincarnation of the Baths of Caracalla – and the Boston Public Library. The effect of their fashionable practice was to divert the stream of American architecture away from what the Chicago School stood for, and into the 'Academic Reaction'. In this attitude they belong firmly to the nineteenth century.

So far in this book we have been able to keep architecture in fairly neat national categories. Now we have to give that up, and describe developments that relate equally to the whole world. One may repudiate the term 'international style' since character and climate may always prevent such a thing, but one must proclaim modern architecture as being part of a world culture. The Renaissance, after its birth in Florence, took nearly two centuries to establish itself truly in England. Today any new idea, any technical advance, is planetary knowledge within a week.

It is generally recognized that, if the prehistory of the modern movement lies in Britain – with such unrepeated *tours de force* as the Crystal Palace – it is to the United States that one must turn for the first large-scale and consistent exploitation of the new principles. Within the United States, it was the architects of the Chicago School – William Le Baron Jenney, William Holabird and Martin Roche, Daniel Burnham and John Wellborn Root, Dankmar Adler and Louis Sullivan – who in the space of some twenty years laid the foundations of modern commercial architecture. In Chicago we find the first use of 'skyscraper construction', the first scientifically planned foundations for high buildings, the first systematization of a type of high office block, and the development of aesthetic programmes to suit the new techniques.

Several things contributed to make Chicago the forcing-ground of modern urban building. One was its

378 Marquette Building, Chicago (1894): Holabird and Roche, at an early date, have here recognized that a new form of structure – steel – needs a new form of architecture. The steel frame is fully proclaimed in the grid-like design, though by law it had to be covered by masonry

379 Marshall Field Wholesale Store, Chicago (1885–7), by H. H. Richardson: a lesson in grandeur, if not in technique

380 Auditorium Building, Chicago (1887–9), by Louis Sullivan: the lesson learned and expanded. This large complex building contains a vast auditorium, a hotel and offices, all successfully in use today

emergence as the capital of the Middle West, the city of the Great Lakes, key to the new east–west commercial axis of New York–San Francisco, as opposed to the old north–south cultural axis of Boston–New Orleans. Another factor was the great fire of 1871 which left the smoking ruins of Chicago wide open to any architect of imagination and power, let alone genius. Finally, there was genius, in the person of Louis Sullivan. Sullivan was a great theoretician of architecture, as well as a great architect. He believed that architecture must be democratic; that architects are as important to a democracy as politicians are. Buildings should serve emotional as well as physical needs.

William L. Jenney's approach was different: a strict functionalist, he was concerned with building cheaply and efficiently, and providing the most possible daylight in his office blocks. This led him in 1883 (in the Home Insurance Building) to 'skyscraper construction': the external cladding is carried entirely by means of metal 'shelves' bolted to a central metal core. Sullivan, Burnham, Holabird and Roche were all in Jenney's office at one time or another, but it was Holabird and Roche who followed his principles most closely. Their Tacoma Building of 1889 had a rivetted rather than bolted frame (thus speeding construction), and floated on concrete rafts; grouting of concrete into unreliable subsoil was here done for the first time. Holabird and Roche's masterpiece, the Marquette Building of 1893–4, is sixteen storeys high; its frame construction is expressed by a grid-like elevation with large horizontal windows – the 'Chicago window' with fixed centre and movable sides. This was a formula which the firm repeatedly applied, reducing the wall area and simplifying details.

Burnham and Root's Montauk Block of 1882 was carefully worked out to meet the requirements of a client who saw clearly that 'tall buildings will pay well in Chicago hereafter, and sooner or later a way will be found to erect them'. Soon the architects reached sixteen storeys; the Monadnock Building (1889–91) marked the culmination of masonry construction, with load-bearing brick walls six feet thick at the base. Though higher buildings were possible – elevators had been commonplace for hoisting goods since 1844 in England, and in New York, for passengers, since 1871 – it was obvious that they would have to be metal-framed. Perhaps the most striking building of the Chicago School made full aesthetic use of the metal frame: the Reliance Building, designed after Root's death, was in fact lower than the Monadnock Building, but its display of manifestly non-bearing walls looked forward to the curtain wall.

The aesthetic inspiration of Louis Sullivan was not a glass-and-iron building, but H. H. Richardson's Marshall Field Wholesale Store of 1885–7. It is boldly rusticated and firmly committed to the masonry construction which was so soon to be superseded by steel. A free paraphrase of an Italian Renaissance palace, simplified and enlarged, it covered an entire city block and rose to seven storeys. What impressed Sullivan was its monumental composition, the fact that a commercial building could have such dignity and vitality. Just how deeply Sullivan was impressed appears in the Auditorium Building (1887–9): here is the Marshall Field Store set on a two-storey plinth, augmented at the back by a tower giving further office space.

In 1890 Adler and Sullivan built the ten-storey Wainwright Building in St Louis, and in 1894 the thirteen-storey Guaranty – now Prudential – Building in Buffalo (the Chicago School and its principles were spreading east and west). The walls are no thicker at the bottom than at the top; in the sense in which the word had been used for thousands of years they were not in fact 'walls' at all. On the whole there is a real and impressive attempt to make the masonry look what it is – veneer.

After breaking with Adler in 1895, Sullivan built the Carson Pirie Scott Store in Chicago, extended round

381 Reliance Building, Chicago (1890–94), by D. H. Burnham and Co. An astonishingly modern design, which completely recognized the aesthetic implications of cage construction: large windows stretch between steel piers sheathed in light terracotta

382 *Carson Pirie Scott Store, Chicago (1899–1904). A few years later than the Reliance Building, this work of Sullivan's, in its light, regular frame and broad fenestration, is more truly modern than any other building of the Chicago School*

383, 384 *Opposite: above, 'L'Innovation' in Brussels (1901), by Victor Horta; below, 'La Samaritaine' in Paris (1905), by Frantz Jourdain. Iron is at the same time structural and decorative, holding the glass and swirling round it*

the corner in 1903–4. By and large this building incredible for its date – could have been designed at ar time in the last fifty years and considered a success. accepts, and indeed exploits, all the implications of i structure. The white terracotta sheathing emphasizes th metal frame behind it. Sullivan designed this buildir with Frank Lloyd Wright, an eager draughtsman thirty, at his elbow and at the drawing-board.

One thing at least links Sullivan with Europe: whi he created a new architecture, he also created a new kir of ornament. In realizing the potentialities of ducti metal and convoluted or tense curves, he made some the finest and most sensual ornament of his time. Th ground floor of the Carson Pirie Scott Store, otherwi so austere, glows with that ornament.

There lay the link with Europe. As far back Matthew Digby Wyatt's traceried iron girders Paddington Station in London, of 1852, the idea alrea

sted that iron might be not only structural or even
nitectural, but could also give rise to its own kind of
oration. We find the idea again in the Eiffel Tower in
7, and in some of the big iron and glass department
es, such as Victor Horta's 'A l'Innovation' in
ssels (1901) and Frantz Jourdain's 'La Samaritaine'
?aris (1905). This was indeed one of the aspects of the
vement we call Art Nouveau. We may say, therefore,
Sullivan existed at two levels. As an architectural
ovator he was of the very greatest significance; as a
orative artist he contributed to an ephemeral fashion.
Art Nouveau was part of the modern movement
far as it rejected historical models. Its favourite
amental motif, the swooning, sensuous double curve,
found in the natural forms of plants, the sea, and
ving hair. While architecture could all too easily
enerate into mere interior decoration, it was at its best
ally free from historicism. Its diversity is shown by the
rk of the four greatest architects of the time: Louis
livan, whom we have already seen, in America;
toni Gaudí in Spain; Victor Horta in Belgium, and
arles Rennie Mackintosh in Scotland.

Antoni Gaudí (1852–1926) was a profoundly
gious man, inspired in his work by the Middle Ages
I by nature. He gradually abandoned historicism for
biological' style, a change apparent in the transept of
Sagrada Familia church in Barcelona. Gaudí was
nmissioned in 1883; his early work is still recognizably
thic, though unorthodox. By the time the tops of the
nwork spires were reached in the 1920s, the forms are
que, surrealist, encrusted with coloured ceramic.
e Casa Batlló (1905–7) is faced with strange, bony
ns; its scaly roof changes colour from left to right like
ridescent fish. The façade of the Casa Milá (1905–10)
bles like the sea, and has curious spiky, seaweedy
conies; its internal plan is entirely free, and highly
gular. Parabolic arches, which appear as the doorways
he Palau Güell (1884–9), are at the basis of Gaudí's

385 Crypt of Santa Coloma de Cervelló, the unfinished chapel of the Colonia Güell (1898–1915). Gaudí used a variety of materials to create a deliberately rough effect, and inclined supports to avoid buttresses. The result is both Surrealist and medieval in quality – organic architecture indeed, though far removed from that envisaged by Frank Lloyd Wright

structural innovations. The tiny chapel of the Colo Güell has self-buttressing inclined columns and wa their angles worked out by means of a complex mo with strings and weights. Throughout his life Gaudí v less a modern engineer-architect than a medieval mas mason, working with his builders and improvising ev new solutions on the site.

Victor Horta (1861–1947) exploited the aesthetic metal and glass construction even more than Sulliv Where Sullivan's iron was either functional or decorati Horta's was both; he made an architecture from lang curves, swirling lines and undisciplined motifs. Van Velde, lecturing in 1894, had said that it should possible to create an ornament 'expressive of joy, lassitu protection': this was the aim of Horta. His 'Innovati store in Brussels has been mentioned. The snake-l curves of the metal stair-rail and of the surface decorat in the Tassel House (1892), and the curved surface the façade of the Solvay House (1895), both in Bruss showed new ways to use materials, but their idiosyncr limited their long-term influence. Horta's masterpie the Maison du Peuple of 1896–9, was the culminatio

is metal and glass aesthetic: the entire façade of iron,
glass and brick was set in curving motion, the iron
exposed and not hidden behind masonry as it had been
– by law – in Chicago. Inside in the large auditorium
the exposed iron was given decorative curves; it was not
yet time to be only functional.

'Si j'étais Dieu!' were the words which the French
International Modern architect, Robert Mallet-Stevens,
placed over his door. 'And if you were God?' he
was asked. 'Then', he said, 'I should design like
Mackintosh.' Indeed in his best work Charles Rennie
Mackintosh (1868–1928) left any form of Art Nouveau
far behind. The houses he built outside Glasgow,
especially Windyhill, Kilmacolm (1898) and Hill
House, Helensburgh (1902), had interiors gleaming in
pastel colours and white, with stencilled decoration, and
slender balusters enclosing the stairs. Their exteriors, by
contrast, are as plain as any of Voysey's; like him,
Mackintosh was steeped in the vernacular tradition. As
a decorator Mackintosh was acclaimed at the Vienna
Secessionist Exhibition of 1900, and his influence was
strong in Austria and Germany. He went largely un-
heeded at home, but it is in Glasgow that his greatest
building stands, the School of Art. It was built in two
stages, 1897–9 and 1907–9. The first part is a straight-

386 The unfinished transept of the
Sagrada Familia in Barcelona (begun
1883) is Gaudi's greatest work. As the
church rose through the years it owed
less and less to its original Gothic inspiration until, in the openwork spires,
we see the personal expression of perhaps
the most extreme individualist in all
architecture

387 Maison du Peuple, Brussels (1896–
99), by Victor Horta: Art Nouveau in
league with new techniques. Like 'L'Innovation', it showed what could be done
in iron and glass

388 *Willow Tea Rooms, Glasgow (1903–4). This view down from the gallery shows Mackintosh's use of a screen to create spatial effects; the highly original character of his ornament appears in the metal railings and plaster frieze*

389 *Frank Lloyd Wright built the open-plan Larkin Building at Buffalo, N.Y., early in his career (1904). The strong horizontal lines and plain brick-work, so superbly used in his later work, are already there*

forward piece of work, surprisingly so for the time: big studio windows are frankly expressed and domin the façade; the only touches of Art Nouveau – and tl not, we must remember, the Art Nouveau of Brussels Paris – are a fantastic little turret over the entrance, segmental curve of the door and the iron finials on railings. The library wing of 1907–9 is even more strikii far removed from the 'Scottish Baronial' houses. T library itself became famous for its complex handling space and the rich, dark angularity of its structu outside it is again the windows that dominate, gi oriels running through several floors, foreshadowi functionalism less than the German Expressionism the twenties.

At the same time, in 1908–9, Peter Behrens (186 1940) was building the Berlin Turbine Factory, the ty of building which until then had been regarded as pur utilitarian, a mere shed. Now the big steel-fram windows are set in splendidly monumental masses concrete masonry – almost the last concession to the h torical prestige of the wall. Four years earlier, in Buffa N.Y., Frank Lloyd Wright had built the Larkin Buil ing, with a large central office, top-lit and surrounded galleries. This building, with sheer walls of unreliev brickwork, was externally impressive and even ruthle Internally it is a miracle of spatial unity; Nikola Pevsner even calls it 'ethereal'. Both the Turbine Factc and the Larkin Building clearly exploited the plain sol wall as something powerful and emblematic of t machine age. It was done so well, and was such a whol some break with the stylistically adorned wall, that v accept it. In fact, however, this Egyptian weight masonry was to be the very thing of which, ultimatel modern structure would rid itself. Lightness, a delica web of steel and glass, was already replacing the wa The structural cage was becoming the sign manual of new architecture. That was the next stage.

A triumphant demonstration of this new architectu

390 Glasgow School of Art. Mackintosh built the first section, on the left, in 1897–9. It has minor touches of Art Nouveau decoration, but its big studio windows are frankly functional. The later section of 1907–9, on the right, makes a more dramatic use of form: the library's long iron-framed windows set in plain stone tower up from the steep street

391 For his purely utilitarian Turbine Factory in Berlin (1908–9) Peter Behrens created a great expression of power. The sides consist only of iron and glass, while the corners are formed by massive pylons of poured concrete below a concrete 'pediment'

392 Fagus Factory, Alfeld (1911). Where Behrens had emphasized the corner, Gropius and Meyer abolished it, showing that steel and glass could achieve delicacy as well as strength

the Fagus Factory at Alfeld, design by Walter Gropius and Adolf Meyer in 1911. This went a stage further than had the Chicago engineers: the floors are cantilevered out slightly from the supporting columns, and the whole structure is therefore set back behind the plane of the glass. The wall had finally disappeared. Massive masonry was seen to be not only unnecessary but also aesthetically irrelevant. At each corner of the Fagus Factory glass butts against glass. Also before the First World War Gropius (1883–1969) had written, in the Werkbund year book of 1913, of the 'majesty' of American dams and silos – an almost shocking statement at that date.

It was in 1919, in the hot-house atmosphere of post-war Germany, that Gropius was allowed to combine the Weimar Art School with the School of Arts and Crafts, thus founding the first Bauhaus. Its teachers were artists, architects and craftsmen. It symbolized in educational form the technical actuality of modernism. Whereas to William Morris and his disciples the machine and all that it implied had been anathema, to Gropius the machine was simply a tool. One must design for it, not against it. Its potentialities must be glorified, not minimized.

In 1925 the Bauhaus – accused of 'degeneracy' and 'bolshevism' – was forced to leave Weimar; it was re-established at Dessau, where Gropius built for it a remarkable complex of buildings. The Bauhaus was never specifically a school of architecture, but architecture was always in the air, every craft subordinated to it. Bauhaus influence on architecture has been incalculable. The second Bauhaus was also doomed, brought to an end by Nazism. In 1937 Walter Gropius accepted the Chair of Architecture at Harvard. The Bauhaus was therefore, indirectly, responsible for the emancipation of American architectural education from bondage to the methods of the Ecole des Beaux-Arts, which had stifled the modernism initiated by Sullivan.

393 Bauhaus, Dessau (1925–6), by Walter Gropius. There are three main interconnecting blocks: in the left background the school of design, in front of it the glass-walled workshops wing, and to the right, linked by the auditorium, a six-storey hostel for the students

394 *In the Müller House, Prague (1930), Adolf Loos married his functional and unornamented architecture to a steep site. The masses reflect the different parts of the open-plan house*

In the thirties Gropius brought a new inspiration from Europe to an architecturally flagging America. In the same way, forty years earlier, Adolf Loos (1870–1933) had returned from America bringing the gospel of Sullivan and the Chicago School to a Vienna in the grip of Art Nouveau. There he found support in the functionalist doctrine of Otto Wagner, and preached that lucid architecture is unornamented architecture, which should above all express its purpose. His Steiner House in Vienna, of 1910, was remarkable for its entirely plain rectangular forms, and for the fact that it was built of reinforced concrete. It was also remarkable for its plan: like Frank Lloyd Wright, Loos was fascinated by the open plan, by the possibility of differentiating rooms by their shapes and levels rather than by doors. In his work these themes reached perfection with the Müller House at Prague (1930).

In America, one architect was the heir of the Chicago School: Louis Sullivan's star pupil, Frank Lloyd Wright. In his earliest buildings heavy, round-arched doorways and ornament à la Sullivan appear. Wright soon abandoned these in favour of the development of open-plan, outward-looking houses with long horizontal

317

395, 396 Frank Lloyd Wright: horizontal emphasis in 1904 and 1949.
Above, the Martin House at Buffalo –
in its marriage of building to landscape,
the essence of Wright's 'organic architecture'. Below, the Research Tower of
S. C. Johnson and Son at Racine; core-
and-cantilever construction, used here for
the first time, allows unbroken bands of
window and floor

rows of windows and far-projecting eaves. Outstanding
among these 'Prairie Houses' are the Martin House in
Buffalo (1904) and the Robie House in Chicago (1909).
The more enclosed, blocky tendency in Wright's early
work appears in the Unity Church at Oak Park,
Illinois, of 1906. Wright claimed that it was the first
true monolithic reinforced concrete structure in the
world. This boxy little building, however, hardly took
account of the possibilities of its material. Thirty years
were to pass before Wright built his two great *tours de
force* in reinforced concrete. (The Imperial Hotel in
Tokyo, begun in 1916, did have a concrete construction
that enabled it to survive the great earthquake of 1923;
this has not saved it from the developers.) The first was
the factory for S. C. Johnson and Son (Johnson Wax)
at Racine, Wisconsin (1936–9). The main office was
designed as a large, high hall – a development of the
Larkin Building. Externally the office is of brick, but the
glass ceiling of the hall is supported by very slender
'Minoan' mushroom columns of concrete, of tremendous
grace and beauty. The second *tour de force*, of the same
date, was Falling Waters, the Kaufmann House at Bear
Run, Pennsylvania. Here the rooms are as it were
extended, by means of big cantilevered balconies or
decks, outwards over a waterfall. The strong horizontal
lines of the balconies are contrasted with the more delicate
verticality of the surrounding birch trees. This was a
poetic concept possible only in modern construction.
Ten years later Frank Lloyd Wright exploited the
cantilever even more daringly: in the Research Tower of
Johnson Wax at Racine, each floor is cantilevered out

397 Unity Church, Oak Park (1906), has the wide eaves of Wright's 'Prairie Houses', combined with severe blocky shapes of Egyptian monumentality. The entire building is of concrete poured in moulds

398 This large open office for S.C. Johnson and Son (Racine, 1936–9) was one of Wright's early masterpieces. The beautifully slender mushroom columns – built in defiance of the general opinion that they would never stand – support a most curiously contrived ceiling of glass tubes

399 Kaufmann House, Bear Run (1936). This probably came nearest, of everything Wright built, to true 'organic architecture'. It makes a full use of concrete, but the broad cantilevered balconies are there also as a foil to the delicate tracery of the birch forest

400, 401 Concrete gave new freedom for decoration and for structural innovation. Below: part of the auditorium of Poelzig's Grosses Schauspielhaus, Berlin (1919). Right: the Solomon R. Guggenheim Museum in New York, designed by Frank Lloyd Wright in 1943 (built 1956–9), a powerful single sculptural unit amidst a wilderness of city blocks

from a central core – a principle now commonly used in skyscraper building.

One of Frank Lloyd Wright's last works, the Solomon R. Guggenheim Museum in New York (designed in 1943, built in 1956–9) demonstrates his unflagging vitality and originality. It shows how reinforced concrete could liberate the designer completely from the past. The building is no longer rectangular: a continuous spiral ramp is substituted for the orthodox picture galleries *en suite*. It remains controversial, but externally the broad masculine simplicity of the Guggenheim is a tribute to the man who, fifty years before, had built the Unity Church.

Frank Lloyd Wright's life embraces so long a span that in speaking of his later works we have had to take the whole story of concrete in modern architecture for granted. That story is of the greatest importance, for in spite of the fact that the same architects could, and did, employ both steel and concrete either separately or in combination, the two techniques tended (if the special opportunities of each were to be fully exploited) to lead in different directions. The result is – to put the position simply – that there are now *two* modern architectures. One is the steel and glass classicism of Gropius and Mies van der Rohe, the other is the *béton brut* of Le Corbusier and the 'New Brutalism'.

The principle that concrete can be a rigid curved slab –
in the strict sense neither a lintel nor an arch – goes back
to 1905 when Maillart was building his first graceful
bridges in Switzerland. Gaudi had made full use of the
freedom that concrete could bring, but as the swooning
curves of Art Nouveau faded from the scene, this freedom
assumed yet another form: Expressionism. In 1919 Hans
Poelzig remodelled the Grosses Schauspielhaus in
Berlin, in which the audience sat beneath a fantastic roof
of stalactites; these stalactites were possible only in reinforced concrete. The next year Erich Mendelsohn –
usually an architect of restraint – designed the Einstein
Observatory Tower near Potsdam. This building, with
its then fashionable streamlining, rounded corners, etc.,
ironically became a popular symbol of modernism:
ironically, because in fact the technique and economics
of reinforced concrete at that date could not cope with
Mendelsohn's freely sketched forms; the building was of
brick plastered over to look like concrete!

During the twenties concrete found an evangelist in
Auguste Perret. In 1922 he designed a church at Le
Raincy, near Paris. He was inspired by the medieval
lantern churches, by such Gothic structures as the Sainte
Chapelle where the tracery windows occupy the whole
wall so that the worshipper is, as it were, within a
coloured casket. At Le Raincy Perret used concrete to
achieve a similar effect. He built vaults of a flat segmental
form resting on very slender columns – a possibility only

*402 Einstein Observatory Tower,
Neubabelsberg (1919–21), by Erich
Mendelsohn: propaganda for new, mainly
streamlined, forms in design rather than
a technical achievement in itself*

*403 Notre Dame, Le Raincy (1922),
by Auguste Perret, a 20th-century
Sainte-Chapelle in concrete*

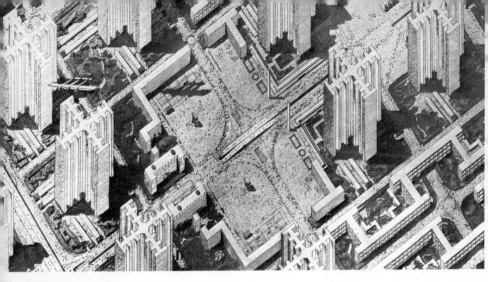

404, 405 Le Corbusier's ideal city, on paper and in 'béton brut'. The 'Plan Voisin' for Paris (1925, detail above) involved building high 'point blocks' – with every wing fully lit – in order to liberate the ground for trees, grass, schools and recreation. At Marseilles he intended the 'Unité' (1947–52, below) to be one of eight similar blocks rising on 'pilotis' among trees

in concrete. He then built the 'walls' as a continuous concrete grille filled with stained glass. The building thus achieves its 'Gothic' objective through what was at that date an advanced use of a new material.

The imaginative use of concrete reaches its climax in the work of Le Corbusier (1887–1965). In 1923 Le Corbusier, virtually proscribed by his colleagues, resorted to his pen. In *Vers une Architecture* and *La Ville Radieuse* he produced two powerful pieces of propaganda. Adolf Loos, years before, had uttered his famous dictum,

'the engineers are our Hellenes'. It was for Le Corbusier to demonstrate the truth of this, to state implicitly what Adolf Loos had only dimly realized, that liners and typewriters were better designed than most architecture. In *La Ville Radieuse* and other books he turned also to the art of town planning. His 'Plan Voisin' for Paris (1925) was a brilliant fantasy – although it seems rather less fantastic now than it did forty years ago – but it was he who saw that skyscrapers might be useful not only because, as in New York, they exploited land values, but because, widely spaced among trees and lakes, they could give back the space they had saved, thus enabling ordinary people to live with light, air and foliage. It was a tremendous idea, scarcely realized even now, although there are a few housing projects in the world – such as London's Roehampton Estate of 1952-9 – where Le Corbusier's theory has been the starting-point of a plan.

Towards the realization of his vision of how men might live in cities, Le Corbusier contributed a number of 'Unités d'Habitation' – in Marseilles (1947-52), Nantes (1952-7), etc. The 'Unité' at Marseilles is a seventeen-storey building, with its own shops, restaurant, roof-top crêche and gymnasium. It has an ingenious arrangement of duplex apartments, on two storeys, with double-height living rooms whose 15-foot-high windows look out either to the Mediterranean or to the mountains: self-contained and private villas in the air. Externally the bare concrete is relieved by a system of squares of primary colour. The whole building is raised on gargantuan pylons or *pilotis*; aesthetically the essence of the design lies in the contrast between the rich textural façade of balconied windows and the primeval scale of these *pilotis*. This indeed is an artist using concrete.

It was in the sculptural quality of his concrete, combined with a great sensitivity for composition, that Le Corbusier ranked as a master; this appears most clearly in his later buildings, such as the Monastery of La Tourette (1957-60) and the Carpenter Center for the

406 Roehampton Estate, London (1952-9), designed by the London County Council Architects' Department, is a practical and economic interpretation of the 'Plan Voisin' and 'Ville Radieuse' theory. Tower blocks, mingled with lower housing, stand far apart in the mature gardens of demolished villas

323

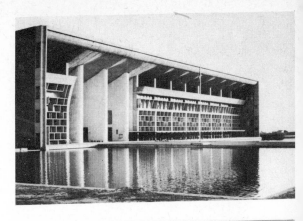

407 In the Law Courts at Chandigarh (1952–6) Le Corbusier used concrete to achieve a pattern of rich textures and forms. The design is also highly functional, the open grilles letting air into the court-rooms

408 The pilgrimage church at Ronchamp (1950–4) is the humblest and perhaps the most moving of Le Corbusier's buildings. The inter-related curves of eaves and walls combine to create a sculptural unity. The concrete is rough ('brut'), the windows placed with a calculated irregularity

Visual Arts at Harvard (1962). Note, for instance, at the Chandigarh Law Courts, the contrast between the large, smooth and well-shaped columns flanking the entrance, and the rich grille which forms the rest of the façade; note the subtly contrasted curves of the walls of the little pilgrimage church at Ronchamp (1950–4) as against the broad outward curve of the eaves, and the tiny irregular windows in the broad white spaces of the concrete. The actual surface of Le Corbusier's concrete is left rough, just as it emerges when the timber shuttering is removed – a rather affected emphasis on how an aesthetic is born of a technique. This mannerism has now become commonplace.

That free and fantastic shapes can be created in concrete does not mean that such shapes are always
appropriate. Concrete can indeed be used with all the
restraint of steel, or stone. In 1932–6, for instance –
contrary to the whole cultural ethos of Fascism –
Giuseppe Terragni built the Casa del Fascio in Como,
one of the simplest, clearest architectural statements
imaginable, worthy of Mies van der Rohe in steel. The
same may be said of the very moving but very subdued
Stockholm Crematorium, in its splendid landscape,
designed by Gunnar Asplund in 1935.

The combination of bold engineering with the
Expressionist shapes made possible by concrete has
produced some of the most exciting buildings of the
modern movement. Pier Luigi Nervi (born 1891)
prefers to call himself an engineer. His stadium at

*409 The Casa del Fascio, Como
(1932–6), by Giuseppe Terragni, not
only defies the pompous stylism of the
Mussolini regime; it also defies the
plastic qualities of concrete in favour of an
absolutely pure geometric statement,
equally appropriate in steel*

410, 411 *Pier Luigi Nervi: archi-tecture born of pure structure. Below right, the Communal Stadium at Florence (1930–2); right, the 'rib-vaulted' hangar at Orbetello (1938)*

412 *In the church of the Miraculous Virgin, Mexico City (1954), Candela used concrete shell vaults of hyperbolic paraboloid form, visually Expressionist but structurally logical: they are self-buttressing (cp. Ill. 385), and need only straight shuttering*

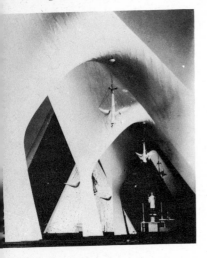

Florence (1930) has a scissor-like structure and a roof cantilevered 50 feet out over the seating. His hangar at Orbetello (1938) is 300 feet long with a 120-foot span, while the first Exhibition Hall at Turin has a span of nearly 300 feet. Nervi's culminating achievement to date is probably the circular covered arena for the Olympic Games in Rome. Most concrete vaults (e.g. Le Raincy, or the factory at Brynmawr in Wales roofed by the Architects' Co-Partnership with nine domes each 90 feet across and 2 inches thick) are poured on to continuous shuttering, and therefore have smooth, unbroken soffits. In Nervi's work, on the other hand, we find that roofs and domes are extremely complicated – a beautiful network of ribs effecting both a saving in shuttering and the pouring of concrete. We can almost say that in the space of a lifetime Nervi has guided this ribbed construction through a process of evolution not unlike that of medieval architecture as, in the course of some four hundred years, it passed from the heavy arches of Romanesque to the delicate tracery of Flamboyant Gothic.

Experiments with concrete vaults, and shapes of all kinds, have been unlimited. Only a few can be noted. Among the most exciting of the vaults – in some ways harking back half a century to Gaudí – are the spiky, macabre, jagged creations of Felix Candela, especially as we see them in his church of the Miraculous Virgin in Mexico City (1953–5). More sober, but very successful, is the big curved canopy which forms the entrance to the railway station in Rome (1951), linking the street with the elegant but more straightforward concourse. In Sweden, at Luleå, Ralph Erskine designed the Sub-Arctic Shopping Center (1963), a large complex containing a most remarkable cinema, a dimly-lit concrete cavern with the projection room suspended within it.

413 Cinema in the Sub-Arctic Shopping Center, Luleå (1963), by Ralph Erskine. A thin, smooth-walled concrete shell, acoustically designed, encloses the audience. Here its light-coloured interior is glimpsed through curved openings in the dark-painted 'ambulatory'. Light effects can be produced on the walls by spotlights near the screen. At the opposite end (right), the projection room is suspended

All over the world are innumerable office and apart-
ment buildings; the vast majority – as in all ages – are
mediocre or routine buildings, but one may mention
the Ministry of Education at Rio de Janeiro, designed in
1937 by Lúcio Costa and Oscar Niemeyer; the
UNESCO Building in Paris by Breuer, Zehrfuss and
Nervi; the Arena at Raleigh, North Carolina (1950)
by Nowicki and Dietrick; the Reynolds Aluminum
Building in Detroit (1959) by Minoru Yamasaki; the
New York State Theater at Lincoln Center, New York
(1962–4) by Philip Johnson; the Tyrone Guthrie
Theatre, Minneapolis (1961–3) by Ralph Rapson;
Dulles International Airport, Washington (1959–6?)
by Eero Saarinen; St Catherine's College, Oxford (196?)
by the Danish architect, Arne Jacobsen; the Art
Building at Yale University (1961–3) by Paul Rudolph;
the Cultural Centre at Wolfsburg in Germany (196?)
by Alvar Aalto; the Philharmonie, Berlin (1964) by
Hans Scharoun; the United States embassies in London
(1955–61) by Eero Saarinen, and in Dublin (1963) by
John M. Johansen. The last two are both built of pre-cast
concrete sections, each section a window unit; both
embassies are unusual in that they attempt – from
diplomatic courtesy – to harmonize their scale with
eighteenth-century cities ... with only qualified success.

Saarinen designed through paper models instead of
the drawing-board: the right angle and the façade have

*414 Ministry of Education, Rio de
Janeiro (1937–43), designed by Costa
and Niemeyer with Le Corbusier as
consultant. This building, with its rich
'brise soleil' grid, shows how refinement
can lift the standardized world office
block to a new level*

*415 The Reynolds Aluminum Build-
ing at Detroit (1959), by Minoru
Yamasaki, shows the enrichment and
glamour given to buildings in the second
generation of the style still popularly
called 'functional'. The screen façade is
virtually a trade-mark of Yamasaki;
here it is, appropriately, of aluminium*

416 *Tyrone Guthrie Theatre, Minneapolis (1961–3). Ralph Rapson here tackled the old problem of how, externally, to give unity to the awkward forms of auditorium and stage, solving it with a symphony of slender concrete planes and fins*

417 *Yale University Art and Architecture Building, New Haven (1961–63), by Paul Rudolph. A forceful composition of towers framing in the big studio windows (compare Mackintosh's solution of a similar problem, Ill. 390). The smoothness of the glass wall is rejected in favour of something more rugged and idiosyncratic*

418 *United States Embassy, Dublin (1963), by John M. Johansen. Another approach to building in concrete: the wall is built up of regular pre-cast sections. It rests, however, on a fortress-like, rusticated basement. The circular plan resolved the problem of an awkward site*

329

419 *TWA Terminal, Kennedy Airport, New York (1956–62). Concrete is here used sculpturally to express movement and spatial freedom. Saarinen made models rather than drawings, realizing that with concrete one no longer designs with walls and arches, but with wings*

lost significance. His TWA Building at Kennedy Airpo is remarkable not only for its wing-shaped roof – seagull in flight – but also internally for its spatial effec It does not have rooms or halls; it has spatial volum flowing into each other. About the same time the Danis architect Jörn Utzon won the competition for Sydne Opera House with a roof consisting of half a dozen va shell-like sails of concrete faced with white mosaic. Th building now rides high like a great galleon above th harbour in which it is reflected.

420 *Sydney Opera House (begun 1959; model). Jörn Utzon uses the wing motif of the TWA Terminal, but not to enclose space. It is used for its own sake, as a medieval builder might use towers, for its tremendous effect on a particular site*

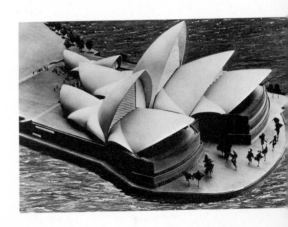

The corresponding list of buildings exploiting the use
of steel must be rather shorter. The greatest master of the
aesthetic of steel is no doubt Mies van der Rohe (born
1888). Like Gropius, Mies was an émigré from the staff
of the Bauhaus. As early as 1929, in the German
Pavilion of the Barcelona Exhibition, we can see the
restraint, austerity and quality of his work. The more
sophisticated but no less austere use of the geometry of
the steel frame is later evident in a whole series of buildings:
the Farnsworth House, Illinois (1950), Lake Shore
Drive Apartments, Chicago (1952), Crown Hall at the
Illinois Institute of Technology, Chicago (1956), the
Seagram Building in New York (1956–8), and the
Bacardi Offices in Mexico City (1963) – all chaste
essays on the theme of the framed rectangle. In the
achievement of beauty by the rejection not only of
ornament but of every superfluity, one recalls Mies van
der Rohe's aphorism, 'Less is More'.

The elegant distinction, the Grecian purity, imparted
to buildings in what one might call the 'Miesian'
tradition is very great; opportunities for variation upon
the theme – let alone violent originality of the Gaudí or
Candela type – are rather less. Second only to Mies van
der Rohe one must place the large American firm of
Skidmore, Owings and Merrill; with big offices in many

421, 422 *Two of Mies van der Rohe's
essays in the use of fine steelwork to
enclose and outline carefully proportioned
and related rectangles. Left, the Bacardi
offices in Mexico City (1963): steel
liberates interior space. Above, the
Seagram Building in New York (designed with Philip Johnson, 1956–8):
major and minor vertical divisions subtly
articulate a vast surface; at ground level
there is no podium, valuable ground being
instead given over to an open plaza*

423 *Lever Building, New York (1952), by Gordon Bunshaft of Skidmore, Owings and Merrill. A Mies-inspired and much-imitated combination of a curtain-walled office tower with a low podium (containing forecourt, restaurant and shops)*

424 *General Motors Technical Center, near Detroit (1951–5), by Saarinen. One of several formal blocks set in a formal landscape*

cities this firm is a phenomenon that would have astounded all earlier centuries. In 1952 one of the partners of this firm, Gordon Bunshaft, gave to New York in the Lever Building its then most distinguished high-rise building; it has great clarity of design, and it incorporates a small but charming garden court which set a precedent that may lift New York to a new level among world capitals. The Lever Building, sheathed in green glass, remained the most distinguished building for five years; it was then excelled by Mies van der Rohe's Seagram Building, sheathed in brown glass and bronze.

To Skidmore, Owings and Merrill we owe the impressive and impressively sited United States Air Force Academy at Colorado Springs, and the chaste even aristocratic, United Airlines Offices at Chicago (1963). Steel and glass houses – ever since Mies' Farnsworth House and the Philip Johnson house at New Canaan, Conn., both in the late forties – have been legion. The most evocative is Craig Elwood's Rosen House at Santa Monica, California (1965) where the rooms are grouped around a small court with an old tree in the centre. The Town Hall at Rødovre, Denmark (1955–6) by Arne Jacobsen is another excellent example of the Miesian clarity and austerity, an essay in pure geometry. The largest building in this idiom is the complex of the General Motors Technical Center near Detroit where, in front of the uncompromising severity of the buildings, Saarinen has designed a broad landscape of lawns, pools and sculpture.

In England a new attitude appeared in the early fifties influenced partly by Le Corbusier's theory and his Unité at Marseille. In their school at Hunstanton (1949–53) Peter and Alison Smithson demonstrated their intention to use steel architecturally, but without the formalism of Mies. The plumbing and engineering are fully exposed on the basis that in great design, whether of ships or cathedrals, technique and art had always been indistinguishable. In fact this school has the beauty of th

425 U.S. Air Force Academy, Colorado Springs (1959). Skidmore, Owings and Merrill here set a large group of buildings of the most austere form on a rocky and mountainous site. One thinks of the Egyptian temple at Deir el-Bahari (Ill. 11)

426 Philip Johnson House, New Canaan (1949). This is the Miesian approach to the purest use of glass and steel: a glass box for living in, justified by its setting in lake and woodland

427 Rødovre Town Hall (1955–6), by Arne Jacobsen. A pure geometric relationship, unelaborated, between the large office building, all glass, and the smaller council chamber, all wall

428 Hunstanton School (1949–53), by Peter and Alison Smithson. This is the Miesian idiom, but with the charm of refinement deliberately omitted to achieve an 'honest' architecture

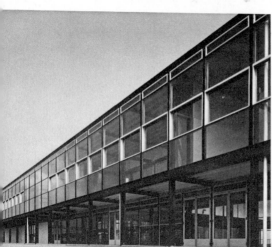

battleship rather than the liner. This gave rise to the phrase 'the New Brutalism' – both a pun on Le Corbusier's *béton brut* (shuttered concrete) and a reference to the Smithsons' anti-formalist principles.

A concise survey of architecture must on the whole limit itself to great buildings designed for great purposes. Two things, however, become obvious. One is that this chapter – the world scene over scarcely more than eighty years – has given us a much more crowded canvas; the other is that throughout history the vernacular – house, cottage, farm and village – had been a craft, with its own skills and traditions, to be considered separately from 'architecture'. Today this is no longer true. Modern techniques, whether steel or concrete, are now being used to solve housing problems all over the world. Great architects are designing for the needs of an expanding population.

It is not possible to deal fully with this separate theme. English legislation, establishing a number of 'New Towns', was probably the first post-war move. It came too soon; it must be recorded that these twelve towns, with one or two exceptions such as Cumbernauld, near Glasgow, merely echo the old pattern of the Garden City of the beginning of the century.

Japan has the most acute population problem in the world. The 1960 project for Tokyo by the Kenzo Tange Team envisages a long-term redevelopment of the city itself, as well as its imaginative expansion on a network of bridges and causeways across Tokyo Bay. Helix City, by Noriaki Kurokawa, is another Tokyo project with helical or corkscrew-shaped towers. Most imaginative of all, however – if still only a hypothesis – is Ocean City by Kiyonori Kikutake, which is conceived as a series of circular towers on artificial off-shore islands . . . poetic and enchanting and surely not impractical.

Cities such as Coventry or Rotterdam are sincere but not very inspired attempts – conceived twenty years ago – to rebuild bombed cities with some separation of cars and

429 Tokyo project (1960), by the Kenzo Tange Team. An interesting attempt to take the Le Corbusier planning concept of 'point blocks' widely spaced, and the U.S. Highway system, and to rationalize them both into a single architectural unity

430 *Ocean City (1958), Kiyonori Kikutake's tremendous project for towers on artificial islands. The circular tower may be the most logical ultimate form of the 'point block' (see the Marina Towers, Chicago), as the ocean may prove to be the logical place for cities of the future*

pedestrians. Cities actually planned *de novo* for th
automobile are Cumbernauld and Brasilia, the nev
capital of Brazil designed by Lúcio Costa and Osca
Niemeyer. Brasilia is still far from complete. Some tw
hundred thousand live in the Federal District, but ther
are still vast empty spaces and arid tracts, planned but nc
built. However the formal and monumental nature c
the finest of the capitals established by *fiat* (the others bein
St Petersburg, Washington, Canberra, New Delhi an
Chandigarh and, in the ancient world, Byzantium
emerges magnificently. The Planalto Palace, with i
graceful loggia of columns like swans' necks around th
central two-level core, is a fine essay in concrete, and wa
the first of the buildings of Brasilia. The main centre c
the city, forming the great panorama, sets in carefu
juxtaposition as well as in geometric contrast the lov
ministry buildings, the tall twin towers of Congress, th

431 *Detail of the Alvorado Palace,
Brasilia, by Oscar Niemeyer. It has a
sculptural concrete loggia like that of the
Planalto Palace, and a chapel shaped
like a shell*

owl and the dome of the arena and the assembly, and
e cathedral. Brasilia has a long way to go before it can
en look finished, but for the next generation it may yet
e the justification of our own.

Lastly, one must ask whether or not, even within this
etwork of world traditions, there is to be found the
mergence of a world style, or at least a world approach.
urely there is. Like all great architectures such a style
ust emerge primarily from the nature of its own epoch,
nly secondarily from the whim or genius of its designers.
strictly scientific analysis of function and human
abits, followed by an architectural interpretation,
hether in concrete or steel, must produce a total solution
a problem. This does not actually necessitate any
gard for tradition or any repudiation of it; one way or
nother the result is certainly a style. It is in fact, despite
s gaucheries, a tremendous style, as brutal as that of
ome, but virile to the last degree. This is a judgement
y which one may stand or fall.

432 *At Brasilia, Niemeyer's buildings
rise upon Costa's sophisticated plan of
1956. Set in a horizontal landscape,
they make use of dramatic contrasts of
form, as in the twin office towers of
Congress set against the 'bowl' housing
the Chamber of Deputies*

A SHORT BIBLIOGRAPHY

General

BACON, E. N. *Design of Cities*. London, 1967
BRIGGS, M. S. *The Architect in History*. Oxford, 1927
FLETCHER, B. *A History of Architecture*, 17th ed. London and New York, 1961
PEVSNER, N. *An Outline of European Architecture*, Jubilee ed. Harmondsworth, 1960

The Ancient World

ANDERSON, W. J. and SPIERS, R. P., rev. W. B. DINSMOOR. *The Architecture of Ancient Greece*. London, 1927
  The Architecture of Ancient Rome. London, 1927
BELL, E. *Hellenic Architecture*. London, 1920
BERVE, H., GRUBER, G. and HIRMER, M. *Greek Temples, Theatres and Shrines* London, 1963
BOWRA, C. M. *The Greek Experience*. London, 1957
CHILDE, G. *What Happened in History*. Harmondsworth, 1942
DINSMOOR, W. B. *The Architecture of Ancient Greece*. London and New York, 1950
GRANT, M. *The World of Rome*. London, 1960
LAWRENCE, A. W. *Greek Architecture*. Harmondsworth, 1957
ROBERTSON, D. S. *A Handbook of Greek and Roman Architecture*, 2nd ed. Cambridge 1943
SMITH, W. S. *The Art and Architecture of Ancient Egypt*. Harmondsworth, 1958
WHEELER, M. *Roman Art and Architecture*. London, 1964

Byzantine, Romanesque and Gothic

BRAUN, H. S. *The English Castle*, 3rd ed. London, 1948
CLAPHAM, A. W. *English Romanesque Architecture*, 2 vols. Oxford, 1930–4
CONANT, K. J. *Carolingian and Romanesque Architecture: 800–1200*. Harmondsworth 1959
DAVIS, J. G. *The Origin and Development of Early Christian Church Architecture*. London 1952
EVANS, J. *Life in Medieval France*, rev. ed. London, 1957
  The Romanesque Architecture of the Order of Cluny. Cambridge, 1938
FRANKL, P. *Gothic Architecture*. Harmondsworth, 1962
GRABAR, A. *Byzantium*. London, 1966
HARVEY, J. *Gothic England*, 2nd ed. London, 1948
  The Gothic World. London, 1950

HEER, F. *The Medieval World 1100–1350*. London, 1961

KRAUTHEIMER, R. *Early Christian and Byzantine Architecture*. Harmondsworth, 1965

LASTEYRIE, R. DE *L'Architecture religieuse en France à l'époque romane*, 2nd ed. Paris, 1929
   L'Architecture religieuse en France à l'époque gothique, 2 vols. Paris, 1926–7

LETHABY, W. R. and SWANSON, H. *The Church of St Sophia*. London, 1894

RICE, D. T. *The Art of Byzantium*. London, 1959

WEBB, G. *Architecture in Britain: The Middle Ages*. Harmondsworth, 1956

Renaissance to Classicism

BLUNT, A. *Art and Architecture in France: 1500–1700*. Harmondsworth, 1953

BURCKHARDT, J. *The Civilisation of the Renaissance in Italy*. London, 1944

HEMPEL, E. *Baroque Art and Architecture in Central Europe*. Harmondsworth, 1965

KAUFMANN, E. *Architecture in the Age of Reason*. Harvard U.P., 1955
   'Three Revolutionary Architects: Boullée, Ledoux and Lequeu', in *Transactions of the American Philosophical Society*, New Series, Vol. 42, 1952

KUBLER, G. and SORIA, M. *Art and Architecture in Spain and Portugal and their American Dominions: 1500–1800*. Harmondsworth, 1959

MURRAY, P. *The Architecture of the Italian Renaissance*, rev. ed. London, 1969

PEVSNER, N. 'The Architecture of Mannerism', in *The Mint,* 1946

PINDER, W. *Deutscher Barock*, 2nd ed. Königstein, 1924

SUMMERSON, J. *Architecture in Britain: 1530–1830*, 3rd ed. Harmondsworth, 1969

WITTKOWER, R. *Architectural Principles in the Age of Humanism*, 3rd ed. London, 1962
   Art and Architecture in Italy: 1600–1750. Harmondsworth, 1958

Nineteenth and Twentieth Centuries

BANHAM, R. *Theory and Design in the First Machine Age*. London, 1960

CLARK, K. *The Gothic Revival*, 2nd ed. Harmondsworth, 1950

CONDIT, C. W. *American Building Art. The Nineteenth Century*. New York, 1960

GIEDION, S. *Space, Time and Architecture*, 3rd ed. Oxford and Harvard U.P., 1954

HATJE, G., ed. *Encyclopedia of Modern Architecture*. London 1963

HITCHCOCK, H. R. *Architecture: Nineteenth and Twentieth Centuries*, 2nd ed. Harmondsworth, 1963
   Early Victorian Architecture in Britain, 2 vols. New Haven and London, 1954

JOEDICKE, J. *A History of Modern Architecture*. London, 1959

JORDAN, R. FURNEAUX *Victorian Architecture*. Harmondsworth, 1966

PEVSNER, N. *Pioneers of Modern Design*, rev. ed. Harmondsworth, 1968

RICHARDS, J. M. *An Introduction to Modern Architecture*, rev. ed. Harmondsworth, 1959
   The Functional Tradition in Early Industrial Buildings. London, 1958

SMITH, G. E. KIDDER *The New Architecture of Europe*. London, 1962

LIST OF ILLUSTRATIONS

Sources of photographs are given in italic

96 Annaberg, Germany; interior of St Anne, looking east; by Conrad Schwarz, Meister Erasmus and Jacob von Schweinfurt, 1499–1525. *Deutsche Fotothek, Dresden*

97 Brixworth (Northamptonshire), England: interior of All Saints' Church, looking west; *c.*680 and after. The Saxon arches (with Roman brick voussoirs) were blocked by Norman masons. *Edwin Smith*

98 Dingle (Co. Kerry) Ireland: Gallarus Oratory; probably 7th C. *Edwin Smith*

99 Venasque (Vaucluse), France: interior of one apse of the baptistery; 6th C. *Jean Roubier*

100 Lorsch, Germany: abbey gatehouse; *c.*800. *Helga Schmidt-Glassner*

101 Aachen, Germany: Palatine Chapel, looking west; 792–805. *Harald Busch*

102 Maria Laach, Germany: view of the abbey church from the north-west; 1093–1156. *Bildarchiv Foto Marburg*

103 Gloucester Cathedral, England: nave, looking east; begun 1087. *Sydney Pitcher, Gloucester*

104 Diagram showing the need for centering in unmoulded and moulded arches. Drawn by Jon Broome

105 Quedlinburg (Saxe-Anhalt), Germany: nave of the abbey church; consecrated 1129. *Harald Busch*

106 Santiago de Compostela Cathedral, Spain: nave; *c.*1075–1150. *Mas*

107 Southwell Minster (Nottinghamshire), England: view south-east in the nave; *c.*1130. *National Monuments Record*

108 Auxerre Cathedral (Yonne), France: interior of the crypt, looking east; *c.*1030. *Bildarchiv Foto Marburg*

109 Mainz Cathedral, Germany: interior, looking east; 11th C. and after 1181. *Martin Hürlimann*

110 St-Martin-du-Canigou (Pyrénées-Orientales), France: monastery from the south; 1001–26. The buildings have since been further restored. *Archives Photographiques*

111 St-Martin-du-Canigou (Pyrénées-Orientales), France: interior of the abbey church, looking east; 1001–26. There are windows only at either end. *Archives Photographiques*

112 Ideal plan for the monastery of St Gall, Switzerland; *c.*820. Redrawn from the original in the Stiftsbibliothek, St Gallen

113 Tournus (Saône-et-Loire), France: plan of the crypt of St-Philibert; *c.*950. From N. Pevsner, *An Outline of European Architecture*, Jubilee ed., 1960, by courtesy of Penguin Books

114 Tournus (Saône-et-Loire), France: detail of St-Philibert, showing vaulting of nave and aisle; vaults early 11th and early 12th C. *Jean Roubier*

115 Cluny (Saône-et-Loire), France: reconstructed plan of the monastery in the 12th C. *By courtesy of Professor Kenneth J. Conant and the Mediaeval Academy of America*

116 Cluny (Saône-et-Loire), France: reconstruction model of the third church, seen from the south-east; begun *c.*1088. *Archives Photographiques*

117 Paray-le-Monial (Saône-et-Loire), France: interior of the abbey church, looking east; *c.*1100. *Jean Roubier*

118 Vézelay (Yonne), France: interior of the abbey church of La Madeleine, looking east; nave *c.*1104–30, choir early 13th C. *Archives Photographiques*

119 Santiago de Compostela Cathedral, Spain: plan; *c.*1075–1150

120 Toulouse (Haute-Garonne), France: St-Sernin from the east; begun *c.*1080. *Giraudon*

121 Pontigny (Yonne), France: Cistercian abbey church from the south-east; 1140–1210. *Jean Roubier*

122 Fontenay (Yonne), France: interior of the Cistercian abbey church, looking east; 1139–47. *Archives Photographiques*

123 Jerichow (Brandenburg), Germany: interior of the Premonstratensian abbey church, looking east; *c.*1200. *Harald Busch*

124 Monreale Cathedral, Sicily: central eastern apse; begun 1174. *Hans Decker*

125 St-Gilles-du-Gard (Gard), France: west portals of the church; finished c. 1170. *Jean Roubier*

126 Jumièges (Seine-Maritime), France: ruins of the abbey church of Notre-Dame, looking west across the transept to the nave; 1037–66. *Jean Roubier*

127 Durham Cathedral, England: nave vaults; c. 1130. *Jean Roubier*

128 Caen (Calvados), France: west front of St-Etienne (Abbaye-aux-Hommes); begun c. 1068. *Bildarchiv Foto Marburg*

129 Ely Cathedral (Cambridgeshire), England: nave; begun c. 1110. *Edwin Smith*

130 Florence, Italy: interior of S. Miniato al Monte, looking east; c. 1073. *Hans Decker*

131 Milan, Italy: interior of S. Ambrogio, looking east; choir c. 940, nave begun c. 1080. *Mansell-Alinari*

132 Rheims Cathedral (Marne), France: detail of south side of the nave; begun c. 1210. *Jean Roubier*

133 Loches (Indre-et-Loire), France: castle from the south-east, showing the curtain wall and keep; c. 1100 and after. From an old photograph

134 Bruges, Belgium: Cloth Hall; 14th–15th C. *Martin Hürlimann*

135 Long Melford (Suffolk), England: stained glass figure of Thomas Peyton from the east window of the church; 15th C. *Alfred Lammer*

136 Rheims Cathedral (Marne), France: west front, before World War I; begun c. 1229. *ND-Giraudon*

137 Kuttenberg (Kutná Horá), Czechoslovakia: vaults in St Barbara; apse vault 1489–1506, continued by Benedikt Ried 1512–47. *Bildarchiv Foto Marburg*

138 Beauvais Cathedral (Oise), France: air view from the south; officially begun 1225, main work begun 1247, left unfinished in 1568. *Aero-Photo, Paris*

139 Diagram showing the development of vaulting. Drawn by Jon Broome

140 St-Denis (near Paris), France: view of the ambulatory and chapels in the abbey church; 1140–3. *Archives Photographiques*

141 St-Denis (near Paris), France: plan of the abbey church; narthex and chevet, c. 1134–44, the rest mid-13th C.

142 Chartres Cathedral (Eure-et-Loir), France: west front; north tower begun 1134, south tower begun 1142, Portail Royal and lancet windows above it c. 1145–50; rose window and gable built after the fire of 1194; north spire 1507. *Bulloz*

143 Chartres Cathedral (Eure-et-Loir), France: north transept, looking north-east; begun 1194. *Martin Hürlimann*

144 Wells Cathedral (Somerset), England: west front; second quarter of the 13th C. *Martin Hürlimann*

145 Amiens (Somme), France: view of the town and cathedral from the west, before World War I. From an old photograph

146 Bourges Cathedral (Cher), France: view of the south side of the nave, showing double aisles; 1192–1266. *Jean Roubier*

147 Noyon Cathedral (Oise), France: interior, looking east; begun c. 1150. *Martin Hürlimann*

148 Beauvais Cathedral (Oise), France: interior of the choir, looking east from the crossing; 1225/47–72 (see Ill. 138), vaults rebuilt after collapse in 1284. *Bulloz*

149–151 Comparative plans to scale of St Elisabeth, Marburg; Amiens Cathedral and Salisbury Cathedral

152 Canterbury Cathedral (Kent), England: choir; by William of Sens and William the Englishman, 1175–84. *Martin Hürlimann*

153 Wells Cathedral (Somerset), England: view north across the nave; cathedral begun c. 1190, nave built in the first third of the 13th C. *A. F. Kersting*

154 Salisbury (Wiltshire), England: air view of the cathedral and close from the south-east; cathedral begun 1220, upper part of tower and spire begun 1334. *Aerofilm Ltd*

155 Salisbury Cathedral (Wiltshire), England: nave, looking east; second quarter of the 13th C. *Edwin Smith*

156 Amiens Cathedral (Somme), France: interior, looking east; upper sections completed *c.*1270. *Martin Hürlimann*

157 Lincoln Cathedral, England: nave, looking east; second quarter of the 13th C. *Martin Hürlimann*

158 Lincoln Cathedral, England: detail of arcade and gallery in the Angel Choir; begun 1256. *Martin Hürlimann*

159 Carlisle Cathedral (Cumberland), England: east window; *c.*1290. *National Monuments Record*

160 Bristol Cathedral, England: choir, looking east; begun 1298, completed by 1337. *A.F. Kersting*

161 Exeter Cathedral (Devon), England: tierceron vault of the nave; mid-14th C., continuing the vaulting scheme of the choir of *c.*1300. *Martin Hürlimann*

162 Bristol Cathedral, England: south aisle of the choir; begun 1298, completed by 1337. *National Monuments Record*

163 Ely Cathedral (Cambridgeshire), England: detail of blind arcading on the north wall of the Lady Chapel; 1321-49. *Martin Hürlimann*

164 Ely Cathedral (Cambridgeshire), England: interior of the octagon from the north-west; probably by William Hurley, the King's Master Carpenter, 1322-42, restored and partially rebuilt by Sir George Gilbert Scott in the 19th C. *Martin Hürlimann*

165 Vendôme (Loir-et-Cher), France: detail of the west front of La Trinité; 1485-1506. *Jean Roubier*

166 Rouen Cathedral (Seine-Maritime), France: 'Tour de Beurre', photographed before World War II: 1485-1500. *Jean Roubier*

167 Freiburg-im-Breisgau Minster, Germany: west tower and spire; *c.*1340. *Helga Schmidt-Glassner*

168 Salzburg, Austria: choir vaults of the Franciscan Church; by Hans von Burghausen, begun *c.*1408. *Landesbildstelle, Salzburg (photo Puschej)*

169 Cologne Cathedral, Germany: interior of the choir, looking east; begun 1248. *Bildarchiv Foto Marburg*

170 Langenstein (Kassel), Germany: skeleton vault in the parish church: probably after 1500. *Bildarchiv Foto Marburg*

171 Nuremberg, Germany: interior of choir of St Lorenz from the south-west; begun 1434. (In the centre, suspended, is Veit Stoss's *Annunciation*; against a pillar to the left, the *Sakramentshaus* (tabernacle) by Adam Krafft.) *Bildarchiv Foto Marburg*

172 Venice, Italy: interior of SS. Giovanni e Paolo, looking east; begun 1246. *Scala*

173 Siena Cathedral, Italy: view from the south-west; 1245-1380 (façade begun 1284 by Giovanni Pisano). *Mansell-Anderson*

174 Venice, Italy: Doge's Palace; late 14th C.-*c.*1457. *Georgina Masson*

175 Toledo Cathedral, Spain: view across transept, looking south; foundation stone laid in 1227 (construction may have begun before then). *Mas*

176 Burgos Cathedral, Spain: ambulatory; begun 1221. *Bildarchiv Foto Marburg*

177 Seville Cathedral, Spain: exterior from the south-west; *c.*1401-1521, with later additions. *A.F. Kersting*

178 Gloucester Cathedral, England: choir, looking east; *c.*1337-57. *National Monuments Record*

179 Cambridge, England: King's College Chapel, looking west in the ante-chapel; by John Wastell, 1508-15. *Royal Commission on Historical Monuments*

180 Paris: interior of the upper church of the Sainte-Chapelle; *c.*1240-8. *Giraudon*

181 Aachen Minster, Germany: interior of the choir; begun 1355. *Bildarchiv Foto Marburg*

182 Canterbury Cathedral (Kent), England: nave looking east; by Henry Yevele, 1379-1403. *Martin Hürlimann*

183 Gloucester Cathedral, England: south cloister walk (on the left is the monks' washing-place); after 1351, chiefly c. 1370. *Edwin Smith*

184 London: roof of Westminster Hall; roof by Hugh Herland, 1394-1402. *Copyright Country Life*

185 Cambridge, England: bird's-eye view of Trinity College. From David Loggan, *Cantabrigia Illustrata*, 1690

186 London: pendant fan vault of Henry VII's Chapel, Westminster Abbey; by Robert and William Vertue, 1503-19. *Edwin Smith*

187 Batalha, Portugal: Claustro Real, built by King Manuel I; c. 1515. *Helga Schmidt-Glassner*

188 Burgos Cathedral, Spain: vault of the Capilla del Condestable; by Simón de Colonia, 1482-94. *Mas*

189 Tomar, Portugal: window of the Chapter House, built by King Manuel I; c. 1520. *Helga Schmidt-Glassner*

190 Venice, Italy: Libreria Vecchia from the lagoon; by Jacopo Sansovino, 1536. *Mansell-Alinari*

191 Florence, Italy: dome of the Cathedral; by Filippo Brunelleschi, 1420-36. *Mansell-Alinari*

192 Florence, Italy: bay of the loggia of the Ospedale degli Innocenti; by Filippo Brunelleschi, 1421-4, with terracotta roundels by Andrea della Robbia, 1463-6. *Mansell-Alinari*

193 Florence, Italy: interior of Sto Spirito, looking east; by Filippo Brunelleschi, 1436-82. *Alinari*

194 Todi, Italy: Sta Maria della Consolazione, from the south; by Cola da Caprarola, begun 1508. *Mansell Collection*

195, 196 Florence, Italy: façade and courtyard of the Palazzo Strozzi; begun 1489 by Benedetto da Maiano, continued by Cronaca, 1497-1507, completed 1536. *Georgina Masson*

197 Florence, Italy: façade of Sta Maria Novella; upper part - above the door - by Leone Battista Alberti, 1456. *Martin Hürlimann*

198 Rimini, Italy: Tempio Malatestiano (S. Francesco); remodelling by Leone Battista Alberti begun 1447, unfinished. *Mansell-Alinari*

199 Mantua, Italy: façade of S. Andrea; by Leone Battista Alberti; 1470-2, unfinished. *Anderson*

200 Mantua, Italy: plan of S. Andrea; by Leone Battista Alberti, 1470-2

201 Rome: part of the façade of the Cancelleria; begun 1486. *Georgina Masson*

202 Rome: Tempietto of S. Pietro in Montorio; by Donato Bramante, 1502. *Georgina Masson*

203 Rome: upper level of the Cortile del Belvedere; by Donato Bramante, begun 1503. The upper storey of the exedra is a later addition. From J. Carcopino, *The Vatican*, London, 1964.

204 Bramante's plan for St Peter's, Rome; 1505/6

205 Michelangelo's plan for St Peter's, Rome; c. 1546

206 Rome: St Peter's, from the south-west (liturgical north-east: the apse is on the left, a transept on the right); begun 1546 by Michelangelo, the dome built by Giacomo della Porta and completed in 1590. *Mansell-Alinari*

207 Rome: interior of St Peter's, looking east from Carlo Maderna's nave of 1606-26. From a painting by G. P. Pannini, 1755. Landesgalerie, Hanover. *Gabinetto Fotografico Nazionale*

208 Rome: part of the façade of Palazzo Vidoni-Caffarelli; by Raphael, c. 1515-20, later altered. *Mansell-Anderson*

209 Florence, Italy: part of the façade of Palazzo Rucellai; by Leone Battista Alberti, 1446-51. *Mansell-Alinari*

210 Rome: interior of the loggia of Villa Madama; designed by Raphael and executed by Giulio Romano, 1516-27. *Georgina Masson*

211 Rome: plan of Palazzo Angelo Massimi and Palazzo Pietro Massimi (Palazzo Massimi alle Colonne); by Baldassare Peruzzi, begun 1535. After Banister Fletcher

212 Rome: entrance to Palazzo Farnese; door by Antonio da Sangallo, window by Michelangelo, 1534–40. *Mansell-Alinari*

213 Rome; façade of Palazzo Massimi alle Colonne; by Baldassare Peruzzi; begun 1535. *Mansell-Alinari*

214 Rome: façade of Palazzo Farnese; by Antonio da Sangallo and Michelangelo, 1534–40. *Georgina Masson*

215 Florence, Italy: Laurentian Library, looking from the vestibule towards the reading room; by Michelangelo, 1524–57. *Alinari*

216 Florence, Italy: Medici Chapel in S. Lorenzo, from the south-east (right, the tomb of Lorenzo de' Medici); by Michelangelo, begun 1521. *Mansell-Anderson*

217 Rome: plan of the Capitol. After Banister Fletcher

218 Rome: the Capitol, with Palazzo del Senatore in the centre; by Michelangelo and Giacomo della Porta, 1538–1612. *A.F. Kersting*

219 Mantua, Italy: detail of courtyard façade of the Palazzo del Te; by Giulio Romano, 1525–35. *Mansell-Alinari*

220 Mantua, Italy: house of Giulio Romano; by Giulio Romano, c.1544. *Alinari*

221 Verona, Italy: Palazzo Bevilacqua; by Michele Sanmicheli; c.1530. *Georgina Masson*

222 Venice, Italy: interior of S. Giorgio Maggiore looking east; by Andrea Palladio, 1565. *Mansell-Anderson*

223 Venice, Italy: air view of the Piazzetta and surrounding buildings (the Bridge of Sighs is at the far right). *Bromostampa, Milan*

224 Rome: façade of the Gesù; by Giacomo Vignola and Giacomo della Porta, begun 1568. *Anderson*

225 Rome: plan of the Gesù; by Giacomo Vignola, begun 1568. From Sandrart, *Insignium Romae Templorum*, 1690

226 Venice, Italy: Sta Maria della Salute; by Baldassare Longhena, 1632. *Mansell-Anderson*

227 Caprarola, Italy: Villa Farnese; basement storey and plan begun 1520s by Antonio da Sangallo and Baldassare Peruzzi, upper part by Giacomo Vignola, 1559–73. *Georgina Masson*

228 Vicenza, Italy: Palazzo Chiericati; by Andrea Palladio, begun 1550. The design is based on Vitruvius' accounts of Roman forum buildings (see *Ill. 36*). *Georgina Masson*

229 Vicenza, Italy: Villa Rotonda; by Andrea Palladio, c.1550–1. *Edwin Smith*

230 Vicenza, Italy: plan of Villa Rotonda; by Andrea Palladio, c.1550–1. From N. Pevsner, *An Outline of European Architecture*, Jubilee ed., 1960, by courtesy of Penguin Books

231 Rome: Basilica and Piazza of St Peter's from the south. Engraving by Lieven Cruyl from *Descriptio faciei variorum locorum ... urbis Romae*, 1694

232 Rome: detail of colonnade of the Piazza of St Peter's; by Gianlorenzo Bernini, begun 1656. *A.F. Kersting*

233 Rome: façade of Sta Susanna; by Carlo Maderna, c.1596–1603. *Anderson*

234 Rome: Cornaro Chapel in Sta Maria della Vittoria; by Gianlorenzo Bernini, 1645–52. From an 18th-C. painting. *Staatliches Museum Schwerin*

235 Rome: Scala Regia in the Vatican; by Gianlorenzo Bernini, 1663–6. *Mansell-Anderson*

236 Rome: façade of the central block of Palazzo Barberini; begun 1628 by Carlo Maderna, completed after his death in 1629 by Gianlorenzo Bernini and Francesco Borromini. *Georgina Masson*

237 Rome: interior of S. Andrea al Quirinale; by Gianlorenzo Bernini, 1658–78. *Anderson*

238 Rome: interior of S. Carlo alle Quattro Fontane; by Francesco Borromini, begun 1633. *Mansell-Alinari*

239 Rome: plan of S. Carlo alle Quattro Fontane; by Borromini, begun 1633, façade 1667

240 Rome: interior of the cupola of S. Ivo della Sapienza; by Borromini, 1642–60. *Bildarchiv Foto Marburg*

241 Rome: façade of S. Carlo alle Quattro Fontane; by Borromini, 1667. *Mansell-Anderson*

242 Rome: lantern of S. Ivo della Sapienza; by Borromini, 1642–60. *Georgina Masson*

243 Rome: façade of Sta Maria della Pace; by Pietro da Cortona, 1656–7. *Georgina Masson*

244 Turin, Italy: interior of the dome of the chapel of the Santissima Sindone; by Guarino Guarini, 1667–90. *Edwin Smith*

245 Rome: façade of S. Agnese in Piazza Navona; by Francesco Borromini, 1652–57. *Mansell-Anderson*

246 Turin, Italy: Palazzo Carignano; by Guarino Guarini, begun 1678. *Mansell-Anderson*

247 Granada, Spain: detail of courtyard of the Palace of Charles V; by Pedro Machuca, begun 1526. *Mas*

248 El Escorial, Spain: general view; begun 1563 by Juan Bautista de Toledo, completed 1567–84 by Juan de Herrera. *Mansell-Anderson*

249 Granada Cathedral, Spain: arch between ambulatory and choir; by Diego de Siloé, c.1529. *Arthur Byne*

250 Blois (Loir-et-Cher), France: staircase in François I wing; 1515–c.1525. *Helga Schmidt-Glassner*

251 Chambord (Loir-et-Cher), France: view of the château; by Pierre Nepveu, 1519–47. *Jean Roubier*

252 Chambord (Loir-et-Cher), France: plan of the château; 1519–47. From Jacques Androuet Ducerceau, *Les plus excellents Bastiments de France*, I, 1576

253 Chenonceau (Indre-et-Loire), France: view of the château; by Thomas Bohier, Philibert de l'Orme and Jean Bullant, 1515–81. *Martin Hürlimann*

254 Paris: rood screen in St-Etienne-du-Mont; probably by Philibert de l'Orme, c.1545. *Giraudon*

255 Paris: detail of Lescot wing in the Cour du Vieux Louvre; by Pierre Lescot, with sculpture by Jean Goujon, begun 1546. *Jean Roubier*

256 Fontainebleau (Seine-et-Marne), France: Galerie François I in the château; by Francesco Primaticcio and Giovanni Battista Rosso ('Rosso Fiorentino'), 1533–7. *Giraudon*

257 Anet (Eure-et-Loir), France: interior of the circular chapel of the château; by Philibert de l'Orme, 1549–52. *Giraudon*

258 Hampton Court (Middlesex), England: base court and great west gatehouse; begun 1515. *National Monuments Record*

259 Nonsuch Palace (Surrey), England: c.1538–58 (demolished 1687). From a drawing by Joris Hoefnagel. British Museum, London

260 London: Strand front of Old Somerset House; 1547–52 (demolished c.1777). From a drawing by John Thorpe. *Courtauld Institute of Art, University of London, by courtesy of the Trustees of Sir John Soane's Museum, London*

261 Longleat House (Wiltshire), England: plan; 1554 and after. After a MS by Robert Smythson at Hatfield. From J. Summerson, *Architecture in Britain: 1530–1830*, 1969, by courtesy of Penguin Books

262 Longleat House (Wiltshire), England: air view; begun 1554, burnt 1567, rebuilt from c.1568 onwards, internal arrangements altered in the 19th C. *Paul Popper*

263 Hatfield House (Hertfordshire), England: interior of the long gallery from the east; begun 1607. *National Monuments Record*

264 Wollaton Hall (Nottinghamshire), England: east front; by Robert Smythson, 1580–8. *A. F. Kersting*

265 Hardwick Hall (Derbyshire), England: plan of ground floor; probably by Robert Smythson, 1590–7

266 Hardwick Hall (Derbyshire), England: entrance front; probably by Robert Smythson, 1590–7. *A. F. Kersting*

267 Hatfield House (Hertfordshire), England: Great Stair; *c.* 1611. *National Monuments Record, by courtesy of B. T. Batsford Ltd*

268 Antwerp, Belgium: façade of the Town Hall; by Cornelis Floris, 1561–5. *ACL*

269 The Hague, Holland: Mauritshuis; by Jacob van Campen, 1633–5. *Rijksdienst v/d Monumentenzorg, The Hague*

270 Paris: Cour du Vieux Louvre, showing Jacques Lemercier's extension, including the Pavillon de l'Horloge; begun 1624. *Bulloz*

271 Third design for the east front of the Louvre, by Gianlorenzo Bernini, 1665. From an engraving by Marot. *Courtauld Institute of Art, University of London*

272 Paris: east front of the Louvre; by Claude Perrault and Louis Le Vau, 1667–70. *A.F. Kersting*

273 Paris: garden front of Palais du Luxembourg; by Salomon de Brosse, begun 1615. *Bulloz*

274 Blois (Loir-et-Cher), France: Orléans wing of the château; by François Mansart, 1635–8. *Copyright Country Life*

275 Paris: Val-de-Grâce; begun 1645 by François Mansart, continued by Jacques Lemercier after Mansart's dismissal, completed 1665. *Giraudon*

276 Vaux-le-Vicomte (Seine-et-Marne), France: plan of the château; by Louis Le Vau, 1657. From N. Pevsner, *An Outline of European Architecture*, Jubilee ed., 1960, by courtesy of Penguin Books

277 Vaux-le-Vicomte (Seine-et-Marne), France: air view of the château; by Louis Le Vau, 1657. *Aerofilms Ltd*

278 Paris: façade of the church of the Invalides; by Jules Hardouin Mansart, designed 1679. *Archives Photographiques*

279 Versailles (Seine-et-Oise), France: garden front of the palace; by Louis Le Vau, 1669 et seq., and Jules Hardouin Mansart, 1678 et seq. *A.F. Kersting*

280 Versailles (Seine-et-Oise), France: air view. *Aerofilms Ltd*

281 Versailles (Seine-et-Oise), France: Galerie des Glaces; by Jules Hardouin Mansart with decorations by Charles Lebrun; 1680. *Mansell-Alinari*

282 Versailles (Seine-et-Oise), France: Petit Trianon; by Jacques-Ange Gabriel; 1763–9. *Giraudon*

283 Versailles (Seine-et-Oise), France: plan of the palace, town and gardens. From J.F. Blondel, *Architecture françoise*, IV, 1756

284 Greenwich, London: Queen's House; by Inigo Jones, 1616–35. *Ministry of Public Buildings and Works*

285 London: Banqueting House, Whitehall; by Inigo Jones, 1619–22. *Ministry of Public Buildings and Works*

286 London: St Paul's, Covent Garden; by Inigo Jones, 1630–1. *National Monuments Record*

287 Wilton House (Wiltshire), England: 'double-cube' room; by Inigo Jones and John Webb; *c.* 1649. *A.F. Kersting*

288 London: plan of St Stephen, Walbrook; by Sir Christopher Wren, 1672–87. From N. Pevsner, *An Outline of European Architecture*, Jubilee ed., 1960, by courtesy of Penguin Books

289 London: interior of St Stephen, Walbrook, from the south-west corner; by Sir Christopher Wren, 1672–87. *National Monuments Record*

290 London: engraved view showing St Paul's Cathedral and Wren's City churches. *By courtesy of the Trustees of the British Museum*

291 London: St Bride's, Fleet Street; by Sir Christopher Wren, 1670–84, spire 1702. *A.F. Kersting*

292 Perspective drawing of Sir Christopher Wren's Great Model for St Paul's Cathedral, London; 1673. From the *Wren Society Report*, XIV, by courtesy of the Trustees of Sir John Soane's Museum, London

293 London: plan of St Paul's Cathedral, as built; by Sir Christopher Wren, 1675–1710

294 London: air view of St Paul's Cathedral; by Sir Christopher Wren, 1675–1710. *Aerofilms Ltd*

325 London: river front of Somerset House; by Sir William Chambers, 1776–8 (wings completed 1835 and 1856). Detail from a 19th-C. engraving by T. A. Prior after T. Allom. County Hall, London. *R.B. Fleming, by courtesy of the Greater London Council*

326 Kedleston Hall (Derbyshire), England: south front; by Robert Adam, 1761–5. *Copyright Country Life*

327 London: library of Kenwood House; by Robert Adam, 1767–8. *Copyright Country Life*

328 London: plan showing, in black, the area laid out by John Nash in 1812–27 (Regent Street and Regent's Park). From J. Summerson, *John Nash, Architect to George IV*, 1935

329 London: Regent Street Quadrant; by John Nash, 1819–20, with the County Fire Office by Robert Abraham (all demolished). From an engraving by Thomas Dale after a drawing by Thomas Shepherd, 1827

330 Williamsburg (Virginia), U.S.A.: Governor's House; 1705, rebuilt 1932. *Wayne Andrews*

331 Westover (Virginia), U.S.A.: house of William Byrd II; by Richard Taliaferro, c.1730. *Wayne Andrews*

332 Boston (Massachusetts), U.S.A.: King's Chapel, looking towards the altar; by Peter Harrison, 1749–58. *Haskell*

333 Monticello (Virginia), U.S.A.: the house of Thomas Jefferson; by Thomas Jefferson, 1769. *United States Information Service*

334 Charlottesville (Virginia), U.S.A.: air view of the University of Virginia; designed by Thomas Jefferson, built 1817–26 by Benjamin Henry Latrobe. *Ralph Thompson*

335 Washington, D.C.: United States Capitol. Central section by William Thornton, Charles Bulfinch and others, 1792–1827; wings and dome by Thomas U. Walter, 1851–65. *Washington Convention and Visitors Bureau, Infoplan*

336 Project for a cenotaph for Newton; by Etienne-Louis Boullée, c.1784. *Bibliothèque Nationale, Paris*

337 Paris: Barrière de la Villette; by Claude-Nicolas Ledoux, 1789. *Giraudon*

338 Section of project for an 'ideal' cemetery – a vast colombarium with four arms radiating from a central sphere; by Claude-Nicolas Ledoux, from his *Architecture considérée . . .*, 1804–6

339 London: breakfast parlour in No. 13 Lincoln's Inn Fields (now Sir John Soane's Museum); by Sir John Soane, 1812. *Sydney W. Newbery, by courtesy of the Trustees of Sir John Soane's Museum, London*

340 London: Consols Office in the Bank of England; by Sir John Soane, 1794. *National Monuments Record, copyright the Bank of England*

341 Baltimore (Maryland), U.S.A.: interior of the Catholic Cathedral; by Benjamin Henry Latrobe, 1805–18. *J.H. Schaefer and Son*

342 Munich, Germany: Glyptothek; by Leo von Klenze, 1815–34. *Lengauer*

343 Edinburgh, Scotland: Royal High School; by Thomas Hamilton, begun 1825. *National Monuments Record of Scotland*

344 Philadelphia (Pennsylvania), U.S.A.: Merchants' Exchange; by William Strickland, 1832–4. *From an old photograph, courtesy the Historical Society of Pennsylvania*

345 Brighton (Sussex), England: detail of Royal Pavilion; by John Nash, 1815–21. *Edwin Smith*

346 Twickenham, near London: library of Strawberry Hill; by John Chute for Horace Walpole, 1754 (house begun 1748). *A.F. Kersting*

347 Berlin: Schauspielhaus; by Karl Friedrich Schinkel, 1819–21. *Dr Franz Stoedtner*

348 Berlin: Altes Museum; by Karl Friedrich Schinkel, 1824–8, restored after World War II. *Staatliche Museen zu Berlin*

349 Brussels: Palais de Justice; by Joseph Poelaert, 1866–83. *ACL*

350 Paris: façade of the Opera House; by Charles Garnier, 1862–75. *Julian Wontner*

351 Paris: grand staircase in the Opera House; by Charles Garnier, 1862–75. *Bulloz*

351

379 Chicago (Illinois), U.S.A.: Marshall Field Wholesale Store; by H. H. Richardson, 1885–7 (demolished). *Chicago Architectural Photographing Company*

380 Chicago (Illinois), U.S.A.: Auditorium Building; by Adler and Sullivan, 1887–9. *Chicago Architectural Photographing Company*

381 Chicago (Illinois), U.S.A.: Reliance Building; by D. H. Burnham and Co., 1890–4

382 Chicago (Illinois), U.S.A.: Carson Pirie Scott Store, in its original state before destruction of the eaves gallery; by Louis Sullivan, lower section at the left 1899–1901, remainder 1903–4. *Chicago Architectural Photographing Company*

383 Brussels: 'A l'Innovation'; by Victor Horta, 1901 (destroyed). *Dr Franz Stoedtner*

384 Paris: detail of façade of 'La Samaritaine'; by Frantz Jourdain, 1905. Only fragments of the design now survive. From *L'Architecture*, pl. X

385 Barcelona, Spain: crypt of Sta Coloma de Cervelló, in the Colonia Güell; by Antoni Gaudí, 1898–1915. Only the crypt of the chapel was ever completed. *Amigos de Gaudí*

386 Barcelona, Spain: façade of the Nativity transept of the Templo Expiatorio de la Sagrada Familia; by Antoni Gaudí, commissioned 1883, pinnacles completed 1930. *Mas*

387 Brussels: façade of the Maison du Peuple; by Victor Horta, 1896–9 (demolished 1965–6). A number of the iron-framed interiors, including the auditorium, were salvaged, and are at present in storage. *Studio Minders*

388 Glasgow, Scotland: view from the gallery into the ground floor front room of the Willow Tea Rooms, Sauchiehall Street; by Charles Rennie Mackintosh, 1903–4. *Annan, Glasgow*

389 Buffalo (New York), U.S.A.: interior of the Larkin Building; by Frank Lloyd Wright, 1904 (demolished 1949). From *A Testament* by Frank Lloyd Wright. Copyright 1957, published by Horizon Press, New York

390 Glasgow, Scotland: School of Art, from the corner of Renfrew Street and Scott Street; by Charles Rennie Mackintosh, 1897–9 and – the last two bays and elevation in the foreground – 1907–9. *Bryan and Shear, by courtesy of the Glasgow School of Art*

391 Berlin: AEG Turbine Factory; by Peter Behrens, 1908–9. *Dr Franz Stoedtner*

392 Alfeld-a.-d.-Leine, Germany: Fagus Factory; by Walter Gropius and Adolf Meyer, 1911–14. *Dr Franz Stoedtner*

393 Dessau, Germany: Bauhaus complex from the south; by Walter Gropius, 1925–6. *Dr Franz Stoedtner*

394 Prague: Müller House; by Adolf Loos, 1930. From L. Münz and G. Künstler, *Adolf Loos, 1966*

395 Buffalo (New York), U.S.A.: Martin House; by Frank Lloyd Wright, 1904. *Jay W. Baxtresser*

396 Racine (Wisconsin), U.S.A.: Research Tower of S. C. Johnson and Son; by Frank Lloyd Wright, completed 1949. *Wayne Andrews*

397 Oak Park (Illinois), U.S.A.: Unity Church; by Frank Lloyd Wright, 1906. *Wayne Anderson*

398 Racine (Wisconsin), U.S.A.: interior of the Administration Building of S. C. Johnson and Son; by Frank Lloyd Wright, 1936–9. *Wayne Andrews*

399 Bear Run (Pennsylvania), U.S.A.: Kaufmann House, 'Falling Waters'; by Frank Lloyd Wright, 1936. *Hedrich-Blessing*

400 New York: Solomon R. Guggenheim Museum; by Frank Lloyd Wright, designed 1943, built 1956–9. *New York State Department of Commerce, Infoplan*

401 Berlin: auditorium of Max Reinhardt's Grosses Schauspielhaus, a remodelled circus; by Hans Poelzig, 1919. *Bildarchiv Foto Marburg*

402 Neubabelsberg, Germany: Einstein Observatory Tower; by Erich Mendelsohn, designed 1919, completed 1921. *Dr Franz Stoedtner*

403 Le Raincy (Seine-et-Oise), France: interior of Notre-Dame, looking east; by Auguste Perret, 1922–3. *Martin Hürlimann*

INDEX